CFA Institute®
CFA Program

# PERFORMANCE MEASUREMENT

CFA® Program Curriculum
2025 • LEVEL III CORE • VOLUME 3

WILEY

ISBN 978-1-961409-44-6 (paper)
ISBN 978-1-961409-56-9 (ebook)
May 2024

SKYDC98D362-5259-489D-8D57-198F9B103506_032324

Please visit our website at
www.WileyGlobalFinance.com.

# CONTENTS

# How to Use the CFA Program Curriculum

The CFA® Program exams measure your mastery of the core knowledge, skills, and abilities required to succeed as an investment professional. These core competencies are the basis for the Candidate Body of Knowledge (CBOK™). The CBOK consists of four components:

> A broad outline that lists the major CFA Program topic areas (www .cfainstitute.org/programs/cfa/curriculum/cbok/cbok)

> Topic area weights that indicate the relative exam weightings of the top-level topic areas (www.cfainstitute.org/en/programs/cfa/curriculum)

> Learning outcome statements (LOS) that advise candidates about the specific knowledge, skills, and abilities they should acquire from curriculum content covering a topic area: LOS are provided at the beginning of each block of related content and the specific lesson that covers them. We encourage you to review the information about the LOS on our website (www.cfainstitute.org/programs/cfa/curriculum/study-sessions), including the descriptions of LOS "command words" on the candidate resources page at www.cfainstitute.org/-/media/documents/support/programs/cfa-and -cipm-los-command-words.ashx.

> The CFA Program curriculum that candidates receive access to upon exam registration

Therefore, the key to your success on the CFA exams is studying and understanding the CBOK. You can learn more about the CBOK on our website: www.cfainstitute .org/programs/cfa/curriculum/cbok.

The curriculum, including the practice questions, is the basis for all exam questions. The curriculum is selected or developed specifically to provide candidates with the knowledge, skills, and abilities reflected in the CBOK.

## CFA INSTITUTE LEARNING ECOSYSTEM (LES)

Your exam registration fee includes access to the CFA Institute Learning Ecosystem (LES). This digital learning platform provides access, even offline, to all the curriculum content and practice questions. The LES is organized as a series of learning modules consisting of short online lessons and associated practice questions. This tool is your source for all study materials, including practice questions and mock exams. The LES is the primary method by which CFA Institute delivers your curriculum experience. Here, candidates will find additional practice questions to test their knowledge. Some questions in the LES provide a unique interactive experience.

## DESIGNING YOUR PERSONAL STUDY PROGRAM

An orderly, systematic approach to exam preparation is critical. You should dedicate a consistent block of time every week to reading and studying. Review the LOS both before and after you study curriculum content to ensure you can demonstrate the knowledge, skills, and abilities described by the LOS and the assigned reading. Use the LOS as a self-check to track your progress and highlight areas of weakness for later review.

Successful candidates report an average of more than 300 hours preparing for each exam. Your preparation time will vary based on your prior education and experience, and you will likely spend more time on some topics than on others.

## ERRATA

The curriculum development process is rigorous and involves multiple rounds of reviews by content experts. Despite our efforts to produce a curriculum that is free of errors, in some instances, we must make corrections. Curriculum errata are periodically updated and posted by exam level and test date on the Curriculum Errata webpage (www.cfainstitute.org/en/programs/submit-errata). If you believe you have found an error in the curriculum, you can submit your concerns through our curriculum errata reporting process found at the bottom of the Curriculum Errata webpage.

## OTHER FEEDBACK

Please send any comments or suggestions to info@cfainstitute.org, and we will review your feedback thoughtfully.

# Performance Measurement

# 1

# Portfolio Performance Evaluation

by Marc A. Wright, CFA, and Charles Mitchell Conover, CFA, CIPM.

*Marc A. Wright, CFA, is at Russell Investments (USA). Charles Mitchell Conover, CFA, CIPM, is at the University of Richmond (USA).*

## LEARNING OUTCOMES

| Mastery | *The candidate should be able to:* |
|---------|------------------------------------|
| ☐ | explain the following components of portfolio evaluation and their interrelationships: performance measurement, performance attribution, and performance appraisal |
| ☐ | describe attributes of an effective attribution process |
| ☐ | contrast return attribution and risk attribution; contrast macro and micro return attribution |
| ☐ | describe returns-based, holdings-based, and transactions-based performance attribution, including advantages and disadvantages of each |
| ☐ | interpret the sources of portfolio returns using a specified attribution approach |
| ☐ | interpret the output from fixed-income attribution analyses |
| ☐ | discuss considerations in selecting a risk attribution approach |
| ☐ | identify and interpret investment results attributable to the asset owner versus those attributable to the investment manager |
| ☐ | discuss uses of liability-based benchmarks |
| ☐ | describe types of asset-based benchmarks |
| ☐ | discuss tests of benchmark quality |
| ☐ | describe the impact of benchmark misspecification on attribution and appraisal analysis |
| ☐ | describe problems that arise in benchmarking alternative investments |
| ☐ | calculate and interpret the Sortino ratio, the appraisal ratio, upside/downside capture ratios, maximum drawdown, and drawdown duration |
| ☐ | describe limitations of appraisal measures and related metrics |
| ☐ | evaluate the skill of an investment manager |

# 1          INTRODUCTION

Performance evaluation is one of the most critical areas of investment analysis. Performance results can be used to assess the quality of the investment approach and suggest changes that might improve it. They are also used to communicate the results of the investment process to other stakeholders and may even be used to compensate the investment managers. Therefore, it is of vital importance that practitioners who use these analyses understand how the results are generated. By gaining an understanding of the details of how these analyses work, practitioners will develop a greater understanding of the insights that might be gathered from the analysis and will also be cognizant of the limitations of those approaches, careful not to infer more than what is explicit or logically implicit in the results.

We will first consider the broad categories of performance measurement, attribution, and appraisal, differentiating between the three and explaining their interrelationships. Next, we will provide practitioners with tools to evaluate the effectiveness of those analyses as we summarize various approaches to performance evaluation. We will cover returns-based, holdings-based, and transactions-based attribution, addressing the merits and shortcomings of each approach and providing guidance on how to properly interpret attribution results. Again, by reviewing how each approach generates its results, we reveal strengths and weaknesses of the individual attribution approaches.

Next, we will turn to the subject of benchmarks and performance appraisal ratios. We will review the long-standing tests of benchmark quality and differentiate market indexes from benchmarks. We will also review different ratios used in performance appraisal, considering the benefits and limitations of each approach.

Lastly, we will provide advice on using these tools to collectively evaluate the skill of investment managers. This advice relies heavily on understanding the analysis tools, the limitations of the approaches, the importance of data to the quality of the analysis, and the pitfalls to avoid when making recommendations.

# 2          PERFORMANCE EVALUATION AND ATTRIBUTION

- [ ] explain the following components of portfolio evaluation and their interrelationships: performance measurement, performance attribution, and performance appraisal
- [ ] describe attributes of an effective attribution process
- [ ] contrast return attribution and risk attribution; contrast macro and micro return attribution
- [ ] describe returns-based, holdings-based, and transactions-based performance attribution, including advantages and disadvantages of each

Performance evaluation includes three primary components, each corresponding to a specific question we need to answer to evaluate a portfolio's performance:

- Performance measurement—what was the portfolio's performance?
- Performance attribution—how was the performance achieved?

- Performance appraisal—was the performance achieved through manager skill or luck?

We will consider each of these components on their own and the interrelationships between them.

Performance measurement provides an overall indication of the portfolio's performance, typically relative to a benchmark. In its simplest form, performance measurement is the calculation of investment returns for both the portfolio and its benchmark. This return calculation is a critical first step in the performance evaluation process, building the foundation on which performance evaluation is based. The investment return tells us what the portfolio achieved over a specific period, irrespective of peer or benchmark performance. For purposes of this reading, we will call this the *absolute return*. But it also provides the basis to understand the difference between the portfolio return and its benchmark return, the **excess return**.

In addition to return, performance measurement must consider the risk incurred to achieve that return. We measure risk using a variety of *ex post* (looking back in time) and *ex ante* (looking forward in time) techniques. For *ex post*, we might consider the volatility or standard deviation of the past returns, along with many other performance appraisal ratios considered later in this reading. The calculation of a portfolio's value at risk (VaR) at a point in time is an example of an *ex ante* measure. These measures of risk allow us to quantify the risk in a portfolio and better assess the performance.

Performance attribution then builds on the foundation of the investment returns and risk, helping us explain *how* that performance was achieved or that risk was incurred. Performance attribution can be used to explain either absolute returns or relative returns. It can be used to understand what portion of returns was driven by active manager decisions and what portion was a result of exposures not specifically targeted by the portfolio manager. Performance attribution can also be used to decompose the excess return into its component sources, where it is used to help explain why a manager over- or underperformed the target benchmark. Similarly, risk attribution can be used to decompose the risk incurred in the portfolio.

The third component of performance evaluation, performance appraisal, makes use of risk, return, and attribution analyses to draw conclusions regarding the *quality* of a portfolio's performance. Performance appraisal attempts to distinguish manager skill from luck. Did the portfolio manager's decisions help achieve a better outcome, or was the outcome due to market changes outside of the manager's control? If superior results can be attributed to skill, there is a higher likelihood that the manager will generate superior performance in the future. The analysis may affirm the management process or may contain insights for improving the process. This is a key feedback loop in the investment management process.

### EXAMPLE 1

## Performance Evaluation

1. Performance attribution:
    A. measures the excess performance of a portfolio.
    B. explains the proportion of returns due to manager skill.
    C. explains how the excess performance or risk was achieved.

### Solution:

C is correct. Performance attribution identifies the drivers of investment returns. A is not correct because measuring the excess performance of a portfolio is the subject of performance measurement. B is not correct because it is performance appraisal that distinguishes skill from luck.

2. Performance appraisal:

    **A.** identifies the sources of under- or outperformance.

    **B.** decomposes a portfolio's risk and return into their constituent parts.

    **C.** uses the results of risk, return, and attribution analyses to assess the quality of a portfolio's performance.

**Solution:**

C is correct. Performance appraisal combines all the techniques of performance measurement and attribution to assess the quality of performance. Both A and B describe performance attribution.

## Performance Attribution

As previously described, performance attribution is a critical component of the portfolio evaluation process. Used by senior management, client relationship specialists, risk controllers, operations staff, portfolio managers, and sales and marketing professionals, attribution analysis provides important insights to the investment decision-making process. Clients and prospects also use attribution analysis as part of their evaluation of that process. Effective performance attribution analysis requires a thorough understanding of the investment decision-making process and should reflect the active decisions of the portfolio manager.

An effective performance attribution process must

- account for *all* of the portfolio's return or risk exposure,
- reflect the investment decision-making process,
- quantify the active decisions of the portfolio manager, and
- provide a complete understanding of the excess return/risk of the portfolio.

If the return or risk quantified by the attribution analysis does not account for all the return or risk presented to the client, then at best the attribution is incomplete and at worst the quality of the attribution analysis is brought into doubt. If the attribution does not reflect the investment decision-making process, then the analysis will be of little value to either the portfolio manager or the client. For example, if the portfolio manager is a genuine bottom-up stock picker who ignores sector benchmark weights, then measuring the impact of sector allocation against these weights is not measuring decisions made as part of the investment process; sector effects are merely a byproduct of the manager's investment decisions.

**Performance attribution** includes return attribution and risk attribution (although in practice, "performance attribution" is often used to mean "return attribution"). **Return attribution** analyzes the impact of active investment decisions on *returns*; **risk attribution** analyzes the *risk* consequences of those decisions. Depending on the purpose of the analysis, risk may be viewed in absolute or benchmark-relative terms. For example, when risk relative to a benchmark is the focus, a risk attribution analysis might identify and evaluate a portfolio's deviations from a benchmark's exposures to risk factors.

Performance attribution provides a good starting point for a conversation with clients, explaining both positive and negative aspects of recent performance. Return attribution analysis is particularly important when performance is weak; portfolio managers must demonstrate an understanding of their performance, provide a rationale for their decisions, and generate confidence in their ability to add value in the future. When it accurately reflects the investment decision-making process, return attribution provides quality control for the investment process and provides senior management with a tool to manage a complex business with multiple investment strategies.

The attribution process described earlier—understanding the drivers of a manager's returns and whether those drivers are consistent with the stated investment process—is a common application of attribution analysis. But attribution can also be conducted to evaluate the asset owner's tactical asset allocation and manager selection decisions (called **macro attribution**) or to evaluate the impact of the portfolio manager's decisions on the performance of the asset owner's total fund (called **micro attribution**). A defined-benefit pension plan makes the decision to allocate a given percentage of the fund to each asset class and decides which manager(s) to hire for each asset class. Macro attribution measures the effect of the sponsor's choice to deviate from the strategic asset allocation, including the effect of "gaps" between the strategic asset allocation and its implementation (e.g., where the sum of the managers' benchmarks is equal to something other than the benchmark index).

Micro attribution measures the impact of portfolio managers' allocation and selection decisions on total fund performance.

Performance attribution may be either returns based, holdings based, or transactions based. The decision to use one set of inputs rather than another depends on the availability of data as well as the investment process being measured.

**Returns-based attribution** uses only the total portfolio returns over a period to identify the components of the investment process that have generated the returns. Returns-based attribution is most appropriate when the underlying portfolio holding information is not available with sufficient frequency at the required level of detail. For example, one might use returns-based attribution to evaluate hedge funds, because it can be difficult to obtain the underlying holdings of hedge funds. Returns-based attribution is the easiest method to implement, but because it does not use the underlying holdings, it is the least accurate of the three approaches and the most vulnerable to data manipulation.

Unlike returns-based attribution, **holdings-based attribution** references the beginning-of-period holdings of the portfolio. Calculated with monthly, weekly, or daily data, the accuracy of holdings-based attribution improves when using data with shorter time intervals. For longer evaluation periods, we link together the attribution results for the shorter measurement periods. Because holdings-based attribution fails to capture the impact of any transactions made during the measurement period, it may not reconcile to the actual portfolio return. For example, in a daily holdings-based attribution, securities are included at the end of the day they are purchased and excluded at the end of the day they are sold. If the transaction price is significantly different from the closing price, the attribution analysis can differ significantly from the actual performance.

The residual caused by ignoring transactions might be described as a timing or trading effect. Holdings-based analysis is most appropriate for investment strategies with little turnover (e.g., passive strategies). Holdings-based analysis may be improved by valuing the portfolio with the same prices used to calculate the underlying benchmark index, removing one potential difference between the portfolio and benchmark returns that is not a management effect.

The third approach, **transactions-based attribution**, uses both the holdings of the portfolio and the transactions (purchases and sales) that occurred during the evaluation period. For transaction-based attribution, both the weights and returns reflect *all transactions* during the period, including transaction costs. Transaction-based attribution is the most accurate type of attribution analysis but also the most difficult and time-consuming to implement. To obtain meaningful results, the underlying data must be complete, accurate, and reconciled from period to period. Because all the data are available, the entire excess return can be quantified and explained. The return used in the attribution analysis will reconcile with the return presented to the client, and attribution analysis can be used as a diagnostic tool to identify errors.

The choice of attribution approach depends on the availability and quality of the underlying data, the reporting requirements for the client, and the complexity of the investment decision-making process.

---

**EXAMPLE 2**

## Performance Attribution

1. Effective attribution analysis must:
   A. use intraday transaction data.
   B. reconcile to the total portfolio return or risk exposure.
   C. measure the contribution of security and sector selection decisions.

### Solution:

B is correct. An effective attribution process accounts for all of the portfolio's return or risk exposure. A is not correct; an attribution analysis is improved with intraday transaction data, but an effective attribution analysis can be produced with a returns- or holdings-based approach. C is not correct because an attribution process that measures the sector selection effects of a bottom-up stock-picker does not measure the effectiveness of the investment decision-making process.

---

2. Which of the following most accurately describes macro attribution?
   A. Attribution analysis at the portfolio level
   B. Attribution analysis of the fund sponsor decisions
   C. Attribution analysis of asset allocation decisions

### Solution:

B is correct. Macro attribution measures the effect of the sponsor's choice to deviate from the strategic asset allocation and the sponsor's manager selection decisions. A is not correct because attribution analysis at the portfolio level may be either macro attribution or micro attribution. C is not correct because macro attribution measures both asset allocation and manager selection decisions of the asset owner.

---

3. Risk attribution differs from return attribution in that it:
   A. is not conducted relative to a benchmark.
   B. quantifies the risk consequences of the investment decisions.
   C. quantifies the investment decisions of the investment manager.

### Solution:

B is correct. Risk attribution, unlike return attribution, attempts to quantify the risk consequences of the investment decisions. A is not correct because risk attribution may be conducted on either an absolute or a relative basis. C is not correct because risk attribution does not capture the return impact of a manager's investment decisions.

4. An analyst is *most likely* to use returns-based attribution when:

   A. the portfolio has a low turnover.

   B. the holdings for the portfolio are not available.

   C. she wants the analysis to be as accurate as possible.

## Solution:

B is correct. Returns-based attribution is typically used when the holdings data are not available. Neither A nor C is correct because returns-based attribution is the least accurate of the three approaches.

# RETURN ATTRIBUTION

3

☐ | interpret the sources of portfolio returns using a specified attribution approach

Return attribution allows us to look across a specific time horizon and identify which investment decisions have either added value to or detracted value from the portfolio, relative to its benchmark. As feedback to the portfolio management process, return attribution quantifies the active decisions of portfolio managers and informs management and clients. In this way, return attribution can be thought of as "backward looking" or *ex post*, meaning that it is used to evaluate the investment decisions for some historical time horizon.

**Return attribution** is a set of techniques used to identify the sources of excess return of a portfolio against its benchmark, quantifying the consequences of active investment decisions.

Specific return attribution approaches have been designed to evaluate particular types of assets. In this section, we will consider two common approaches for equity attribution: Brinson–Fachler and factor-based attribution. We will also review the output and findings from a typical fixed-income attribution approach.

Practitioners may also encounter the concept of geometric attribution and arithmetic attribution, two approaches to measuring attribution effects over longer periods. **Arithmetic attribution** approaches are designed to explain the **excess return**, the arithmetic difference between the portfolio return, $R$, and its benchmark return, $B$.

When using an arithmetic attribution approach, the attribution effects will sum to the excess return. Arithmetic approaches are straightforward for a single period, for which there is no difference between the sum of the attribution effects and the excess return. However, when combining multiple periods, the sub-period attribution effects will *not* sum to the excess return. Because the excess return is calculated by *geometrically* linking the sub-period returns, adjustments must be made to "smooth" the *arithmetic* sub-period attribution effects over time. Multiple smoothing approaches exist in the industry, including algorithms suggested by David Cariño (1999) and Jose Menchero (2000).

Geometric attribution approaches extend the arithmetic approaches by attributing the geometric excess return ($G$), as defined below:

$$G = \frac{1+R}{1+B} - 1 = \frac{R-B}{1+B}$$

Note that the geometric excess return is simply the arithmetic excess return divided by the wealth ratio of the benchmark (1 plus the return on the benchmark during the period).

In a geometric attribution approach, the attribution effects will compound (multiply) together to total the geometric excess return. Because the attribution effects compound together to exactly equal the geometric excess return, the compounding works across multiple periods. Therefore, no smoothing is required to adjust the geometric attribution effects across multiple periods.

Practitioners typically choose arithmetic attribution approaches when they want to use the attribution analysis with non-practitioner clients or in marketing reports. With results that add up to the total excess return for all periods, arithmetic approaches are more intuitively understood. Geometric approaches tend to be limited to practitioners who understand the approach and who appreciate that they do not have to adjust the attribution effects over time.

## A Simple Return Attribution Example

Suppose a portfolio's return for the past year was 5.24% and the portfolio's benchmark return for that same period was 3.24%. In this case, the portfolio achieved a positive arithmetic excess return of 2.00% (5.24% – 3.24% = 2.00%) over the past year.

To understand how the 2.00% was achieved, we apply return attribution. In this example, return attribution will quantify two typical sources of excess return: *security selection* and *asset allocation*. Security selection answers the question, Was the return achieved by selecting securities that performed well relative to the benchmark or by avoiding benchmark securities that performed relatively poorly? Asset allocation answers the question, Was the return achieved by choosing to overweight an asset category (e.g., economic sector or currency) that outperformed the total benchmark or to underweight an asset category that underperformed the total benchmark? (The term "allocation" is used somewhat differently here. It is not measuring the plan sponsor's asset allocation decision but, rather, the *manager's* decision to allocate among countries, sectors, or, in cases where the manager has a broad mandate, asset classes.)

Models of equity return attribution often attempt to separate the investment process into those two key decisions—selection and allocation—assigning each a magnitude and direction (plus or minus) for both decisions. For instance, for the portfolio referenced previously, we might calculate the return attribution results shown in Exhibit 1:

### Exhibit 1: Total Portfolio Return Attribution Analysis (Time Period: Past 12 Months)

| Portfolio Return | Benchmark Return | Excess Return | Allocation Effect | Selection Effect |
|---|---|---|---|---|
| 5.24% | 3.24% | 2.00% | −0.50% | 2.50% |

As we noted, the investment decisions generated a positive excess return of 200 basis points (bps) relative to the benchmark. We use the "return attribution analysis" to see how this 200 bps was generated. First, note that the *negative* allocation effect indicates that the allocation decisions over the past 12 months, whatever they were, had a negative impact on the total portfolio performance. They *subtracted* 50 bps from the excess return. In contrast, the *positive* selection effect indicates that the security selection decisions—decisions to overweight or underweight securities relative to their benchmark weights—*added* 250 bps to the excess return. Our return attribution analysis implies that the portfolio manager's security selection decision was far superior to his or her asset allocation decision for the past 12 months.

## Equity Return Attribution—The Brinson–Hood–Beebower Model

The foundations of return attribution were established in two articles, one written by Brinson and Fachler (1985) and the other by Brinson, Hood, and Beebower (1986). The Brinson–Fachler model is more widely used in performance attribution today, but we introduce the Brinson–Hood–Beebower (BHB) model first to lay an important foundation.

BHB is built on the assumption that the total portfolio and benchmark returns are calculated by summing the weights and returns of the sectors within the portfolio (Equation 1) and the benchmark (Equation 2):

$$\text{Portfolio return } R = \sum_{i=1}^{i=n} w_i R_i \tag{1}$$

$$\text{Benchmark return } B = \sum_{i=1}^{i=n} W_i B_i \tag{2}$$

where

$w_i$ = weight of the $i$th sector in the portfolio

$R_i$ = return of the portfolio assets in the $i$th sector

$W_i$ = weight of the $i$th sector in the benchmark

$B_i$ = return of the benchmark in the $i$th sector

$n$ = number of sectors or securities

The sum of the weights in both the portfolio and the benchmark must equal 100%. The presence of leverage would require a position with a negative weight (borrowings or short positions) to balance to 100%.

Attribution analysis quantifies each of the portfolio manager's active decisions that explain the difference between the portfolio return, $R$, and the benchmark return, $B$. Note that for this example, we are concerned with only single-period, single-currency return attribution models.

Exhibit 2 provides data for a three-sector domestic equity portfolio, used to illustrate the BHB model.

### Exhibit 2: BHB Model Illustration—Portfolio and Benchmark Data

| Sector | Portfolio Weight | Benchmark Weight | Portfolio Return | Benchmark Return |
|---|---|---|---|---|
| Energy | 50% | 50% | 18% | 10% |
| Health care | 30% | 20% | –3% | –2% |
| Financials | 20% | 30% | 10% | 12% |
| **Total** | **100%** | **100%** | **10.1%** | **8.2%** |

Total portfolio return $R = (50\% \times 18\%) + (30\% \times -3\%) + (20\% \times 10\%) = 10.1\%$

Total benchmark return $B = (50\% \times 10\%) + (20\% \times -2\%) + (30\% \times 12\%) = 8.2\%$

Thus, the excess return is 1.9% (10.1% − 8.2% = 1.9%), or 190 bps.

We will use the weights and returns data shown in Exhibit 2 to calculate the basic attribution effects using the BHB model, including the allocation effect, the security selection effect, and the interaction effect. The allocation effect refers to the value the portfolio manager adds (or subtracts) by having portfolio sector weights that are different from the benchmark sector weights. A sector weight in the portfolio greater than the benchmark sector weight would be described as *overweight*, and a sector weight less than the benchmark sector weight would be described as *underweight*.

To calculate allocation, we first calculate the contribution to allocation ($A_i$) for each sector. The contribution to allocation in the $i$th sector is equal to the portfolio's sector weight minus the benchmark's sector weight, times the benchmark sector return:

$$A_i = (w_i - W_i)B_i \tag{3}$$

Using the data from Exhibit 2, we calculate individual sector allocation effects as follows:

- Energy: (50% − 50%) × 10% = 0.0%
- Health care: (30% − 20%) × −2.0% = −0.2%
- Financials: (20% − 30%) × 12% = −1.2%

To find the total portfolio allocation effect, $A$, we sum the individual sector contributions to allocation:

$$A = \sum_{i=1}^{i=n} A_i \tag{4}$$

Total allocation effect = 0.0% − 0.2% − 1.2% = −1.4%

We can then use the results to state the following conclusions:

- The portfolio weight in the energy sector is equal to the benchmark weight; therefore, there is no contribution to allocation in energy.
- In health care, the portfolio manager held a higher weight than the benchmark (30% versus 20%), but the sector underperformed the aggregate benchmark (−2.0% versus 8.2%). Therefore, the decision to overweight health care lowered the overall excess return; the contribution to allocation is −0.2%.
- In financials, the portfolio manager chose to underweight versus the benchmark (20% versus 30%). But because financials outperformed the aggregate benchmark (12% versus 8.2%), the decision to underweight financials also lowered the overall excess return; the contribution to allocation is −1.2%.
- Overall, the combined allocation effect for this portfolio was −1.4%, demonstrating that the weighting decisions negatively contributed to the performance of the portfolio.

The other attribution effect in the BHB model is security selection—the value the portfolio manager adds by holding individual securities or instruments within the sector in different-from-benchmark weights.

To calculate selection, we first calculate the contribution to selection ($S_i$) for each sector. The contribution to selection in the $i$th sector is equal to the benchmark sector weight times the portfolio's sector return minus the benchmark's sector return.

$$S_i = W_i(R_i - B_i) \tag{5}$$

Using the data from Exhibit 2, we calculate individual sector selection effects as follows:

- Energy: 50% × (18% − 10%) = 4.0%

- Health care: 20% × (−3% − −2.0%) = −0.2%
- Financials: 30% × (10% − 12%) = −0.6%

To find the total portfolio selection effect, $S$, we sum the individual sector contributions to selection:

$$S = \sum_{i=1}^{i=n} S_i \qquad (6)$$

Total selection effect = 4.0% + −0.2% + −0.6% = 3.2%

We can use the results to state the following conclusions:

- The portfolio's energy sector outperformed the benchmark's energy sector by 800 bps (18% − 10%); 800 bps times the benchmark weight of 50% for this sector results in a 4.0% contribution to selection.
- The portfolio's health care sector underperformed the benchmark's health care sector by 100 bps [(−3%) − (−2%)]; 100 bps times the benchmark weight of 20% for this sector results in a contribution of −0.2%.
- The portfolio's financials sector underperformed the benchmark's financials sector by 200 bps (10% − 12%); 200 bps times the benchmark weight of 30% to this sector results in a contribution of −0.6%.
- Overall, the combined selection effect for this portfolio was 3.2%.

In the BHB model, selection and allocation do not completely explain the arithmetic difference. For example, in the attribution analysis based on Exhibit 2, allocation (−1.4%) and selection (3.2%) together represent just 1.8% of the arithmetic difference between the portfolio return of 10.1% and the benchmark return of 8.2%; 0.1% is missing. To explain this remaining difference in the excess return, the BHB model uses a third attribution effect, called "interaction." The **interaction effect** is the effect resulting from the interaction of the allocation and selection decisions combined.

To calculate interaction, we first calculate the contribution to interaction for each sector. The contribution to interaction in the $i$th sector is equal to the portfolio sector weight minus the benchmark sector weight, times the portfolio sector return minus the benchmark sector return:

$$I_i = (w_i − W_i)(R_i − B_i) \qquad (7)$$

Using the data from Exhibit 2, we calculate individual sector selection effects as follows:

- Energy: (50% − 50%) × (18% − 10%) = 0.0%
- Health care: (30% − 20%) × (−3% − −2.0%) = −0.1%
- Financials: (20% − 30%) × (10% − 12%) = 0.2%

To find the total portfolio interaction effect, we sum the individual sector contributions to interaction:

$$I = \sum_{i=1}^{i=n} I_i \qquad (8)$$

Total interaction effect = 0.0% + −0.1% + 0.2% = 0.1%

We can use the results to state the following conclusions:

- For the energy sector, the portfolio weight equals the benchmark weight and thus there is no contribution to interaction.
- Because the manager had an overweight to a sector in which selection was negative, the contribution from interaction in health care was also negative, −0.1%.

- In the financials sector, the manager was underweight by 10% and selection was negative. The effect of being underweight in a sector in which the manager underperforms leads to a contribution from interaction of +0.2%.

- Total contribution from interaction is +0.1%, representing the combined effect of the interaction of the selection and allocation effects.

---

**EXAMPLE 3**

## Interpreting the Results of a BHB Attribution

**BHB Attribution Analysis Results Table**

| Region | Portfolio Return | Benchmark Return | Portfolio Weight | Benchmark Weight | Allocation | Selection | Inter-action | Total |
|--------|------------------|------------------|------------------|------------------|------------|-----------|--------------|-------|
| Americas | 2.80% | 1.20% | 30% | 30% | 0.00% | 0.48% | 0.00% | 0.48% |
| APAC | −1.50% | −0.50% | 20% | 30% | 0.05% | −0.30% | 0.10% | −0.15% |
| EMEA | 0.70% | 1.50% | 50% | 40% | 0.15% | −0.32% | −0.08% | −0.25% |
| Total | **0.89%** | **0.81%** | **100%** | **100%** | **0.20%** | **−0.14%** | **0.02%** | **0.08%** |

Use the table above to answer the following questions.

1. Why is the contribution to selection for Europe, the Middle East, and Africa (EMEA) negative?

    A. The total benchmark return is less than the total portfolio return.

    B. The manager selected securities in EMEA that underperformed the benchmark.

    C. The manager underweighted an outperforming sector.

**Solution:**

B is correct. The manager selected securities that underperformed the benchmark, with a portfolio return for EMEA of 0.7% versus a benchmark return for EMEA of 1.5%.

2. Why is the contribution to allocation for Asia Pacific (APAC) equal to +5 bps?

    A. The benchmark weight and the portfolio weight are equal.

    B. The manager has an overweight position in an overperforming region.

    C. The manager has an underweight position in an underperforming region.

**Solution:**

C is correct. The manager is underweight in APAC, 20% versus a benchmark weight of 30%. The APAC portion of the portfolio underperformed, with a −0.50% benchmark return versus the total benchmark return of 0.81%.

3. Which of the following conclusions from the above attribution analysis is *most* correct?

    A. The manager's security selection decisions were better in the Americas than in APAC.

## Brinson–Fachler Model

The Brinson–Fachler (BF) model differs from the BHB model only in how individual sector allocation effects are calculated.

In the BHB model, all overweight positions in sectors with positive returns will generate positive allocation effects irrespective of the overall benchmark return, whereas all overweight positions in negative markets will generate negative allocation effects. Thus, overweighting a sector $i$ that earns a positive return, $B_i > 0$, results in a positive allocation effect, $A_i = (w_i - W_i)B_i > 0$, even when the sector return is less than the overall benchmark return (i.e., $B_i < B$). When the sector return is negative, $0 > B_i$, overweighting produces a negative allocation effect, $A_i = (w_i - W_i)B_i < 0$.

Clearly, if the portfolio manager is overweight in a negative market that has outperformed the overall benchmark, the effect should be positive.

The BF model solves this problem by modifying the asset allocation factor to compare returns with the overall benchmark as follows:

$$B_S - B = \sum_{i=1}^{i=n} (w_i - W_i) B_i = \sum_{i=1}^{i=n} (w_i - W_i) (B_i - B) \qquad (9)$$

Because $\sum_{i=1}^{i=n} w_i = \sum_{i=1}^{i=n} W_i = 1$, the constant $B$ can be introduced. The contribution to asset allocation in the $i$th sector is now:

$$A_i = (w_i - W_i) (B_i - B) \qquad (10)$$

Note that in Equation 10, the allocation effect at the portfolio level, $B_S - B$, is unchanged from the BHB model.

The contribution to arithmetic excess return from sector allocation for the portfolio data shown in Exhibit 2 is $B_S - B = 6.8\% - 8.2\% = -1.4\%$. Revised BF sector allocation effects are calculated for the portfolio data in Exhibit 2 as follows, using $A_i = (w_i - W_i)(B_i - B)$:

| Energy | $(50\% - 50\%) \times (10\% - 8.2\%) = 0.0\%$ |
| Health care | $(30\% - 20\%) \times (-2.0\% - 8.2\%) = -1.02\%$ |
| Financials | $(20\% - 30\%) \times (12\% - 8.2\%) = -0.38\%$ |
| **Total** | $0.0\% - 1.02\% - 0.38\% = -1.4\%$ |

The impact in health care is much greater. In addition to being overweight in a negative market, which costs –0.2%, the portfolio manager is correctly penalized the opportunity cost of not being invested in the overall market return of 8.2%, generating a further cost of $10\% \times -8.2\% = -0.82\%$ and resulting in a total impact of –1.02%. To describe it another way, the portfolio is 10% overweight in a market that is underperforming the overall market by –10.2% (i.e., –2.0% – 8.2%) and generating a loss of –1.02%

The impact in financials is much smaller. Although being underweight in a positive market cost –1.2%, we must add back the opportunity cost of being invested in the overall market return of 8.2%, generating a contribution of $-10\% \times -8.2\% = 0.82\%$ and resulting in a total impact of –0.38%. To describe it another way, the portfolio is 10% underweight in an industry that is outperforming the overall market by 3.8% (i.e., 12.0% – 8.2%), generating a loss of –0.38%. As expected, at the portfolio level, the allocation effect of –1.4% remains the same as that calculated with the BHB model.

The revised attribution effects are summarized in Exhibit 3.

**Exhibit 3: BF Return Attribution Results**

|  | Portfolio Weight | Benchmark Weight | Portfolio Return | Benchmark Return | Allocation | Selection | Interaction |
|---|---|---|---|---|---|---|---|
| Energy | 50% | 50% | 18% | 10% | 0.0% | 4.0% | 0.0% |
| Health care | 30% | 20% | –3% | –2% | –1.02% | –0.2% | –0.1% |
| Financials | 20% | 30% | 10% | 12% | –0.38% | –0.6% | 0.2% |
| Total | 100% | 100% | 10.1% | 8.2% | –1.4% | 3.2% | 0.1% |

**EXAMPLE 4**

## Allocation Using the BF Model

**Exhibit 4: Sample Portfolio Data**

|  | Portfolio Weight | Benchmark Weight | Portfolio Return | Benchmark Return |
|---|---|---|---|---|
| Technology | 20% | 30% | –11.0% | –10.0% |
| Telecommunications | 30% | 40% | –5.0% | –8.0% |
| Utilities | 50% | 30% | –8.0% | –5.0% |
| Total | 100% | 100% | –7.7% | –7.7% |

1. Using the BF method, the allocation effect of utilities based on the portfolio data in Exhibit 4 is:

   A. –1.50%.

   B. 0.54%.

   **C.** 1.35%.

## Solution:

B is correct: $(w_i - W_i)(B_i - B) = (50\% - 30\%)(-5.0\% + 7.7\%) = 0.54\%$. The portfolio is 20% overweight in a sector outperforming the overall benchmark by 2.7%, therefore contributing 0.54% to the overall allocation effect.

A is incorrect: $W_i B_i = 30\% \times -5.0\% = -1.5\%$ is the contribution to the benchmark return from utilities.

C is incorrect: $w_i(B_i - B) = 50\% \times (-5.0\% + 7.7\%) = +1.35\%$. Only the portfolio weight of 50% has been used, not the overweight position of 20%.

# FACTOR-BASED AND FIXED-INCOME RETURN ATTRIBUTION

4

<table>
<tr><td>☐</td><td>interpret the sources of portfolio returns using a specified attribution approach</td></tr>
<tr><td>☐</td><td>interpret the output from fixed-income attribution analyses</td></tr>
</table>

As we have seen, return attribution allows us to analyze a portfolio's excess return by comparing the accounting information (weights and returns) in the portfolio with the information in the benchmark. The Brinson–Fachler model focuses on security selection, asset allocation, and the interaction of selection and allocation. But what if we want to assess other decisions within the investment process?

Another type of return attribution uses fundamental factor models to decompose the contributions to excess return from *factors*. Fundamental factor analysis allows us to quantify the impact of specific active investment decisions within the portfolio, showing how they add or remove value relative to the benchmark. We want to remove the effects of the market to identify the excess return generated by the active investment decisions. To do that, we return to our definition of excess return: Excess return = $R - B$.

Many different factor models can be used to decompose excess returns. The choice of factor model is driven by which aspects of the investment process you want to measure. One of the factor models commonly used in equity attribution analyses is the Carhart four-factor model, or simply the **Carhart model**, given in Equation 11 (Carhart 1997). The Carhart model explains the excess return on the portfolio in terms of the portfolio's sensitivity to a market index (RMRF), a market-capitalization factor (SMB), a book-value-to-price factor (HML), and a momentum factor (WML).

$$R_p - R_f = a_p + b_{p1}\text{RMRF} + b_{p2}\text{SMB} + b_{p3}\text{HML} + b_{p4}\text{WML} + E_p \tag{11}$$

where

$R_p$ and $R_f$ = the return on the portfolio and the risk-free rate of return, respectively

$a_p$ = "alpha" or return in excess of that expected given the portfolio's level of systematic risk (assuming the four factors capture all systematic risk)

$b_p$ = the sensitivity of the portfolio to the given factor

RMRF = the return on a value-weighted equity index in excess of the one-month T-bill rate

SMB = small minus big, a size (market-capitalization) factor (SMB is the average return on three small-cap portfolios minus the average return on three large-cap portfolios)

HML = high minus low, a value factor (HML is the average return on two high-book-to-market portfolios minus the average return on two low-book-to-market portfolios)

WML = winners minus losers, a momentum factor (WML is the return on a portfolio of the past year's winners minus the return on a portfolio of the past year's losers)

$E_p$ = an error term that represents the portion of the return to the portfolio, $p$, not explained by the model

By analyzing the results of a factor return attribution analysis, we can identify the investment approach and infer the relative strengths and/or weaknesses of the investment decisions. For example, using the Carhart factor model, we calculate the following results for a hypothetical manager.

### Exhibit 5: Sample Carhart Factor Model Attribution

| | Factor Sensitivity | | | | Contribution to Active Return | |
|---|---|---|---|---|---|---|
| | Portfolio | Benchmark | Difference | Factor Return | Absolute | Proportion of Total |
| Factor | (1) | (2) | (3) | (4) | (3) × (4) | Active |
| RMRF | 0.95 | 1.00 | −0.05 | 5.52% | −0.28% | −13.30% |
| SMB | −1.05 | −1.00 | −0.05 | −3.35% | 0.17% | 8.10% |
| HML | 0.40 | 0.00 | 0.40 | 5.10% | 2.04% | 98.40% |
| WML | 0.05 | 0.03 | 0.02 | 9.63% | 0.19% | 9.30% |
| | | | | A. Factor tilts return = | 2.12% | 102.40% |
| | | | | B. Security selection = | −0.05% | −2.40% |
| | | | | C. Active return (A + B) = | 2.07% | 100.00% |

This attribution analysis yields information about this portfolio's investment approach, how the manager generated excess return, and his or her ability to consistently add value relative to the benchmark.

Let's first look at the analysis of the benchmark (column 2). The sensitivity to RMRF of 1 indicates that the assigned benchmark has average market risk, consistent with it being a broad-based index. The benchmark's negative sensitivity to SMB indicates a large-cap orientation. Assuming, of course, that the benchmark is a good fit for the manager's stated strategy, we can describe the approach as large cap without a value/growth bias (HML is zero) or a momentum bias (WML is close to zero).

Let's now look at where the portfolio manager's approach differed from that of the benchmark. Based on the factor sensitivities shown in column 1 (positive sensitivity to HML of 0.40) and the differences relative to the benchmark shown in column 3, we can see that the manager likely had a value tilt but was otherwise relatively neutral to the benchmark. We would expect the portfolio to hold more value-oriented stocks than the benchmark, and we would want to evaluate the contribution of this tilt.

We can examine the effects of this decision by looking at the balance of the table. Positive active exposure to the HML factor—the bet on value stocks—contributed 204 bps to the realized active return, about 98% of the 207 bps of total realized active return. The manager's minor active exposures to small stocks and momentum also contributed positively to return, whereas the active exposure to RMRF was a drag on performance. However, because the magnitudes of the exposures to RMRF, SMB, and WML were relatively small, the effects of those bets were minor compared with the value tilt (HML).

What about the manager's ability to contribute return through stock selection? Again, assuming that the benchmark is a good fit for the manager's investment process, the overall active return from security selection is the portion of return not explained by factor sensitivities. In this period, the contribution from selection was slightly negative (−0.05%).

In the aggregate, the manager's positive active return was largely the result of the large active bet on HML (+0.40) and a high return to that factor during the period (+5.10%). Is this type of tilt consistent with the manager's stated investment process? If yes, the manager can be credited with an active decision that contributed positively to return. If no, then the excess return in the period is unlikely to result from manager skill but, rather, is a byproduct of luck. What does the manager's investment process say about the role of security selection? If the manager does not profess skill in security selection but instead focuses on sector or factor allocation, then the minimal contribution of security selection should not be perceived as a negative reflection on manager skill.

## EXAMPLE 5

## Factor-Based Attribution

Use the data from Exhibit 5 to answer the following questions.

1. Which of the following statements is *not* correct?

    A. The manager's slight small-cap tilt contributed positively to return.

    B. The manager's slight momentum tilt contributed positively to return.

    C. The manager's below-benchmark beta contributed negatively to return.

### Solution:

A is the correct answer. The negative coefficient on SMB indicates that the manager had a slight large-cap bias relative to the benchmark. The slight tilt on WML (+0.02) combined with a positive return to the factor resulted in a positive contribution to return. The below-benchmark beta of RMRF

(−0.05) combined with a positive return to the factor resulted in a negative contribution to return.

2. What investment approach, not taken by the portfolio manager, could have delivered more value to the portfolio during the investment period?

   A.  A momentum-based approach

   B.  A growth-oriented approach

   C.  A small-cap-based approach

### Solution:

A is correct. Had the manager overweighted momentum stocks during the period, the momentum factor (WML) return of 9.63% would have contributed significant positive performance to the portfolio.

## Fixed-Income Return Attribution

Fixed-income portfolios are driven by decisions made with respect to credit risk and positioning along the yield curve. Building on work by Groupe de Reflexion en Attribution de Performance, or GRAP, outlined in Giguère (2005) and Murira and Sierra (2006), we will discuss three typical approaches to fixed-income attribution:

- Exposure decomposition—duration based
- Yield curve decomposition—duration based
- Yield curve decomposition—full repricing based

Candidates are not responsible for *calculating* fixed-income attribution but should be able to interpret the results of a fixed-income attribution analysis.

### *Exposure Decomposition—Duration Based*

Exposure decomposition is a top-down attribution approach that seeks to explain the active management of a portfolio relative to its benchmark, typically working through a hierarchy of decisions from the top to the bottom. These decisions might include portfolio duration bets, yield curve positioning or sector bets, each relative to the benchmark. The term "exposure decomposition" relates to the decomposition of portfolio risk exposures by means of grouping a portfolio's component bonds by specified characteristics (e.g., duration, bond sector). The term "duration based" relates to the typical use of duration to represent interest rate exposure decisions.

Models that take an exposure decomposition approach are similar to Brinson-type equity attribution models, where we might group the portfolio by its market value weights in different economic sectors. In this case, however, we group the portfolio by its market value weights in duration buckets (i.e., exposure to different ranges of duration). This approach simplifies the data requirements and allows straightforward presentation of results relative to other fixed-income approaches. For these reasons, the exposure decomposition approach is used primarily for marketing and client reports, where an important benefit is that users can easily understand and articulate the results of active portfolio management.

### Yield Curve Decomposition—Duration Based

The duration-based yield curve decomposition approach to fixed-income attribution can be either executed as a top-down approach or built bottom-up from the security level. This approach estimates the return of securities, sector buckets, or years-to-maturity buckets using the known relationship between duration and changes in yield to maturity (YTM), as follows:

% Total return = % Income return + % Price return,

where % Price return ≈ –Duration × Change in YTM.

Duration measures the sensitivity of bond price to a change in the bond's yield to maturity. So, the percentage price return of a bond will be approximately equal to the negative of its duration for each 100 bp change in yields. The change in yield to maturity of the portfolio or instrument can be broken down into yield curve factors and spread factors to provide additional insights. These factors represent the changes in the risk-free government curve (e.g., changes in level, slope, and curvature) and in the premium required to hold riskier sectors and bonds. When they are combined and applied to the duration, we can determine a percentage price change for each factor.

For example, a manager may have a view as to how the yield curve factors will change over time. We can use the attribution analysis to determine the value of the yield curve views as they unfold over time.

This approach is applied to both the portfolio and the benchmark to identify contributions to total return from changes in the yield to maturity. Comparing the differences between the benchmark's return drivers and the portfolio's return drivers gives us the *effect of active portfolio management decisions*.

In this regard, this group of models is quite different from the exposure decomposition. One consequence of this difference is that we require more data points to calculate the separate absolute attribution analyses for the portfolio and the benchmark. Thus, the yield decomposition approach exchanges better transparency for more operational complexity. These models are typically used when preparing reports for analysts and portfolio managers, rather than in marketing or client reports.

### Yield Curve Decomposition—Full Repricing

Instead of estimating price changes from changes in duration and yields to maturity, bonds can be repriced from zero-coupon curves (spot rates). Recall that a bond's price is the sum of its cash flows discounted at the appropriate spot rate for each cash flow's maturity. The discount rate to compute the present value depends on the yields offered on the market for comparable securities and represents the required yield an investor expects for holding that investment. Typically, we discount each cash flow at a rate from the spot curve that corresponds to the time the cash flow will be received.

As with the duration-based approaches, instruments can be repriced following incremental changes in spot rates, whether resulting from changes in overall interest rates, spreads, or bond-specific factors. This bottom-up security-level repricing can then be translated into a contribution to a security's return and aggregated for portfolios, benchmarks, and active management.

This full repricing attribution approach provides more precise pricing and allows for a broader range of instrument types and yield changes. It also supports a greater variety of quantitative modeling beyond fixed-income attribution (e.g., *ex ante* risk). This approach is better aligned with how portfolio managers typically view the instruments. However, it requires the full capability to reprice all financial instruments in the portfolio and the benchmark, including the rates and the characteristics of the instrument. Its complex nature can make it more difficult and costly to administer operationally and can make the results more difficult to understand, particularly for non-fixed-income professionals.

All three approaches can be applied to single-currency and multi-currency portfolios. We can most clearly demonstrate the principles of fixed-income attribution by using a single-currency domestic portfolio, without digressing into the relative merits of the various multi-currency approaches. Therefore, this example is a single-currency example.

### Fixed-Income Attribution—Worked Example

Let's begin with an example of exposure decomposition analysis.

Exhibit 6 shows a breakdown of the portfolio and the benchmark by weights, duration, and each bucket's contribution to duration, aggregated by sector and duration buckets. For this example, the short-, mid-, and long-duration buckets are defined as follows:[1]

| Bucket | Duration |
|--------|----------|
| Short | Less than or equal to 5 |
| Mid | Greater than 5 and less than or equal to 10 |
| Long | Greater than 10 |

---

1 Note that the practitioner should take care when selecting the upper and lower bands of each duration bucket. By grouping bonds of different durations in the same bucket, one is measuring the combined impact of those bonds relative to the combined impact of similar bonds in the benchmark. In this example (Exhibit 6 and the related discussion), for instance, a bond with a duration of 5.5 is treated the same as a bond with a duration of 9.5 in terms of its relative impact on the portfolio versus its benchmark.

**Exhibit 6: Sample Exposure Decomposition: Relative Positions of Portfolio and Benchmark**

| | Portfolio Weights | | | | Portfolio Duration | | | | Portfolio Contribution to Duration | | | |
|---|---|---|---|---|---|---|---|---|---|---|---|---|
| | Short | Mid | Long | Total | Short | Mid | Long | Total | Short | Mid | Long | Total |
| Government | 10.00% | 10.00% | 20.00% | 40.00% | 4.42 | 7.47 | 10.21 | 8.08 | 0.44 | 0.75 | 2.04 | 3.23 |
| Corporate | 10.00% | 20.00% | 30.00% | 60.00% | 4.40 | 7.40 | 10.06 | 8.23 | 0.44 | 1.48 | 3.02 | 4.94 |
| Total | 20.00% | 30.00% | 50.00% | 100.00% | 4.41 | 7.42 | 10.12 | 8.17 | 0.88 | 2.23 | 5.06 | 8.17 |

| | Benchmark Weights | | | | Benchmark Duration | | | | Benchmark Contribution to Duration | | | |
|---|---|---|---|---|---|---|---|---|---|---|---|---|
| | Short | Mid | Long | Total | Short | Mid | Long | Total | Short | Mid | Long | Total |
| Government | 20.00% | 20.00% | 15.00% | 55.00% | 4.42 | 7.47 | 10.21 | 7.11 | 0.88 | 1.49 | 1.53 | 3.91 |
| Corporate | 15.00% | 15.00% | 15.00% | 45.00% | 4.40 | 7.40 | 10.06 | 7.29 | 0.66 | 1.11 | 1.51 | 3.28 |
| Total | 35.00% | 35.00% | 30.00% | 100.00% | 4.41 | 7.44 | 10.14 | 7.19 | 1.54 | 2.60 | 3.04 | 7.19 |

| | Portfolio Weights | | | | Portfolio Returns | | | | Portfolio Contribution to Return | | | |
|---|---|---|---|---|---|---|---|---|---|---|---|---|
| | Short | Mid | Long | Total | Short | Mid | Long | Total | Short | Mid | Long | Total |
| Government | 10.00% | 10.00% | 20.00% | 40.00% | −3.48% | −5.16% | −4.38% | −4.35% | −0.35% | −0.52% | −0.88% | −1.74% |
| Corporate | 10.00% | 20.00% | 30.00% | 60.00% | −4.33% | −6.14% | −5.42% | −5.48% | −0.43% | −1.23% | −1.63% | −3.29% |
| Total | 20.00% | 30.00% | 50.00% | 100.00% | −3.91% | −5.81% | −5.00% | −5.03% | −0.78% | −1.74% | −2.50% | −5.03% |

| | Benchmark Weights | | | | Benchmark Returns | | | | Benchmark Contribution to Return | | | |
|---|---|---|---|---|---|---|---|---|---|---|---|---|
| | Short | Mid | Long | Total | Short | Mid | Long | Total | Short | Mid | Long | Total |
| Government | 20.00% | 20.00% | 15.00% | 55.00% | −3.48% | −5.16% | −4.38% | −4.34% | −0.70% | −1.03% | −0.66% | −2.39% |
| Corporate | 15.00% | 15.00% | 15.00% | 45.00% | −4.33% | −6.14% | −5.86% | −5.44% | −0.65% | −0.92% | −0.88% | −2.45% |
| Total | 35.00% | 35.00% | 30.00% | 100.00% | −3.84% | −5.58% | −5.12% | −4.83% | −1.35% | −1.95% | −1.54% | −4.83% |

From Exhibit 6, we can make the following inferences regarding the manager's investment decisions:

- With a higher duration than the benchmark (8.17 compared with 7.19 for the benchmark), the manager likely expected the rates to fall and took a bullish position on long-term bonds (interest rates) by increasing exposure to the long end of the interest rate curve (e.g., investing 50% of the portfolio in the longest-duration bucket versus 30% for the benchmark).

- Based on the overweight in the corporate sector (60% versus the 45% benchmark weight), the manager likely expected credit spreads to narrow.[2] Notice that this bet increases the 4.94 contribution to duration of the corporate sector in the portfolio compared with the 3.28 contribution to duration for the benchmark. This allocation makes the portfolio more exposed to market yield fluctuations in the corporate sector.

---

2 If corporate yields were at a historically large spread with respect to governments, the overweight to corporates might also have been a yield bet. Even if spreads do not narrow, the higher-yielding corporates are likely to outperform the government bonds in the portfolio.

- The total portfolio return is –5.03%, relative to a total benchmark return of –4.83%, showing an underperformance of –0.20% over the period.

We can then use the portfolio and benchmark information from Exhibit 6 to calculate the portfolio's attribution results. These results are summarized in Exhibit 7. (Note that candidates are expected to be able to interpret, but not calculate, these results.)

Total interest rate allocation is the contribution from active management resulting from the manager's active exposures to changes in the level and shape of the yield curve. This can be decomposed into the duration effect (the contribution to active management from taking a different-from-benchmark aggregate duration position) and the curve effect (the specific points along the yield curve at which the manager made his benchmark-relative duration bets).

Sector allocation measures the effect of the manager's decision to overweight corporate bonds, whereas the selection effect measures the impact of the manager's decision to hold non-benchmark bonds in the portfolio. The hypothetical portfolio underlying this example contains only one bond that is not in the benchmark—a long-duration corporate bond, Corp. (P). Accordingly, there is no selection effect in the other duration buckets.

**Exhibit 7: Sample Exposure Decomposition: Attribution Results**

| Duration Bucket | Sector | Duration Effect | Curve Effect | Total Interest Rate Allocation | Sector Allocation | Bond Selection | Total |
|---|---|---|---|---|---|---|---|
| Short | Government | | | | | 0.00% | 0.00% |
| | Corporate | | | | 0.04% | 0.00% | 0.04% |
| | *Total* | *0.40%* | *0.12%* | *0.52%* | *0.04%* | *0.00%* | *0.56%* |
| Mid | Government | | | | | 0.00% | 0.00% |
| | Corporate | | | | –0.05% | 0.00% | –0.05% |
| | *Total* | *0.23%* | *0.03%* | *0.26%* | *–0.05%* | *0.00%* | *0.21%* |
| Long | Government | | | | | 0.00% | 0.00% |
| | Corporate | | | | –0.22% | 0.13% | –0.09% |
| | *Total* | *–1.25%* | *0.37%* | *–0.88%* | *–0.22%* | *0.13%* | *–0.97%* |
| Total | | **–0.62%** | **0.52%** | **–0.10%** | **–0.23%** | **0.13%** | **–0.20%** |

Using the results from Exhibit 7, we can draw the following conclusions about the investment decisions made by this manager:

- The portfolio underperformed its benchmark by 20 bps.
- 62 bps were lost by taking a long-duration position during a period when yields increased (benchmark returns were negative in each duration bucket).
- 52 bps were gained as a result of changes in the shape of the yield curve. Given the manager's overweighting in the long-duration bucket, we can infer that the yield curve flattened.
- 23 bps were lost because the manager overweighted the corporate sector during a period when credit spreads widened (the benchmark corporate returns in each duration bucket were less than the government returns in those same duration buckets).
- 7 bps were added through bond selection.

Exhibit 8 provides an example of a sample duration-based yield curve decomposition attribution analysis. Again, we do not include the calculations for this analysis but instead present the results and suggested interpretations.

### Exhibit 8: Yield Curve Decomposition—Duration Based: Active Return Contribution

| Bond | Yield | Roll | Shift | Slope | Curvature | Spread | Specific | Residual | Total |
|------|-------|------|-------|-------|-----------|--------|----------|----------|-------|
| Gov't. 5% 30 June 21 | −0.19% | −0.04% | 0.43% | 0.01% | 0.15% | 0.00% | 0.00% | −0.01% | 0.35% |
| Gov't. 7% 30 June 26 | −0.22% | −0.03% | 0.71% | 0.04% | 0.04% | 0.00% | 0.00% | −0.03% | 0.52% |
| Gov't. 6% 30 June 31 | 0.12% | 0.01% | −0.48% | 0.05% | 0.09% | 0.00% | 0.00% | −0.01% | −0.22% |
| Corp. 5% 30 June 21 | −0.11% | −0.02% | 0.21% | 0.05% | 0.05% | 0.04% | 0.02% | −0.02% | 0.22% |
| Corp. 7% 30 June 26 | 0.12% | 0.01% | −0.35% | −0.02% | −0.02% | −0.07% | 0.00% | 0.02% | −0.31% |
| Corp. (B) 6% 30 June 31 | −0.39% | −0.03% | 1.41% | −0.26% | −0.11% | 0.30% | 0.00% | −0.04% | 0.88% |
| Corp. (P) 6% 30 June 31 | 0.78% | 0.06% | −2.82% | 0.52% | 0.33% | −0.60% | 0.15% | −0.05% | −1.63% |
| Total | 0.11% | −0.04% | −0.89% | 0.39% | 0.53% | −0.33% | 0.17% | −0.14% | −0.20% |
| | *Time:* | *0.08%* | *Curve Movement:* | | *0.03%* | | | | |

*Note:* There may be minor differences due to rounding in this table.

Using the data from Exhibit 6 and Exhibit 8, we can infer the following about the portfolio investment process over this period:

- *Yield*: The portfolio overweighted corporate bonds and longer-term maturities relative to the benchmark (from Exhibit 6), which generally offer higher yield than government bonds and short-term maturities. This decision contributed 11 bps to the excess return (from Exhibit 8).

- *Roll*: The portfolio overweighted longer maturities (from Exhibit 6). Because of the shape of the yield curve, bonds with longer maturities generally sit on a flatter part of the yield curve, where the roll return is limited. The over-weighting of the longer maturities reduced the portfolio roll return by 4 bps.

- *Shift*: The portfolio overall duration of 8.17 is greater than the benchmark duration of 7.19 (from Exhibit 6), which reduced the portfolio return by 89 bps.

- *Slope*: The slope flattening caused the long-term yields to increase less than yields on shorter terms to maturity. The overweight at the long end of the curve contributed 39 bps to the excess return.

- *Curvature*: The reshaping of the yield curve resulted in a larger yield increase at the five-year maturity point. The manager underweighted that part of the yield curve. This decision contributed 53 bps to the excess return.

- *Spread*: The manager overweighted the corporate sector, which resulted in a 33 bp reduction in return because corporate spreads widened.

- *Specific spread*: Looking at the bond-specific spreads in Exhibit 8, the corporate 5% 30 June 2021 bond added 2 bps of selection return and the corporate (P) 6% 30 June 2031 bond added 15 bps of selection return. These decisions added a total of 17 bps to active return.

- *Residual*: A residual of −0.14% is unaccounted for because duration and convexity can only *estimate* the percentage price variation. It is not an accurate measure of the true price variation. The residual becomes more important during large yield moves, which is the case here, with a +1% yield shift.

**EXAMPLE 6**

## Fixed-Income Return Attribution

Use the data in Exhibit 7 and Exhibit 8 to answer the following questions.

1. Which decision had the most positive effect on the overall performance of the portfolio?

   A. Taking a long-duration position

   B. Security selection of bond issues

   C. Overweighting the long end of the yield curve

**Solution:**

C is correct: 52 bps were gained by overweighting the long end of the yield curve during a period when the slope of the yield curve flattened.

2. Explain the contribution of the long-duration bucket to overall portfolio performance.

**Solution:**

The long-duration bucket cost the portfolio 97 bps of relative return. From Exhibit 7, the curve and selection effects were positive (37 bps and 7 bps, respectively) whereas the duration and sector allocation effects were negative (–125 bps and –16 bps, respectively). The negative duration effect indicates that the manager took a longer-than-benchmark-duration position in the long-duration bucket, a decision that hurt performance because interest rates rose. The positive curve effect implies that the manager's specific positioning along the long end of the yield curve benefited from changes in the shape of the yield curve. This implication is further supported by the positive slope effect shown in Exhibit 8. Taken together, the duration and curve effects accounted for the majority of the manager's underperformance relative to the benchmark. In the long-duration bucket, the manager overweighted corporate bonds relative to the benchmark. This decision penalized returns because credit spreads widened, which can be inferred from the weaker performance of the long-duration corporate segment of the benchmark (–5.42%) relative to the long-duration government segment (–4.38%). The positive selection effect of 7 bps implies that the manager's specific bond selections added to return. This implication is supported by the specific spread contribution reflected in Exhibit 8.

# 5    RISK ATTRIBUTION

☐ | discuss considerations in selecting a risk attribution approach

Performance attribution, on its own, is typically insufficient to evaluate the investment process. In addition to performance, we need to understand the impact of exposure to risk by including risk attribution.

Risk attribution identifies the sources of risk in the investment process. For absolute mandates, it identifies the sources of portfolio volatility. For benchmark-relative mandates, it identifies the sources of tracking risk. Managers seek opportunities for profit by taking specific exposures to risk (e.g., portfolio volatility or tracking risk). Risk attribution identifies these risks taken and, together with return attribution, quantifies the contributions to both the return and risk of the investment manager's active decisions.

Risk attribution should reflect the investment decision-making process. Exhibit 9 classifies investment decision-making processes and suggests appropriate risk attribution approaches. The columns indicate whether the focus is absolute risk or benchmark-relative risk. The rows categorize investment decision-making processes as bottom up, top down, or factor based. A bottom-up approach focuses on individual security selection. Top-down approaches focus first on macro decisions, such as allocations to economic sectors, and then on security selection within sectors. A factor-based approach looks for profits by taking different-from-benchmark exposures to the risk factors believed to drive asset returns.

**Exhibit 9: Selecting the Appropriate Risk Attribution Approach**

| Investment Decision-Making Process | Type of Attribution Analysis | |
|---|---|---|
| | Relative (vs. Benchmark) | Absolute |
| Bottom up | Position's marginal contribution to tracking risk | Position's marginal contribution to total risk |
| Top down | Attribute tracking risk to relative allocation and selection decisions | Factor's marginal contribution to total risk and specific risk |
| Factor based | Factor's marginal contribution to tracking risk and active specific risk | |

For portfolios that are managed against benchmarks, a common measure of risk is tracking risk (TR), also often called tracking error. The objective of an attribution model for a benchmark-relative portfolio is to quantify the contribution of active decisions to TR. For bottom-up benchmark-relative investment processes, each position's marginal contribution to TR multiplied by its active weight gives the position's contribution to TR. For benchmark-relative top-down investment processes, the active return is explained first by the allocation decisions. Risk attribution, accordingly, will identify the total contribution of allocation and selection to TR.

For absolute mandates, the risk of the portfolio is explained by exposures to the market, size and style factors, and the specific risk due to stock selections. The attribution model quantifies the contribution of each exposure and of specific risk. Suppose that the manager follows an absolute bottom-up process where the measure of risk is the volatility (standard deviation) of returns. In this case, we want to measure the contribution of selection decisions to overall portfolio risk. To do this, we need to know the marginal contribution of each asset to the portfolio risk—the increase or decrease in the portfolio standard deviation due to a slight increase in the holding of that asset. If we know the marginal contribution of a security to absolute portfolio risk, we can then calculate the overall risk contribution of the portfolio manager's selection decisions.

In all cases, risk attribution explains only where risk was introduced into the portfolio. It needs to be combined with return attribution to understand the full impact of those decisions. For example, if a manager has added to excess return through asset allocation (e.g., positive return attribution allocation effect), we use risk attribution to understand whether those allocation decisions introduced additional risk. As such, risk attribution complements the return attribution by evaluating the risk consequences of the investment decisions.

---

### EXAMPLE 7

## Risk Attribution

Manager A is a market-neutral manager following a systematic investment approach, scoring each security on a proprietary set of risk factors. He seeks to maximize the portfolio score on the basis of the factor characteristics of individual securities. He has a hurdle rate of T-bills plus 5%.

Manager B has a strong fundamental process based on a comprehensive understanding of the business model and competitive advantages of each firm. He also uses sophisticated models to make explicit three-year forecasts of the growth of free cash flow to determine the attractiveness of each security's current valuation. His objective is to outperform the MSCI World ex-US Index by 200 bps.

Manager C specializes in timing sector exposure and generally avoids idiosyncratic risks within sectors. Using technical analyses and econometric methodologies, she produces several types of forecasts. The manager uses this information to determine appropriate sector weights. The risk contribution from any single sector is limited to 30% of total portfolio risk. She hedges aggregate market risk and seeks to earn T-bills plus 300 bps.

1. Which risk attribution approach is most appropriate to evaluate Manager A?

   **A.** Marginal contribution to total risk

   **B.** Marginal contribution to tracking risk

   **C.** Factor's marginal contributions to total risk and specific risk

### Solution:

A is correct. Manager A is a bottom-up manager with an absolute return target. B is incorrect because tracking risk is not relevant to an absolute return mandate. C is incorrect because, as a market-neutral manager, Manager A is not seeking to take different-from-market exposures.

---

2. Which risk attribution approach is most appropriate to evaluate Manager B?

   **A.** Marginal contribution to total risk

   **B.** Marginal contribution to tracking risk

   **C.** Factor's marginal contributions to total risk and specific risk

### Solution:

B is correct. Manager B is a bottom-up manager with a relative return target. A and C are incorrect because they are best suited to absolute return mandates.

---

3. Which risk attribution approach is most appropriate to evaluate Manager C?

   **A.** Marginal contribution to total risk

   **B.** Marginal contribution to tracking risk

   **C.** Factor's marginal contributions to total risk and specific risk

> **Solution:**
>
> C is correct. Manager C is a top-down manager with an absolute return
> target. A factor-based attribution is best suited to evaluate the effectiveness
> of the manager's sector decisions and hedging of market risk.

# RETURN ATTRIBUTION ANALYSIS AT MULTIPLE LEVELS

6

☐ identify and interpret investment results attributable to the asset
owner versus those attributable to the investment manager

To this point, the return attribution presented in the Brinson examples focused on the
bottom-up approach, where we calculated attribution effects at security and sector
levels and summed those effects to determine their impact at the total portfolio and
fund levels. We can use a similar return attribution approach at multiple levels of the
decision process to evaluate the impact of different decisions.

## Macro Attribution—An Example

Consider an example in which the top level is the fund sponsor (e.g., a university
endowment or a defined-benefit pension plan sponsor). At the fund sponsor level, the
first decision might be to allocate a certain weight to asset classes—the strategic asset
allocation. If the fund sponsor does not manage funds internally, it would delegate
a second investment decision to the investment managers to decide on any tactical
deviations from the strategic asset allocation. The sponsor might also select multiple
portfolio managers to manage against specific mandates within a given asset class.

The attribution analysis that we use to determine the impact of these fund sponsor
decisions is sometimes called macro attribution. The attribution of the individual
portfolio manager decisions is sometimes called micro attribution.

Assume our hypothetical fund sponsor has the following total equity benchmark:

- 50% large-cap value equities
- 25% small-cap value equities
- 25% large-cap growth equities

The fund sponsor hires two investment managers to manage the equity portion
of the fund. Value Portfolio Manager manages the large-cap and small-cap value
allocations, and Growth Portfolio Manager manages the growth equity allocation.
The investment returns are shown in Exhibit 10.

### Exhibit 10: Performance of Value and Growth Equity Managers

|  | Fund Weight | Fund Return | Benchmark Weight | Benchmark Return |
|---|---|---|---|---|
| Total | 100% | 0.95 | 100% | −0.03 |
| Value Portfolio Manager | 78% | 0.99 | 75% | 0.32 |

| | Fund Weight | Fund Return | Benchmark Weight | Benchmark Return |
|---|---|---|---|---|
| *Small-cap value equities* | 20% | 2.39 | 25% | 1.52 |
| *Large-cap value equities* | 58% | 0.51 | 50% | −0.28 |
| Growth Portfolio Manager | 22% | 0.82 | 25% | −1.08 |
| *Large-cap growth equities* | 22% | 0.82 | 25% | −1.08 |

To evaluate the decisions of the fund sponsor, we perform a return Brinson–Fachler attribution analysis using the set of weight and return data in Exhibit 10. "Allocation" measures the tactical asset allocation decision of the sponsor against its own strategic benchmark. In this example, the fund sponsor overweighted value equities and under-weighted growth equities. "Selection" measures the fund sponsor's manager selection decision: Did the selected managers add value relative to their assigned benchmarks?

For the decision to hire the Value Portfolio Manager, we would calculate the effects as follows:

Allocation = (78% − 75%)[0.32 − (−0.03)] = 0.01

- The fund sponsor overweighted value equities (78% − 75%).
- Value equities outperformed the fund's aggregate benchmark [0.32 − (−0.03)].
- The decision to overweight value equities added to portfolio return.

Selection + Interaction = [(75%)(0.99 − 0.32)] + [(78% − 75%)(0.99 − 0.32)] = 0.52

- The value manager outperformed the value benchmark (0.99 − 0.32). Thus, the fund sponsor's manager selection decision, independent of the decision to overweight value equities, added value.
- The fund sponsor overweighted a manager who outperformed his benchmark [(78% − 75%)(0.99 − 0.32)]. This is the interaction effect. (For simplicity, we combine interaction with selection, rather than showing interaction separately. By combining with selection, we assume that the selection decisions include the interaction and leave the allocation decision separate.) The interaction effect was positive.

For the decision to hire the Growth Portfolio Manager, we would calculate the effects as follows:

Allocation = (22% − 25%)[−1.08 − (−0.03)] = 0.03

- The fund sponsor underweighted growth equities (22% − 25%)
- Growth equities underperformed the fund's aggregate benchmark (−1.08 versus −0.03)
- The decision to underweight growth equities added to portfolio return

Selection + Interaction = [(25%)(0.82 − (−1.08)] + [(22% − 25%)(0.82 − (−1.08)] = 0.42

- The growth manager outperformed the growth benchmark (+0.82 versus −1.08). Thus, the fund sponsor's manager selection decision, independent of the decision to underweight growth equities, added value.

- The fund sponsor underweighted a manager who outperformed his benchmark $[(-3\%)(0.82 - (-1.08)]$. The interaction effect was negative.

The results are summarized in Exhibit 11.

**Exhibit 11: Macro Attribution**

| Return Attribution (Plan Sponsor Level) | Selection + Interaction | Allocation | Total |
|---|---|---|---|
| Total | 0.94 | 0.04 | 0.98 |
| Value Portfolio Manager | **0.52** | **0.01** | **0.53** |
| Growth Portfolio Manager | **0.42** | **0.03** | **0.45** |

Return attribution analysis is most often calculated with reference to the portfolio's agreed-upon benchmark. But it is entirely possible to attribute one portfolio against another when both are using the same or a similar investment strategy. The purpose of such analysis might be to explain an unexpected difference in return between two portfolios managed by the same portfolio manager using the same investment decision-making process.

## Micro Attribution—An Example

Using the same return data, we now move to the next level of the investment decision-making process and will evaluate the impact of the portfolio managers' decisions on total fund performance. We calculate the return attribution effects using the Brinson–Fachler approach at the segment level (i.e., small-cap value, large-cap value, and large-cap growth):

Allocation $= (w_i - W_i)(B_i - B)$

Selection + Interaction $= W_i(R_i - B_i) + (w_i - W_i)(R_i - B_i)$

We calculate the attribution effects for the small-cap value equities:

Allocation $= (20\% - 25\%)[1.52 - (-0.03)] = -0.08$

Selection + Interaction $= [(25\%)(2.39 - 1.52)] + [(20\% - 25\%)(2.39 - 1.52)]$

$= 0.17$

Using the same approach for large-cap value equities and large-cap growth equities yields the results shown in Exhibit 12. (Note that the numbers are rounded to two decimal places and may not sum because of this rounding.)

**Exhibit 12: Segment-Level Return Attribution**

| Return Attribution (Segment Level) | Fund Weight | Selection + Interaction | Allocation | Total |
|---|---|---|---|---|
| Total | 100% | 1.05 | −0.07 | 0.98 |
| Value Portfolio Manager | 78% | 0.63 | −0.10 | 0.53 |
| *Small-cap value equities* | *20%* | *0.17* | *−0.08* | *0.10* |
| *Large-cap value equities* | *58%* | *0.46* | *−0.02* | *0.44* |

| Return Attribution (Segment Level) | Fund Weight | Selection + Interaction | Allocation | Total |
|---|---|---|---|---|
| Growth Portfolio Manager | 22% | 0.42 | 0.03 | 0.45 |
| *Large-cap growth equities* | *22%* | *0.42* | *0.03* | *0.45* |

In Exhibit 12, the attribution results in italics are calculated at the segment level. The attribution results at the next level above, the Value Portfolio Manager and Growth Portfolio Manager, are sums of the segment-level results. For example, the allocation effect for the Value Portfolio Manager is equal to the sum of the small-cap and large-cap segments: −0.08 + −0.02 = −0.10.

Summing up the segment-level results for each manager, we reach the following conclusions:

- The total outperformance at the overall fund level of 98 bps is almost entirely the result of positive security selection decisions (105 bps in total).
- The decision of the Value Portfolio Manager to underweight small cap in favor of large cap detracted from total fund performance because the small-cap value benchmark outperformed the total benchmark (1.52% versus −0.03%), leading to an allocation effect of −0.10.
- The large-cap value benchmark underperformed the total benchmark (−1.08% versus −0.03%). Because the portfolio was underweight large-cap value, this led to a positive allocation effect of 0.03.
- In total, allocation decisions contributed −7 bps.

Note that in using the total fund benchmark in this analysis, we are evaluating the *impact* of the Value Portfolio Manager's decision on the performance of the total fund.

We can extend the attribution analysis down another level and examine the investment manager's results relative to the investment process. The manager may have an investment process that specifically targets country allocations.[3] At this level of analysis, the same allocation formula will calculate the impact of country allocation decisions within the manager's portfolio and the selection formula will calculate the impact of selection decisions within each country.

If the portfolio manager has an investment process that specifically targets sector allocations within each country, the allocation formula can be used to calculate the impact of sector selection decisions within countries and the selection decisions within sectors.

Whatever the level of analysis, the return attribution must reflect the decision-making process of the portfolio manager. For example, a eurozone investment strategy might use a country allocation process with security selection within each country or a sector allocation process with security selection within each industrial sector. Exhibit 13 and Exhibit 14 illustrate the different results that might be reached from an analysis based on the investment process. In each case, an arithmetic Brinson approach has been used.

**Exhibit 13: Country Allocation**

| | Portfolio Weight | Benchmark Weight | Portfolio Return | Benchmark Return | Allocation | Selection + Interaction |
|---|---|---|---|---|---|---|
| France | 20% | 30% | 8.0% | 6.0% | 0.15% | 0.40% |
| Germany | 20% | 35% | 8.0% | 7.0% | 0.07% | 0.20% |

3 For some portfolios, the next level may be asset classes (as an example).

| | Portfolio Weight | Benchmark Weight | Portfolio Return | Benchmark Return | Allocation | Selection + Interaction |
|---|---|---|---|---|---|---|
| Holland | 20% | 10% | 9.0% | 15.0% | 0.76% | −1.20% |
| Italy | 30% | 15% | 10.0% | 9.0% | 0.23% | 0.30% |
| Spain | 10% | 10% | 3.0% | 3.5% | 0.00% | −0.05% |
| **Total** | **100%** | **100%** | **8.3%** | **7.45%** | **1.20%** | **−0.35%** |

### Exhibit 14: Industry Sector Allocation

| | Portfolio Weight | Benchmark Weight | Portfolio Return | Benchmark Return | Allocation | Selection + Interaction |
|---|---|---|---|---|---|---|
| Energy | 25% | 30% | 18.0% | 12.0% | −0.23% | 1.50% |
| Health care | 30% | 20% | −3.0% | −6.0% | −1.35% | 0.90% |
| Financial | 20% | 30% | 10.0% | 12.0% | −0.46% | −0.40% |
| Transportation | 10% | 15% | 12.0% | 8.0% | −0.03% | 0.40% |
| Metals and mining | 15% | 5% | 10.0% | 5.0% | −0.25% | 0.75% |
| **Total** | **100%** | **100%** | **8.3%** | **7.45%** | **−2.30%** | **3.15%** |

Exhibit 13 suggests that the manager demonstrated good country allocation but negative security selection within countries, whereas Exhibit 14 suggests that the manager demonstrated poor sector allocation but strongly positive security selection within industrial sectors. This apparent "contradiction" illustrates the importance of designing an attribution approach around the investment decision-making process used by the manager.

Drilling down to the lowest level, the same allocation and selection formulas can be used to calculate the contribution of individual security decisions within sectors. For example, the allocation formula can be used to determine the impact of over- or underweighting individual securities, whereas the selection formula can be used to determine the contribution arising from a difference in the return of a security in the portfolio and the return of the same security in the benchmark. If the pricing sources used in the portfolio and the benchmark are identical, then any difference in return will be caused by transaction activity. Transaction activity because of trading expenses and bid–offer spreads will negatively affect returns, but occasionally because of timing, the portfolio manager may be able to trade at advantageous prices during the day and recover all the transaction costs by the end of the day, resulting in a positive effect.

Exhibit 15 shows the security-level return attribution effects for a small portfolio of oil stocks against a customized benchmark consisting of the same oil stocks. This approach would be used by a pure stock picker, the only decisions in the portfolio being individual stock weighting and timing decisions.

### Exhibit 15: Security-Level Return Attribution Effects of Pure Stock Picker

| | Portfolio Weight | Benchmark Weight | Portfolio Return | Benchmark Return | Allocation | Transaction Costs and Timing Effects |
|---|---|---|---|---|---|---|
| Chevron | 24% | 30% | 10% | 10% | −0.18% | 0.00% |
| ConocoPhillips | 21% | 25% | 8% | 8% | −0.04% | 0.00% |
| ExxonMobil | 41% | 35% | 5% | 6% | −0.06% | −0.41% |

| | Portfolio Weight | Benchmark Weight | Portfolio Return | Benchmark Return | Allocation | Transaction Costs and Timing Effects |
|---|---|---|---|---|---|---|
| Marathon Oil | 6% | 5% | 4% | 4% | −0.03% | 0.00% |
| Newfield Expl. | 8% | 5% | −5% | −5% | −0.36% | 0.00% |
| Total | 100% | 100% | 5.97% | 7.05% | −0.67% | −0.41% |

The arithmetic allocation effects of each security using the Brinson approach are as follows:

| Chevron | $(24\% - 30\%) \times (10\% - 7.05\%) = -0.18\%$ |
|---|---|
| ConocoPhillips | $(21\% - 25\%) \times (8.0\% - 7.05\%) = -0.04\%$ |
| ExxonMobil | $(41\% - 35\%) \times (6.0\% - 7.05\%) = -0.06\%$ |
| Marathon Oil | $(6\% - 5\%) \times (4.0\% - 7.05\%) = -0.03\%$ |
| Newfield Exploration | $(8\% - 5\%) \times (-5.0\% - 7.05\%) = -0.36\%$ |

Allocation in this context measures the value added from individual security selection. Transactions occur for only one security during the period—ExxonMobil. Therefore, the only selection effects (transaction costs and timing) occur for this security. The calculation is as follows:

| ExxonMobil | $41\% \times (5.0\% - 6.0\%) = -0.41\%$ |
|---|---|

### EXAMPLE 8

## Macro Attribution

1. AAA Asset Management runs a fixed-income fund of funds. The fund's benchmark is a blended benchmark comprising 80% Bloomberg Barclays Global Aggregate Index and 20% Bloomberg Barclays Global Treasury Index (both in US dollars, unhedged). Two internal investment teams have been selected to manage the fund's assets. The allocations to the two products are determined by the firm's chief fixed-income strategist. The fund has under-performed its benchmark in each of the last three years. You are a member of the board of directors, which is meeting to determine what action should be taken. Based solely on the data in the table below, which of the following courses of action would you recommend? Justify your response.

   A. Terminate the manager of Product A.

   B. Terminate the manager of Product B.

   C. Remove the chief fixed-income strategist as manager of the fund of funds.

| | Fund-of-Funds Return | | | |
|---|---|---|---|---|
| | Year 1 | Year 2 | Year 3 | Cumulative Return |
| Total Fund | 3.72% | −3.00% | −0.13% | 0.47% |
| *Benchmark:* | 3.84% | −2.94% | 0.07% | 0.86% |

| | Product Returns | | | | | |
|---|---|---|---|---|---|---|
| | Year 1 | | Year 2 | | Year 3 | |
| | Weight | Return | Weight | Return | Weight | Return |
| Product A | 0.7 | 4.45% | 0.75 | −2.50% | 0.8 | −0.10% | 1.74% |
| *Benchmark: Bloomberg Barclays Global Aggregate* | | 4.32% | | −2.60% | | 0.29% | 1.90% |
| Product B | 0.3 | 2.00% | 0.25 | −4.50% | 0.2 | −0.25% | −2.83% |
| *Benchmark: Bloomberg Barclays Global Treasury* | | 1.93% | | −4.30% | | −0.79% | −3.22% |

## Solution:

C is correct. Based solely on the information provided, the chief fixed-income strategist's allocation decision was the main driver of the fund's underperformance. Product A modestly underperformed its benchmark over the three-year period (−16 bps). Product B outperformed its benchmark (+39 bps). The strategist's allocation decisions were strongly negative in Years 1 and 2, when he overweighted the Treasury allocation and the Treasury index underperformed the aggregate fund benchmark. The results of the attribution analysis are shown below:

**AAA Asset Management Fixed-Income Fund-of-Funds Attribution Analysis**

| | Year 1 | | Year 2 | | Year 3 | |
|---|---|---|---|---|---|---|
| | Allocation | Selection | Allocation | Selection | Allocation | Selection |
| Product A | −0.05% | 0.10% | −0.02% | 0.08% | 0.00% | −0.31% |
| Product B | −0.19% | 0.01% | −0.07% | −0.04% | 0.00% | 0.11% |
| Total | −0.24% | 0.12% | −0.09% | 0.04% | 0.00% | −0.20% |

# ASSET- AND LIABILITY-BASED BENCHMARKS

**7**

- [ ] discuss uses of liability-based benchmarks
- [ ] describe types of asset-based benchmarks

An investment benchmark is typically a collection of securities that represents the pool of assets available to the portfolio manager. For example, an investor in Japanese small-cap stocks might have a benchmark consisting of a broad portfolio of small-cap Japanese equities. A benchmark should reflect the investment process and the constraints that govern the construction of the portfolio. If the benchmark does not reflect the investment process, then the evaluation and analysis that flow from the comparison with the benchmark are flawed.

Benchmarks communicate information about the set of assets that may be considered for investment and the investment discipline. They provide investment managers with a guidepost for acceptable levels of risk and return and can be a powerful influence on investment decision making.

In investment practice, we use benchmarks as

- reference points for segments of the sponsor's portfolio,
- communication of instructions to the manager,
- communication with consultants and oversight groups (e.g., a board of directors),
- identification and evaluation of the current portfolio's risk exposures,
- interpretations of past performance and performance attribution,
- manager selection and appraisal,
- marketing of investment products, and
- demonstrations of compliance with regulations, laws, or standards.

Benchmarks help analysts measure the effectiveness of a manager's decisions to depart from benchmark weights.

When considering benchmarks, we need to understand the differences between a "benchmark" and a "market index." A market index represents the performance of a specific security market, market segment, or asset class. For example, the FTSE 100 Index is constructed to represent the broad performance of large-cap UK equities. The S&P US Aggregate Bond Index is designed to measure the performance of publicly issued US dollar-denominated investment-grade debt. The constituents of these indexes are selected for their appropriateness in representing the target market, market segment, or asset class.

A market index may be considered for use as a benchmark or a comparison point for an investment manager. Consider the case of passive managers, who typically invest in portfolios designed to closely track the performance of market indexes. For example, the iShares Core S&P 500 ETF seeks investment results, before fees and expenses, that correspond to the price and yield performance of US large-cap stocks as represented by the S&P 500 Index. Because the investment objective of the iShares Core S&P 500 ETF is to track the performance of the S&P 500, the S&P 500 is the appropriate benchmark for the iShares Core S&P 500 ETF.

However, the most appropriate benchmark for an investment manager is not necessarily a market index. Many active managers follow specific investment disciplines that cannot be adequately described by a security market index. For example, market-neutral long–short managers typically have absolute return benchmarks—a specific minimum rate of return or a specified spread over a risk-free rate. Benchmarks must be suitable to the specific needs of the asset owner and any investment manager hired to manage money; market indexes are typically meant to serve the general public's purposes and to have broad appeal. Nonetheless, indexes can sometimes serve as valid benchmarks.

Another category of benchmarks is liability-based benchmarks, which focus on the cash flows that the asset must generate. Liability-based benchmarks are most often used when the assets are required to pay a specific future liability (e.g., as in a defined benefit pension plan). They allow the asset owner to track the fund's progress toward fully funded status (assets greater than or equal to liabilities) or, if fully funded, to track the performance of assets relative to the changes in liabilities. The performance relative to liabilities is important because it would be possible for the portfolio to outperform a market index but still not meet its liabilities. Furthermore, a market-value-weighted index would likely be an inappropriate benchmark because the liability often has a targeted asset allocation and risk exposures that are different from those of the index.

As an example, consider the fixed-income portion of a pension fund. A cap-weighted index is typically not a suitable benchmark because the duration of the index is usually shorter than the duration of most pension plans' liabilities. Furthermore, many fixed-income indexes are heavily weighted toward corporate bonds in the short maturities, which may represent a greater degree of credit risk than the plan desires. As an alternative, a well-diversified portfolio of individual bonds that minimizes idiosyncratic risk could be used as the benchmark. A more recent innovation is liability-driven investment (LDI) indexes. The Bloomberg Barclays LDI Index Series is a series of six investible indexes designed specifically for portfolios intended to hedge pension liabilities. However, they may not describe a plan's liability structure as accurately as a benchmark constructed specifically for the plan.

To best determine how a liability-based benchmark should be constructed, the manager first needs to understand the nature of the plan's liabilities and the plan's projected future cash flows. Although each plan will have its own unique characteristics, the following plan features will influence the structure of the liability:

- the average number of years to retirement in the workforce,
- the percentage of the workforce that is retired,
- the average participant life expectancy,
- whether the benefits are indexed to inflation,
- whether the plan offers an early retirement option,
- whether the sponsor could increase its plan contributions (e.g., whether the sponsor is profitable and diversified),
- the correlation between plan assets and the sponsoring company's operating assets (a lower correlation is desired so that the sponsor can make contributions when the plan requires funds), and
- whether the plan is a going concern (e.g., plans will eventually terminate if the sponsor has exited its business).

These characteristics influence the composition of the pension plan portfolio and hence its liability-based benchmark. Nominal bonds, real return bonds, and common shares are the assets most commonly found in liability-driven portfolios. The allocation to each asset class is driven by the proportion of accrued versus future obligations, whether the benefits are inflation indexed, and whether the plan is growing. A younger workforce means that more is allocated to equities. Greater inflation indexing of the benefits would imply more inflation-indexed bonds. If the fund's managers outperform the benchmark constructed according to these principles, the pension obligations should be met. Risk and noise that cannot be modeled in the benchmark may require additional future contributions.

### EXAMPLE 9

## Liability-Based Benchmarks

1. Which of the following portfolios is most likely to use a liability-based benchmark?

    **A.** A portfolio managed for a private client with a goal of capital appreciation

    **B.** An intermediate-duration fixed-income portfolio managed for a defined benefit pension fund

    **C.** The total portfolio for a defined benefit pension fund with an asset allocation of 80% fixed income/20% equity

### Solution:

C is correct. A liability-based benchmark is most likely to be used for the total pension fund portfolio as the plan sponsor tracks its funded status.

2. Which of the following most accurately describes a liability-based benchmark?

    **A.** It focuses on the cash flows that the benchmarked asset must generate.

    **B.** It represents the performance of a specific security market, market segment, or asset class.

    **C.** It is a collection of securities that represents the pool of assets available to the portfolio manager.

### Solution:

A is correct. A liability-based benchmark is constructed according to the cash flows that the benchmarked asset must generate.

## Asset-Based Benchmarks

Benchmarks are an important part of the investment process for both institutional and private wealth clients. In the following discussion, we introduce the types of benchmarks based on the discussion in Bailey, Richards, and Tierney (2007). The seven types of benchmarks introduced in this section are

- absolute (including target) return benchmarks,
- broad market indexes,
- style indexes,
- factor-model-based benchmarks,
- returns-based (Sharpe style analysis) benchmarks,
- manager universes (peer groups), and
- custom security-based (strategy) benchmarks.

An **absolute return benchmark** is a minimum target return that the manager is expected to beat. The return may be a stated minimum (e.g., 9%), stated as a spread above a market index (e.g., the Euro Interbank Offered Rate + 4%), or determined from actuarial assumptions. An example of an absolute return benchmark is 20% per annum return for a private equity investment. Market-neutral long–short equity funds often have absolute return benchmarks. Such funds consist of long and short positions in perceived undervalued and overvalued equities. Overall, the portfolio is expected to be insensitive to broad equity market movements (i.e., market neutral with a market beta of zero). Therefore, market-neutral fund benchmarks may be specified as a three-month Treasury bill return; the investment objective is often to outperform the benchmark consistently by a given number of basis points.

Broad market indexes are measures of broad asset class performance, such as the JP Morgan Emerging Market Bond Index (EMBI) for emerging market bonds or the MSCI World Index for global developed market equities. Broad market indexes are well known, readily available, and easily understood. The performance of broad market indexes is widely reported in the popular media.

Market indexes have also been more narrowly defined to represent investment styles within asset classes, resulting in style indexes. An **investment style** is a natural grouping of investment disciplines that has some predictive power in explaining the future dispersion of returns across portfolios.[4] In the late 1970s, researchers found that stock valuation (e.g., the price-to-earnings ratio) and market capitalization explained much of stock return variation. In response, many index providers created various style versions of their broad market indexes (e.g., the Russell 2000 Value and Russell 1000 Growth Indexes).

**Factor-model-based benchmarks** can be constructed to more closely capture the investment decision-making process. Building a factor model identifies the relative explanatory powers of each factor in the portfolio return. Examples of factors include broad market index returns, industry exposure, and financial leverage. To determine the factor sensitivities, the portfolio's return is regressed against the factors believed to influence returns. The general form of a factor model is:

$$R_p = a_p + b_1 F_1 + b_2 F_2 \dots b_k F_k + \varepsilon_p \tag{12}$$

where

$R_p$ = the portfolio's periodic return

$a_p$ = the "zero-factor" term, which is the expected portfolio return if all factor sensitivities are zero

$b_k$ = the sensitivity of portfolio returns to the factor return

$F_k$ = systematic factors responsible for asset returns

$\varepsilon_p$ = residual return due to nonsystematic factors

The sensitivities ($b_k$) are then used to predict the return the portfolio should provide for given values of the systematic-risk factors. Earlier, we discussed the four-factor Carhart model, but any key element of the investment process can be considered for inclusion in a factor model. As an example, if the investment manager believes that interest rates are inversely related to security prices, then the model can incorporate an interest rate factor. If interest rates unexpectedly rise, then security returns can be expected to fall by an amount determined by the security's sensitivity ($b_k$) to interest rate changes.

**Returns-based benchmarks** (Sharpe style analysis) are like factor-model-based benchmarks in that portfolio returns are related to a set of factors that explain portfolio returns. With returns-based benchmarks, however, the factors are the returns for various style indexes (e.g., small-cap value, small-cap growth, large-cap value, and large-cap growth). The style analysis produces a benchmark of the weighted average of these asset class indexes that best explains or tracks the portfolio's returns. Unlike the investment-style indexes previously discussed, returns-based benchmarks *view style on a continuum*. For example, a portfolio may be characterized as 60% small-cap

---

4 Brown and Goetzmann (1997).

value and 40% small-cap growth. To create a returns-based benchmark using Sharpe style analysis, we use an optimization procedure to force the portfolio's sensitivities (analogous to the $b_k$'s in factor-model-based benchmarks) to be non-negative and sum to 1.

A **manager universe**, or **manager peer group**, is a broad group of managers with similar investment disciplines. Although not a benchmark, per se, a manager universe allows investors to make comparisons with the performance of other managers following similar investment disciplines. Managers are typically expected to beat the universe's median return. Manager universes are typically formed by asset class and the investment approach within that class.

Peer groups as benchmarks suffer from some significant weaknesses. Although managers within a peer group may all nominally be classified as "large-cap value" or "small-cap growth," for example, they may not truly be substitutable for one another. Some may have tilts or constraints that create an investment product very different from that of the median manager. A manager's ranking within the peer group might change considerably with very small changes in performance, often in response to factors outside of the manager's control: A change in the ranking may be driven not by something he did but by the actions of others in the peer group (e.g., other managers in the peer group may have chosen to overweight a "hot" sector, whereas the target manager's investment discipline constrains him from making a similar bet).

Lastly, **custom security-based benchmarks** are built to more precisely reflect the investment discipline of an investment manager. Such benchmarks are developed through discussions with the manager and an analysis of past portfolio exposures. After identifying the manager's investment process, the benchmark is constructed by selecting securities and weightings consistent with that process and client restrictions. If an allocation to cash is a key component of the investment process, an appropriate cash weight will be incorporated into the benchmark. The benchmark is rebalanced on a periodic basis to ensure that it stays consistent with the manager's investment practice. Custom security-based benchmarks are also referred to as *strategy benchmarks* because they should reflect the manager's strategy. Custom security-based benchmarks are particularly appropriate when the manager's strategy cannot be closely matched to a broad market index or style index. These benchmarks are costly to calculate and maintain.

## 8    BENCHMARK SELECTION

☐    discuss tests of benchmark quality

☐    describe the impact of benchmark misspecification on attribution and appraisal analysis

The choice of benchmark often has a significant effect on the assessment of manager performance. Investment managers should be compared only with benchmarks that reflect the universe of securities available to them. A valid benchmark must satisfy certain criteria. We examine the characteristics of a valid benchmark by using the definitive list from Bailey and Tierney (1998).

- *Unambiguous*—The individual securities and their weights in a benchmark should be clearly identifiable. For example, we should be able to identify whether Nestlé is included in a global equity benchmark and its weight.

- *Investable*—It must be possible to replicate and hold the benchmark to earn its return (at least gross of expenses). The sponsor should have the option of moving assets from active management to a passive benchmark. If the benchmark is not investable, it is not a viable investment alternative.

- *Measurable*—It must be possible to measure the benchmark's return on a reasonably frequent and timely basis.

- *Appropriate*—The benchmark must be consistent with the manager's investment style or area of expertise.

- *Reflective of current investment opinions*—The manager should be familiar with the securities that constitute the benchmark and their factor exposures. Managers should be able to develop an opinion regarding their attractiveness as investments; they should not be given a mandate of obscure securities.

- *Specified in advance*—The benchmark must be constructed prior to the evaluation period so that the manager is not judged against benchmarks created after the fact.

- *Accountable*—The manager should accept ownership of the benchmark and its securities and be willing to be held accountable to the benchmark. The benchmark should be fully consistent with the manager's investment process, and the manager should be able to demonstrate the validity of his or her benchmark. Through acceptance of the benchmark, the sponsor assumes responsibility for any discrepancies between the targeted portfolio for the fund and the benchmark. The manager becomes responsible for differences between the benchmark and her performance.

The properties outlined by Bailey and Tierney help ensure that a benchmark will serve as a valid instrument for the purposes of evaluating the manager's performance. Although these qualities for a desirable benchmark may seem straightforward, we will show later that many commonly used benchmarks do not incorporate them.

---

**EXAMPLE 10**

## Benchmarks

1. You have hired a bond manager to run an intermediate-duration government fixed-income portfolio. Which type of benchmark is most suitable for this portfolio?

    **A.** A broad market index

    **B.** A liability-based benchmark

    **C.** A factor-model-based benchmark

### Solution:

A is correct. A broad market index is a suitable benchmark for a government bond portfolio provided the maturity and duration characteristics of the benchmark align with those of the investment mandate.

---

2. You have hired a top-down quantitative equity manager who has built a proprietary process based on timing the fund's exposures to systematic risks. Which type of benchmark is most suitable for this portfolio?

    **A.** A broad market index

    **B.** A liability-based benchmark

**C.** A factor-model-based benchmark

**Solution:**

C is correct. Factors represent systematic risks. The manager's approach attempts to create alpha by timing the portfolio's exposure to factors. A factor-model-based benchmark can be constructed to represent the manager's investment approach.

3. You are on the board of a pension fund that is seeking to close the gap between its assets and its liabilities. What is the most appropriate benchmark against which to measure the performance of the plan's outsourced chief investment officer?

**A.** A broad market index

**B.** A liability-based benchmark

**C.** A factor-model-based benchmark

**Solution:**

B is correct. The primary investment objective of the pension portfolio is to close the gap between assets and liabilities. The performance of the pension fund's manager should be evaluated relative to this objective.

4. You are a portfolio manager at JEMstone Capital. Your firm has been hired to run a global small-cap developed market equity portfolio. The agreement with the client sets a minimum market cap of US$500 million and a liquidity constraint that states that a portfolio holding is capped at 5 times its average daily liquidity over the past 12 months. Most portfolios managed by the firm are managed without constraint against the MSCI ACWI Small Cap Index, which has an average market cap of approximately $1.2 billion and a median market cap of approximately $650 million. A stock is eligible for inclusion in the index if the shares traded over the prior three months are equal to at least 20% of the security's free-float-adjusted market capitalization.[5] Your team is discussing the suitability of the MSCI ACWI Small Cap Index for this portfolio. Discuss the validity of this benchmark using the Richards and Tierney framework.

**Solution:**

- The benchmark meets the criteria of *unambiguous*. The individual securities and their weights are clearly identifiable.
- The benchmark most likely meets the criteria of *investable*. The shares in the index are freely tradeable.
- The benchmark meets the criteria of *measurable*. Index returns are published daily.
- The benchmark *does not* meet the criteria of *appropriate*. The liquidity and capitalization constraints imposed by the client are not consistent with the manner in which the manager runs other portfolios managed by the firm.

---

5 This is a very abbreviated representation of the liquidity constraint used in the construction of the MSCI indexes. For a more complete description of the liquidity requirements, refer to "MSCI Global Investable Market Indexes Methodology": www.msci.com/eqb/methodology/meth_docs/MSCI_GIMIMethodology_Nov2018.pdf (accessed 5 December 2019).

- The benchmark meets the criteria of *reflective of current investment opinions.* The benchmark was selected by the manager and is presumed to be representative of the manager's investment process.

- The benchmark meets the criteria of *specified in advance.* The benchmark is not created after the fact.

- The manager may choose to be *accountable* to this index if the liquidity and capitalization constraints are not expected to interfere with the ability to execute the investment strategy. The client should be made aware of the discrepancies between the portfolio constraints and the benchmark.

## Evaluating Benchmark Quality: Analysis Based on a Decomposition of Portfolio Holdings and Returns

Once a benchmark is constructed, we can evaluate its quality using tests. To understand these tests, it helps to first decompose the benchmark's returns. Using the decomposition from Bailey et al. (2007), we can first state the identity where a portfolio's return (P) is equal to itself:

$$P = P \tag{13}$$

Then, add an appropriate benchmark (B) to, and subtract this benchmark from, the right-hand side of the equation:

$$P = B + (P - B) \tag{14}$$

The term P − B is the result of the manager's active management decisions, which we denote as A. Thus, we have

$$P = B + A \tag{15}$$

From Equations 13–15, we see that the portfolio return is a function of the benchmark and the manager's active decisions.

Next, add the market index return (M) to and subtract it from the right-hand side of the equation:

$$P = M + (B - M) + A \tag{16}$$

The difference between the benchmark return and the market index (B − M) is the manager's style return, which we denote as S:

$$P = M + S + A \tag{17}$$

Equation 17 states that the portfolio return (P) is a result of the market index return (M), a style return (S), and the active management return (A).

If the manager's portfolio is a broad market index where S = 0 and A = 0, then the portfolio earns the broad market return: P = M.

If the benchmark is a broad market index, then S is assumed to be zero and the prediction is that the manager earns the market return and a return to active management: P = M + A. However, if the benchmark is a broad market index and the manager *does* have style differences from the benchmark, the analysis using the broad market benchmark is incorrect. In this case, any style return (S) will be lumped together with the measured active management component (A), such that an analysis of a manager's true added value will be obscured.

We can use these benchmark building blocks to further search for systematic biases between the active management return and the style return, identified through correlation. For instance, if we measure the correlation between active management return, A = (P − B), and style return, S = (B − M), we can identify whether the manager's active selection decisions align with the style currently favored by the market. A good benchmark should not reflect these systematic biases, where the correlation between A and S should not be statistically different from zero. Likewise, we define the difference between the portfolio and the broad market index as E = (P − M). When a manager's style (S) is in (out of) favor relative to the market, we expect both the benchmark and the account to outperform (underperform) the market. Therefore, a good benchmark will have a statistically significant positive correlation coefficient between S and E.

---

### EXAMPLE 11

## Decomposition of Portfolio Return

---

1. Assume that the Courtland account has a return of −5.3% in a given month, during which the portfolio benchmark has a return of −5.5% and the market index has a return of −2.8%.

   A. Calculate the Courtland account's return due to the manager's style.

   B. Calculate the Courtland account's return due to active management.

### Solution:

   A. The return due to style is S = B − M = −5.5% − (−2.8%) = −2.7%.

   B. The return due to active management is A = P − B = −5.3% − (−5.5%) = 0.2%.

---

2. Assume that Mr. Kuti's account has a return of 5.6% in a given month, during which the portfolio benchmark has a return of 5.1% and a market index has a return of 3.2%.

   A. Calculate the return due to the manager's style for Mr. Kuti's account.

   B. Calculate the return due to active management for Mr. Kuti's account.

### Solution:

   A. The return due to style is S = B − M = 5.1% − 3.2% = 1.9%.

   B. The return due to active management is A = P − B = 5.6% − 5.1% = 0.5%.

---

3. An actively managed mid-cap value equity portfolio has a return of 9.24%. The portfolio is benchmarked to a mid-cap value index that has a return of 7.85%. A broad equity market index has a return of 8.92%. Calculate the return due to the portfolio manager's style.

### Solution:

   The return due to style is the style-specific benchmark return of 7.85% minus the broad market return of 8.92%: −1.07%.

---

4. A US large-cap value portfolio run by Anderson Investment Management returned 18.9% during the first three quarters of 2019. During the same time period, a US large-cap value index had a return of 21.7% and a broad US equity index returned 25.2%.

   A. Calculate the return due to style.

   B. Calculate the return due to active management.

> **C.** Using your answers to A and B, discuss Anderson's performance rela-
> tive to the benchmark and relative to the market.
>
> **Solution:**
>
> **A.** The return due to style is the difference between the benchmark and
> the market index, or S = (B − M) = (21.7% − 25.2%) = −3.5%.
>
> **B.** The return due to active management is the difference between the
> portfolio and the benchmark, or A = (P − B) = (18.9% − 21.7%) =
> −2.8%.
>
> **C.** Anderson's underperformance relative to the broad US equity index is
> partly a function of style and partly a function of the manager's weak
> performance within the style. Given that the US large-cap value index
> underperformed the US market index by 3.5%, we can infer that large-
> cap value was out of favor during the period measured. Provided the
> US large-cap value index is an appropriate benchmark for Anderson,
> the manager's underperformance bears further investigation. The cli-
> ent would want to understand the specific drivers of the underperfor-
> mance and relate those decisions to the manager's stated investment
> process.

## Importance of Choosing the Correct Benchmark

As we have described, performance evaluation and attribution require appropriate
benchmarks. When benchmarks are misspecified, subsequent performance measurement will be incorrect; both the attribution and the appraisal analyses will be useless.

For example, consider a manager who invests in Japanese stocks. The sponsor uses
the MSCI Pacific Index to evaluate the manager. Japanese stocks constitute most of
the MSCI Pacific, but the index also includes four other developed markets (Australia,
New Zealand, Hong Kong SAR, and Singapore). Thus, the MSCI Japan Index more
closely represents the manager's normal portfolio. The returns were as follows:

- Manager return: 18.0%

- MSCI Pacific (investor's benchmark) return: 20.0%

- MSCI Japan (normal portfolio) return: 9.0%

Although the manager *underperformed* the investor's benchmark (18.0% for the
manager versus 20.0% for the MSCI Pacific), the manager *outperformed* when correctly
benchmarked against the normal portfolio (18.0% for the manager versus 9.0% for the
normal portfolio). In summary,

- True Active Return = Mgr Return − Normal Portfolio Return = 18.0 − 9.0 =
  9.0%

- Investor (Mismeasured) Active Return = Mgr Return − Investor Benchmark
  return = (Mgr Return - Normal portfolio Return) + (Normal Portfolio
  Return - Investor Benchmark return) = True Active Return + Misfit Active
  Return = 18.0 − 20.0 = -9.0 + (−11.0) = −2.0%

Measuring the manager's results against the normal portfolio instead of the investor's benchmark more accurately evaluates the manager's performance. The manager's
negative "true" active return indicates that the manager outperformed the normal
portfolio. Fundamentally, any further performance attribution against the investor's
benchmark will also be useless. By using the incorrect benchmark, the attribution
would attempt to explain an underperformance, rather than the true active return,
which contributed positively to the investor's return.

Peer group benchmarking is particularly susceptible to selection problems. For example, practitioners must select the appropriate peers without suggesting to the portfolio managers that median peer group performance is the target. Peer group benchmarks provide an incentive not to underperform the peer group median, often leading to herding around the median return. As a result, the investment decisions of the fund manager can be biased by the structure of the benchmarks chosen.

Sometimes, benchmarks are chosen for the wrong reasons. Underperforming managers have been known to change benchmarks to improve their measured excess return, which is both inappropriate and unethical.

Benchmark misspecification can lead to mismeasurement of the value added by the portfolio managers. A "normal portfolio" or "normal benchmark" is the portfolio that most closely represents the manager's typical positions in his investment universe. The manager's "true" active return is equal to his return minus his normal portfolio return.

Most investors, however, tend to use a broad market benchmark for manager evaluation. The manager's active return is thus measured as the manager's return minus the investor's benchmark return. There is a mismatch between the broad market benchmark and the manager's "normal" portfolio or benchmark; this is not the manager's "true" active return but is more appropriately termed the "misfit active return" (see, e.g., Gastineau, Olma, and Zielinski 2007). Using a broad market index typically misses the manager's style (i.e., creates style bias). This decomposition is useful for understanding the impact of a misspecified benchmark on performance appraisal.

For example, consider a manager who invests in US value stocks. The sponsor uses the broad Russell 3000 equity index (the "investor's benchmark") to evaluate the manager. However, the manager's normal portfolio is better represented by his or her universe of value stocks. In this example, the manager returns 15%, the Russell 3000 (the investor's benchmark) return is 10%, and the manager's normal portfolio return is 18%. Although the manager has outperformed the investor's benchmark (15% versus 10%), the manager has underperformed when correctly benchmarked against the normal portfolio (15% versus 18%).

# 9    BENCHMARKING ALTERNATIVE INVESTMENTS

☐ | describe problems that arise in benchmarking alternative investments

Performance evaluation for alternative asset classes presents many challenges. The selection of an appropriate benchmark is stymied by the lack of high-quality, investible market indexes, the frequent use of leverage in many strategies, the limited liquidity and lack of readily available market values for many underlying assets, and the use of internal rates of return rather than time-weighted rates of return.

In the following sections addressing each of the major alternative asset classes, we will consider how these challenges affect performance evaluation.

## Benchmarking Hedge Fund Investments

Hedge funds do not represent an asset class, such as equities or fixed income. Rather, hedge funds encompass a broad range of possible strategies designed to exploit market inefficiencies. Hedge funds may have an unlimited investment universe, vary substantially from one to another, and can vary their asset allocations over time.

Hedge funds also use leverage, sell assets short, take positions in derivatives, and may be opportunistic in their choice of strategy. These characteristics make it difficult to create a single standard against which hedge funds should be judged.

Some hedge funds lever many times their capital base, which increases their expected return and risk. Short positions and derivatives used in long–short strategies can increase return or reduce risk. A manager's use of style, leverage, short positions, and derivatives may change over time. Hedge funds also typically lack transparency, are difficult to monitor, and are often illiquid.

These characteristics of hedge funds make it clear that broad market indexes are unsuitable as hedge fund benchmarks.

The risk-free rate (e.g., Treasury yield) plus a spread (e.g., 3%–6%) is sometimes advocated as a hedge fund benchmark for arbitrage-based hedge fund strategies. The argument for using the risk-free rate is that investors desire a positive return and that arbitrage strategies are risk free, with the spread reflecting the active management return and management costs.

However, most funds, even those that target market-neutral strategies, are not completely free of systematic risk, and the use of leverage could magnify that systematic risk. In this case, the spread relative to the risk-free rate should be adjusted upward.

Both broad market indexes and the risk-free rate will be weakly correlated or uncorrelated with hedge fund returns, thus failing the benchmark quality test of Bailey et al. (2007) that states that portfolio and benchmark factor sensitivities should be similar.

Because of the shortcomings of broad market indexes and the risk-free rate, hedge fund manager universes from such providers as CSFB/Tremont are often used as hedge fund benchmarks. Hedge fund peer universes are subject to a number of limitations:

1. The risk and return characteristics of a strategy peer group is unlikely to be representative of the approach taken by a single fund.

2. Hedge fund peer groups suffer from survivorship and backfill bias. Backfill bias occurs when the index provider adds a manager to the index and imports the manager's entire return history.

3. Hedge fund performance data are often self-reported and typically not confirmed by the index provider. A fund's reported net asset value may be a managed value. Even if the manager has no intention to misreport the data, hedge funds hold illiquid assets that require some subjectivity in pricing. If the previous period's price is used as the current price or an appraisal is used, then the data will be smoothed. The presence of stale pricing will result in downward-biased standard deviations and temporal instability in correlations, with hedge funds potentially given larger portfolio allocations as a result.

## Benchmarking Real Estate Investments

There are numerous private real estate indexes offered by industry associations, large and small index providers, investment consultants, and others who collect real estate data. There are indexes and sub-indexes for nearly all the major developed countries, major sectors, investment styles, and structures (open-end and closed-end funds). Choosing the appropriate real estate benchmark requires careful consideration and an understanding of the limitations of such benchmarks—and their relevance to the investment strategy under evaluation. The following are some limitations of the available real estate benchmarks:

1. The benchmarks are based on a subset of the real estate opportunity set and, therefore, are not fully representative of the asset class.

2.  Index performance is likely to be highly correlated with the returns of the largest fund data contributors.

3.  Benchmark returns are based on manager-reported performance and may be inherently biased.

4.  Benchmarks weighted by fund or asset value may place a disproportionate emphasis on the most expensive cities and asset types.

5.  Valuations of the underlying properties are typically based on appraisals because there are few transactions to measure. Appraisals are infrequent, they smooth changes in property values, and they can lag underlying property performance. Transaction-based indexes are becoming more readily available.

6.  Some benchmark returns are unlevered, whereas others contain varying degrees of leverage based on the structure used by the investor that contributed the data.

7.  Real estate indexes do not reflect the high transaction costs, limited transparency, and lack of liquidity that drive performance for actual real estate investments.

Further complicating the performance evaluation of real estate funds is the selection of the appropriate return measure. Open-end funds, for which the contributions and withdrawals are at the discretion of the investor, generally use time-weighted rates of return. Closed-end funds, however, for which the timing of the contributions and withdrawals is at the discretion of the fund manager, generally report using internal rates of return.

## Benchmarking Private Equity

When measuring the performance of a private equity investment, investors typically calculate an internal rate of return (IRR) based on cash flows since inception of the investment and the ending valuation of the investment (the net asset value or residual value). Similarly, major venture capital benchmarks, such as those of Cambridge Associates, provide IRR estimates for private equity funds that are based on fund cash flows and valuations. Major indexes serving as benchmarks for US and European private equity include those provided by Cambridge Associates, Preqin, and LPX.

These benchmarks can be used to compare the managers' individual funds with an appropriate peer group, normally defined by subclass, geography, and vintage year of the underlying fund. Benchmarks commonly used for this purpose include ones prepared by Burgiss, Cambridge Associates, and the Institutional Limited Partners Association.

Although relative performance measures help an investor understand how a fund performs relative to peers or a relevant public index, there are several limitations to be aware of when comparing returns among managers:

1.  The valuation methodology used by the managers may differ.

2.  A fund's IRR can be meaningfully influenced by an early loss or an early win in the portfolio.

3.  The data are from a specific point in time, and the companies in a fund can be at different stages of development.

The public market equivalent (PME) methodology has been developed to allow comparisons of private equity IRRs with returns of publicly traded equity indexes. The methodology uses cash flow data to replicate the general partner's capital calls and distributions, assuming these same cash flows were invested in the chosen equity index. Comparing the performance of the PME index with the net IRR of the fund reveals the extent of over- or underperformance of the PME index relative to the public index. Several PME methodologies exist, the most common being Long–Nickels PME, PME+, Kaplan and Schoar PME, and Direct Alpha PME. It is important to choose the appropriate PME for each private equity fund; a poorly chosen PME raises the risk of leading the investor to an incorrect conclusion.

## Benchmarking Commodity Investments

Commodity benchmarks tend to use indexes based on the performance of futures-based commodity investments. These include the Reuters/Jefferies Commodity Research Bureau (RJ/CRB) Index, the S&P Goldman Sachs Commodity Index (GSCI), and the Bloomberg Commodity Index (BCOM). However, because the indexes use futures, rather than actual assets, they attempt to replicate the returns available to holding long positions in commodities. The S&P GSCI, the BCOM, and the RJ/CRB Index provide returns comparable to those of passive long positions in listed futures contracts. Because the cost-of-carry model ensures that the return on a fully margined position in a futures contract mimics the return on an underlying spot deliverable, futures contract returns are often used as a surrogate for cash market performance.

These indexes are considered investable. The major indexes contain some common groups of underlying assets. For example, the RJ/CRB Index, the BCOM, and the S&P GSCI all include energy (oil and gas), metals (industrial and precious), grains (corn, soybeans, and wheat), and soft commodities (cocoa, coffee, cotton, and sugar). However, beyond these basic groupings, they and other commodity indexes vary greatly in their composition and weighting schemes. A market-cap-weighting scheme, so common for equity and bond market indexes, cannot be carried over to indexes of commodity futures. Because every long futures position has a corresponding short futures position, the market capitalization of a futures contract is always zero.

Benchmarking of commodity investments presents similar challenges to other alternatives, including

1. the use of derivatives to represent actual commodity assets,
2. varying degrees of leverage among funds, and
3. the discretionary weighting of exposures within the index.

## Benchmarking Managed Derivatives

Because market indexes do not exist for managed derivatives, the benchmarks are typically specific to a single investment strategy. For example, the Mount Lucas Management Index takes both long and short positions in many futures markets based on a technical (moving-average) trading rule that is, in effect, specific to an active momentum strategy.

Other derivative benchmarks are based on peer groups. For example, the BarclayHedge and CISDM CTA trading strategy benchmarks are based on peer groups of commodity trading advisers (CTAs). The CISDM CTA Equal Weighted Index reflects manager returns for all reporting managers in the CISDM CTA database. These indexes suffer from the known limitations of peer group–based benchmarks, including survivorship bias.

## Benchmarking Distressed Securities

Distressed securities are illiquid and almost non-marketable at the time of purchase, making it very difficult to find suitable benchmarks. If the companies' prospects improve, the values of the distressed securities may go up gradually and liquidity may improve. Typically, it takes a relatively long time for this strategy to play out; thus, valuing the holdings may be a challenge. It is difficult to estimate the true market values of distressed securities, and stale pricing is almost inevitable.

One possible strategy is to use market indexes, such as the Barclay Distressed Securities Index. This index is constructed from fund managers who invest in distressed securities. Because this index is constructed from multiple strategies, however, it is difficult to discern whether the index is suitable for a given investment approach. In addition, because the valuations for the member funds are calculated at random intervals, it doesn't necessarily correct for the valuation issues noted previously.

# 10    PERFORMANCE APPRAISAL: RISK-BASED MEASURES

☐    calculate and interpret the Sortino ratio, the appraisal ratio, upside/downside capture ratios, maximum drawdown, and drawdown duration

☐    describe limitations of appraisal measures and related metrics

Investment performance appraisal identifies and measures investment skill, providing the information to assess how effectively money has been invested given the risks that were taken. (Risk-adjusted past performance is just one of many considerations when choosing investment managers. Qualitative considerations, although not within the scope of this reading, are also very important.)

Performance appraisal is most often concerned with ranking investment managers who follow similar investment disciplines. Return attribution provides information that can complement a performance appraisal analysis by providing more details about the consequences of managerial decisions. Performance attribution identifies and quantifies the sources of added value, whereas performance appraisal seeks to ascertain whether added value was a result of managerial skill.

Skill in any profession can be thought of as the ability to influence outcomes in desired directions. We define active investment management skill as the ability of a portfolio manager to add value on a risk-adjusted basis through investment analysis and insights. In everyday language, active investment skill is typically viewed as the ability to "beat the market" or an assigned benchmark with some consistency. The evaluation of active management skill is the focus of performance appraisal and this reading.

## Distinguishing Investment Skill from Luck

An investment manager's record for any specific period will reflect good luck (unanticipated good developments) and bad luck (unanticipated bad developments). One reason that luck should be considered important when appraising investment performance is the paradox of skill. As people become more knowledgeable about an activity, the difference between the worst and the best performers becomes narrower. Thus, the ever-increasing aggregate skill level of investment managers, supplemented by massive computing power and access to "big data," may lead to narrower investment performance differentials and a greater likelihood that these differentials can be explained by luck.

Deciding whether a portfolio manager has or lacks active investment skill on the basis of past returns is difficult and always subject to error. Financial market returns have a large element of randomness. Some of this randomness reflects the impact of news and information that relate directly or indirectly to asset values. Trading motivated by liquidity needs and by the emotions of investors adds to return volatility.

When we observe the historical performance of an investment portfolio, we see only one out of a potentially unlimited number of outcomes for a manager applying the same investment discipline but with different luck. Perhaps we gain additional insight into skill by examining the consistency of performance over time. But the hypothesis that the manager's underlying mean return exceeds the benchmark's mean return may require many years of observations to confirm with a reasonably high degree of confidence.[6]

## Appraisal Measures

The academic and the professional investment literatures have developed several returns-based measures to assess the value of active management. Important measures include the following:

- Sharpe ratio
- Treynor ratio
- Information ratio
- Appraisal ratio
- Sortino ratio
- Capture ratios

The selection of an appropriate appraisal measure requires an understanding of which aspect of risk is most important given the role of the investment in the client's total portfolio. It is also important to understand the assumptions a measure makes about the probability distribution of possible returns and any assumptions regarding the underlying theoretical pricing model. The Sharpe, information, and Treynor ratios are covered elsewhere in the curriculum and are not covered in depth here. This section will focus primarily on the remaining measures.

### The Sharpe Ratio

The **Sharpe ratio** measures the additional return for bearing risk above the risk-free rate, stated per unit of return volatility. In performance appraisal, this additional return is often referred to as **excess return**. This use contrasts with how "excess return" is used in return performance attribution—that is, as a return in excess of a benchmark's return.

The Sharpe ratio is commonly used on an *ex post* basis to evaluate historical risk-adjusted returns, as in

$$S_A = \frac{\overline{R}_A - \overline{r}_f}{\hat{\sigma}_A} \tag{18}$$

---

6 Can you be lucky once and correctly pick the flip of a fair coin? Of course! How about four times in a row? Yes, although this outcome is much less likely. Can a portfolio manager be lucky enough to generate 15 continuous years of superior investment performance? This outcome is very unlikely, but with hundreds or even thousands of portfolio managers, a few might succeed solely because of luck. One problem faced in investment performance appraisal is that many investment management performance records are only a few years long, making it difficult to distinguish between luck and skill.

One weakness of the Sharpe ratio is that the use of standard deviation as a measure of risk assumes investors are indifferent between upside and downside volatility. For example, for an investor looking for a potentially high-rewarding investment, volatility on the upside is not necessarily a negative. Similarly, risk-averse investors concerned about the preservation of capital are clearly most concerned with downside risk.

### The Treynor Ratio

The Treynor ratio (Treynor 1965) measures the excess return per unit of systematic risk. With the Treynor ratio, as well as the systematic-risk-based appraisal measures that follow, we must carefully choose an efficient market benchmark against which to measure the systematic risk of the manager's fund. In contrast, the Sharpe ratio can be compared among different funds without the explicit choice of a market benchmark.

$$T_A = \frac{\bar{R}_A - r_f}{\hat{\beta}_A} \tag{19}$$

The usefulness of the Treynor ratio depends on whether systematic risk or total risk is most appropriate in evaluating performance. Because of its reliance on beta, the Treynor ratio shows how a fund has performed in relation not to its own volatility but to the volatility it would bring to a well-diversified portfolio. Thus, a ranking of portfolios based on the Treynor ratio is most useful if the portfolios whose performance is being evaluated are being combined in a broader, fully diversified portfolio. The ratio is most informative when the portfolios being evaluated are compared with the same benchmark index.

### The Information Ratio

The information ratio (IR) is a simple measure that allows the evaluator to assess performance relative to the benchmark, scaled by risk. The implicit assumption is that the chosen benchmark is well matched to the risk of the investment strategy. The IR is calculated by dividing the portfolio's mean excess return relative to its benchmark by the variability of that excess return, as shown in Equation 18. The denominator of the information ratio, $\sigma(r_p - r_B)$, is the portfolio's tracking risk, a measure of how closely a portfolio follows the index to which it is benchmarked. (Many writers use "tracking error" in the sense of "tracking risk," although, confusingly, tracking error is also used to refer to simply the return difference between a passive portfolio and its benchmark.)

$$IR = \frac{E(r_p) - E(r_B)}{\sigma(r_p - r_B)} \tag{20}$$

### The Appraisal Ratio

The appraisal ratio (AR) is a returns-based measure, like the IR. It is the annualized alpha divided by the annualized residual risk. In the appraisal ratio, both the alpha and the residual risk are computed from a factor regression. Although the AR can be computed using any factor model appropriate for the portfolio, the measure was first introduced by Treynor and Black (1973) using Jensen's alpha and the standard deviation of the portfolio's residual or non-systematic risk. Treynor and Black argued that security selection ability implies that deviations from benchmark portfolio weights can be profitable and showed that the optimal deviations from the benchmark holdings for securities depend on what they called an "appraisal ratio." The appraisal ratio is also referred to as the *Treynor–Black ratio* or the *Treynor–Black appraisal ratio*.

The appraisal ratio measures the reward of active management relative to the risk of active management (alpha from a factor model):

$$AR = \frac{\alpha}{\sigma_\varepsilon} \tag{21}$$

where $\sigma_\varepsilon$ equals the standard deviation of $\varepsilon_t$, commonly denoted as the "standard error of regression," which is readily available from the output of commonly used statistical software.

### The Sortino Ratio

The Sortino ratio is a modification of the Sharpe ratio that penalizes only those returns that are lower than a user-specified return. The Sharpe ratio penalizes both upside and downside volatility equally.

Equation 22 presents the *ex ante* Sortino ratio, where $r_T$ is the minimum acceptable return (MAR), which is sometimes referred to as a *target rate of return*.[7] Instead of using standard deviation in the denominator, the Sortino ratio uses a measure of downside risk known as target semi-standard deviation or target semideviation, $\sigma_D$, as shown in Equation 23. By using this value, the Sortino ratio penalizes managers only for "harmful" volatility and is a measure of return per unit of downside risk.

$$SR_D = \frac{E\left(r_p\right) - r_T}{\sigma_D} \tag{22}$$

$$\widehat{SR}_D = \frac{\bar{r}_p - \bar{r}_T}{\hat{\sigma}_D} \tag{23}$$

$$\sigma_D = \left[\frac{\sum_{t=1}^{N} \min\left(r_t - r_T, 0\right)^2}{N}\right]^{1/2} \tag{24}$$

Assume a portfolio has an MAR of 4.0%. The portfolio's returns over a 10-year period are given in Exhibit 16. The numerator of the Sortino ratio is the average portfolio return minus the target return: $\bar{r}_p - \bar{r}_T = 6.0\% - 4.0\% = 2.0\%$. The calculation of target semi-standard deviation is reported in Exhibit 16. Based on the information in the table, the Sortino ratio is approximately 0.65.

### Exhibit 16: Sortino Ratio Using Target Semi-Standard Deviation

| Year | Rate of Return: $r_t$ | Target Return: $r_T = 4\%$ $\min(r_t - r_T, 0)^2$ |
|------|------|------|
| 1 | 6.0% | 0 |
| 2 | 8.0% | 0 |
| 3 | −1.0% | 0.0025 |
| 4 | 18.0% | 0 |
| 5 | 12.0% | 0 |
| 6 | 3.0% | 0.0001 |
| 7 | −4.0% | 0.0064 |
| 8 | 5.0% | 0 |
| 9 | 2.0% | 0.0004 |
| 10 | 11.0% | 0 |

---

7 The MAR is the lowest rate of return at which an investor will consider investing. For example, an MAR set equal to the expected rate of inflation would be associated with capital preservation in real terms. It is possible to use the benchmark return as the MAR. The MAR does not determine intrinsic value. Rather, it is a constraint or decision criterion that applies to all investment considerations.

| | | Target Return: $r_T$ = 4% |
|---|---|---|
| Year | Rate of Return: $r_t$ | $\min(r_t - r_T, 0)^2$ |

$$\sum_{t=1}^{N} \min(r_t - r_T, 0)^2 = 0.0094$$

$$\sigma_D = \left[ \frac{\sum_{t=1}^{N} \min(r_t - r_T, 0)^2}{N} \right]^{1/2} \qquad = \left( \frac{0.0094}{10} \right)^{1/2} = 3.07\%$$

More so than traditional performance measures, the Sortino ratio offers the ability to accurately assess performance when return distributions are not symmetrical. For example, because of its underlying assumption of normally distributed returns, the Sharpe ratio would not effectively distinguish between strategies with greater-than-normal upside volatility (positively skewed strategies, such as trend following) and strategies with greater-than-normal downside volatility (negatively skewed strategies, such as option writing). Both types of volatility are penalized equally in the Sharpe ratio. The Sortino ratio is arguably a better performance metric for such assets as hedge funds or commodity trading funds, whose return distributions are purposefully skewed away from the normal.

The Sortino ratio formula is not a risk premium. It is the return a portfolio manager generates that is greater than what is minimally acceptable to the investor. Essentially, the Sortino ratio penalizes a manager when portfolio return is lower than the MAR; it is most relevant when one of the investor's primary objectives is capital preservation.

Although there are arguments in favor of both the Sharpe ratio and the Sortino ratio, the Sharpe ratio has been much more widely used. In some cases, this preference may reflect a certain comfort level associated with the use of standard deviation, which is a more traditional measure of volatility. Also, cross-sectional comparisons of Sortino ratios are difficult to make applicable to every investor, because the MAR is investor-specific.

## EXAMPLE 12

## Performance Appraisal Measures

1. Portfolio B delivered 10.0% annual returns on average over the past 60 months. Its average annual volatility as measured by standard deviation was 14.0%, and its downside volatility as measured by target semi-standard deviation was 8.0%. Assuming the target rate of return is 3.0% per year, the Sortino ratio of portfolio B is closest to:

   A. 0.66.

   B. 0.77.

   C. 0.88.

### Solution:

C is correct.

$$\widehat{SR}_D = \frac{\bar{r}_p - \bar{r}_T}{\hat{\sigma}_D} = \frac{0.10 - 0.03}{0.08} = 0.88$$

2.  Why might a practitioner use the Sortino ratio, rather than the Sharpe ratio, to indicate performance?

    **A.** He is measuring option writing.

    **B.** The return distributions are not symmetrical.

    **C.** The investor's primary objective is capital preservation.

    **D.** All of the above

## Solution:

D is correct, because the Sortino ratio is more relevant when return distributions are not symmetrical, as with option writing. The Sortino ratio is also preferable when one of the primary objectives is capital preservation.

3.  Portfolio Y delivered an average annualized return of 9.0% over the past 60 months. The annualized standard deviation over this same time period was 20.0%. The market index returned 8.0% per year on average over the same time period, with an annualized standard deviation of 12.0%. Portfolio Y has an estimated beta of 1.40 versus the market index. Assuming the risk-free rate is 3.0% per year, the appraisal ratio is *closest* to:

    **A.** −0.8492.

    **B.** −0.0922.

    **C.** −0.0481.

## Solution:

B is correct. Jensen's alpha is −1.0%: $\alpha_p$ = 9.0% − [3.0% + 1.40(8.0% − 3.0%)] = −1.0% = −0.01. Non-systematic risk is 0.011776: $\sigma_{\varepsilon_p}^2 = 0.20^2 - 1.40^2(0.12^2)$ = 0.011776. The appraisal ratio is approximately −0.0922: $\widehat{AR} = \frac{-0.01}{\sqrt{0.011776}} =$ −0.0922.

4.  The appraisal ratio is the ratio of the portfolio's alpha to the standard deviation of its:

    **A.** total risk.

    **B.** systematic risk.

    **C.** non-systematic risk.

## Solution:

C is correct. The appraisal ratio is the ratio of the portfolio's alpha to the standard deviation of the portfolio's non-systematic risk. Essentially, this ratio allows an investor to evaluate whether excess returns warrant the additional non-systematic risk in actively managed portfolios.

5.  Assume a target return of 3.0%. Annual returns over the past four years have been 6.0%, −3.0%, 7.0%, and 1.0%. The target semi-standard deviation is *closest* to:

    **A.** 1.33%.

    **B.** 3.16%.

    **C.** 4.65%.

## Solution:

B is correct.

|       |                      | Target Return: $r_T = 3\%$ |
|-------|----------------------|----------------------------|
| Year  | Rate of Return: $r_t$ | $\min(r_t - r_T, 0)^2$     |
| 1     | 6.0%                 | 0                          |
| 2     | –3.0%                | 0.0036                     |
| 3     | 7.0%                 | 0                          |
| 4     | 1.0%                 | 0.0004                     |

$$\sum_{t=1}^{N} \min(r_t - r_T, 0)^2 = \quad\quad 0.004$$

$$\sigma_D = \left[\frac{\sum_{t=1}^{N} \min(r_t - r_T, 0)^2}{N}\right]^{1/2} = \quad \left(\frac{0.004}{4}\right)^{1/2} \approx 0.0316 = 3.16\%$$

## 11  PERFORMANCE APPRAISAL: CAPTURE RATIOS AND DRAWDOWNS

☐   calculate and interpret the Sortino ratio, the appraisal ratio, upside/downside capture ratios, maximum drawdown, and drawdown duration

☐   describe limitations of appraisal measures and related metrics

In investing, we understand that large losses require proportionally greater gains to reverse or offset. Performance measures used to monitor this aspect of manager performance include capture ratios and drawdowns. Capture ratios have several variations that reflect various aspects of the manager's gain or loss relative to the gain or loss of the benchmark. Capture ratios also help assess manager suitability relative to the investor, especially in relation to the investor's time horizon and risk tolerance. **Drawdown** is the loss in value incurred in any continuous period of negative returns. A manager who experiences larger drawdowns may be less suitable for an investor with a shorter time horizon. This section reviews capture ratios and drawdowns, their implications for performance, and their use in evaluating manager performance and suitability.

### Capture Ratios

Capture ratios measure the manager's participation in up and down markets—that is, the manager's percentage return relative to that of the benchmark. The upside capture ratio, or upside capture (UC), measures capture when the benchmark return is positive. The downside capture ratio, or downside capture (DC), measures capture when the benchmark return is negative. Upside capture greater (less) than 100% generally suggests outperformance (underperformance) relative to the benchmark, and downside capture less (greater) than 100% generally suggests outperformance (underperformance) relative to the benchmark. Practitioners should note that when the manager and benchmark returns are of the opposite sign, the ratio will be negative— for example, a manager with a 1% return when the market is down 1% will have a downside capture ratio of −100%.

The expressions for upside capture and downside capture are

$$UC(m,B,t) = R(m,t)/R(B,t) \text{ if } R(B,t) \geq 0$$

$$DC(m,B,t) = R(m,t)/R(B,t) \text{ if } R(B,t) < 0$$

where

$UC(m,B,t)$ = upside capture for manager $m$ relative to benchmark $B$ for time $t$

$DC(m,B,t)$ = downside capture for manager $m$ relative to benchmark $B$ for time $t$

$R(m,t)$ = return of manager $m$ for time $t$

$R(B,t)$ = return of benchmark $B$ for time $t$

The upside/downside capture, or simply the capture ratio (CR), is the upside capture divided by the downside capture. It measures the asymmetry of return and, as such, is like bond convexity and option gamma. A capture ratio greater than 1 indicates positive asymmetry, or a convex return profile, whereas a capture ratio less than 1 indicates negative asymmetry, or a concave return profile. Exhibit 17 illustrates what is meant by concave and convex return profiles. The dotted-line curve for a concave return profile resembles a downward-facing bowl, and the solid-line curve for a convex return profile resembles an upward-facing bowl. The horizontal and vertical axes are, respectively, benchmark returns [$R(B)$] and portfolio returns [$R(m)$]. As benchmark returns increase (i.e., moving to the right on the horizontal axis), portfolio returns increase—but at a *decreasing* rate for a concave return profile and at an *increasing* rate for a convex return profile. The expression for the capture ratio is

$$CR(m,B,t) = UC(m,B,t)/DC(m,B,t)$$

where

$CR(m,B,t)$ = capture ratio for manager $m$ relative to benchmark $B$ for time $t$

**Exhibit 17: Convex and Concave Return Profiles**

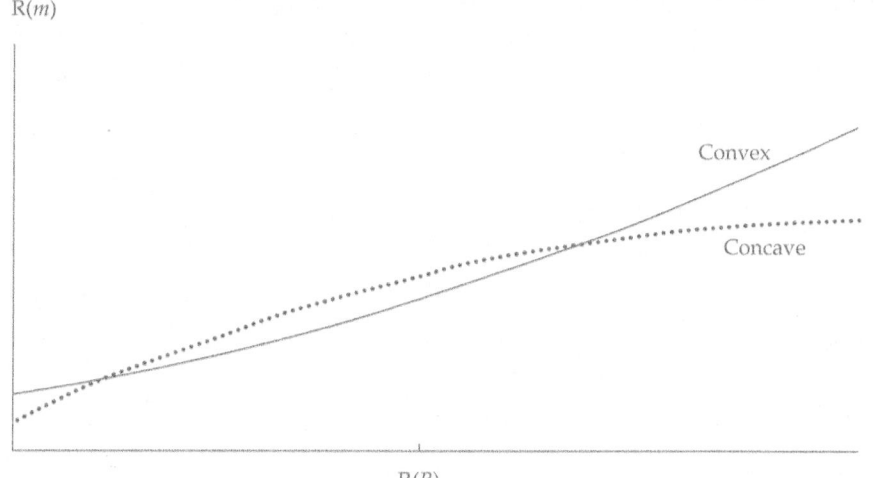

Consider the following return series for the manager, R($m$), and the benchmark, R($B$), shown in Exhibit 18. The upside columns calculate the cumulative return for the manager, Cum R($m$), and the benchmark, Cum R($B$), for those periods when the benchmark return is positive. The downside columns calculate the cumulative returns when the benchmark return is negative.

## Exhibit 18: Capture Ratio

| | | | Upside Return | | | | Downside Return | | | |
|---|---|---|---|---|---|---|---|---|---|---|
| $t$ | R($m$) | R($B$) | R($m$) | R($B$) | Cum R($m$) | Cum R($B$) | R($m$) | R($B$) | Cum R($m$) | Cum R($B$) |
| 1 | 0.6% | 1.0% | 0.6% | 1.0% | 0.60% | 1.00% | | | 0.00% | 0.00% |
| 2 | −0.3% | −0.5% | | | 0.60% | 1.00% | −0.3% | −0.5% | −0.30% | −0.50% |
| 3 | 1.0% | 1.5% | 1.0% | 1.5% | 1.61% | 2.52% | | | −0.30% | −0.50% |
| 4 | 0.1% | 0.2% | 0.1% | 0.2% | 1.71% | 2.72% | | | −0.30% | −0.50% |
| 5 | −1.0% | −2.0% | | | 1.71% | 2.72% | −1.0% | −2.0% | −1.30% | −2.49% |
| 6 | 0.5% | 0.6% | 0.5% | 0.6% | 2.22% | 3.34% | | | −1.30% | −2.49% |
| 7 | 0.2% | 0.1% | 0.2% | 0.1% | 2.42% | 3.44% | | | −1.30% | −2.49% |
| 8 | −0.8% | −1.0% | | | 2.42% | 3.44% | −0.8% | −1.0% | −2.09% | −3.47% |
| 9 | 0.8% | 1.0% | 0.8% | 1.0% | 3.24% | 4.47% | | | −2.09% | −3.47% |
| 10 | 0.4% | 0.5% | 0.4% | 0.5% | 3.65% | 5.00% | | | −2.09% | −3.47% |
| Geometric average | | | 0.51% | 0.70% | | | −0.70% | −1.17% | | |
| Upside capture | | | 0.51%/0.70% = 72.8% | | | | Downside capture | | −0.70%/−1.17% = 59.8% | |
| Capture ratio | | | 72.8%/59.8% = 121.7% | | | | | | | |

During up markets, the geometric average return is 0.51% for the manager and 0.70% for the benchmark, giving an upside capture of 72.8%. During down markets, the geometric average return is −0.70% for the manager and −1.17% for the benchmark, giving a downside capture of 59.8%. The manager's capture ratio is 1.217, or 121.7%. Exhibit 19 shows a graph of the cumulative upside and downside returns.

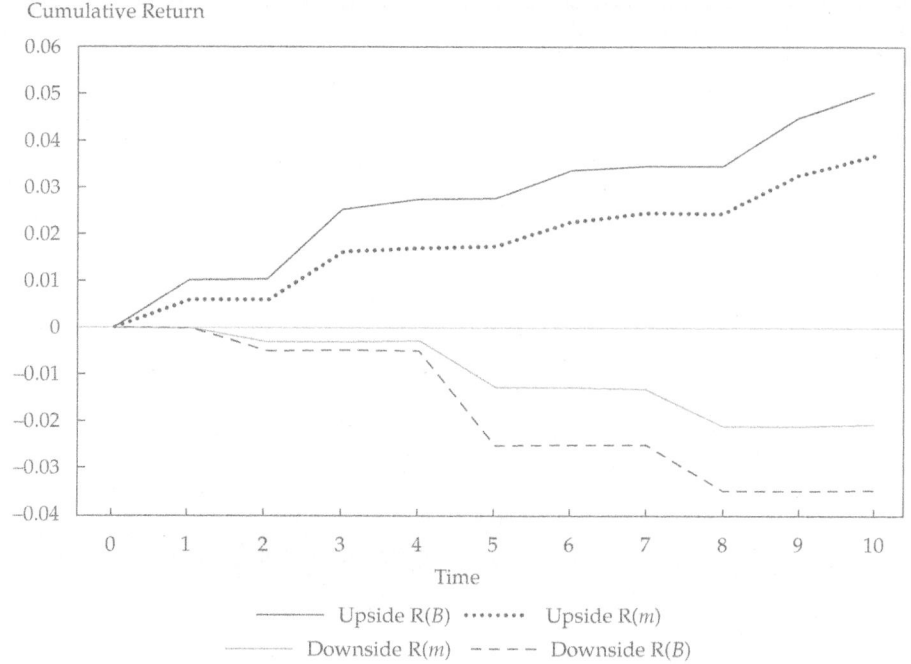

**Exhibit 19: Cumulative Upside and Downside Returns**

## Drawdown

Drawdown is measured as the cumulative peak-to-trough loss during a continuous period. Drawdown duration is the total time from the start of the drawdown until the cumulative drawdown recovers to zero, which can be segmented into the drawdown phase (start to trough) and the recovery phase (trough-to-zero cumulative return).

$$\text{Maximum DD}(m,t) = \min([V(m,t) - V(m,t^*)]/V(m,t^*), 0)$$

where

$V(m,t)$ = portfolio value of manager $m$ at time $t$

$V(m,t^*)$ = peak portfolio value of manager $m$

$t > t^*$

Consider the return on the S&P 500 Index at the start of the global COVID-19 outbreak (from November 2019 to February 2020, shown in Exhibit 20 and Exhibit 21. The drawdown is 0% until January 2020, when the return is −0.04% and the drawdown continues to worsen, reaching a maximum of −19.6% in March 2020. The strong positive returns from April to July 2020 reverse the drawdown. The total duration of the drawdown was 7 months, with a 4-month recovery period.

### Exhibit 20: Drawdown

| Month | R(m) | Cumulative R(m) | Drawdown | Cumulative Drawdown | |
|---|---|---|---|---|---|
| November 2019 | 3.63% | 7.86% | | 0.00% | |
| December 2019 | 3.01% | 11.10% | | 0.00% | |
| January 2020 | −0.04% | 11.05% | −0.04% | −0.04% | Drawdown begins |
| February 2020 | −8.23% | 1.91% | −8.23% | −8.27% | |
| March 2020 | −12.35% | −10.67% | −12.35% | −19.60% | Maximum drawdown |
| April 2020 | 12.82% | 0.78% | | −9.30% | |
| May 2020 | 4.76% | 5.58% | | −4.98% | |
| June 2020 | 1.99% | 7.67% | | −3.09% | |
| July 2020 | 5.64% | 13.75% | | 0.00% | Recovery begins |

### Exhibit 21: Drawdown

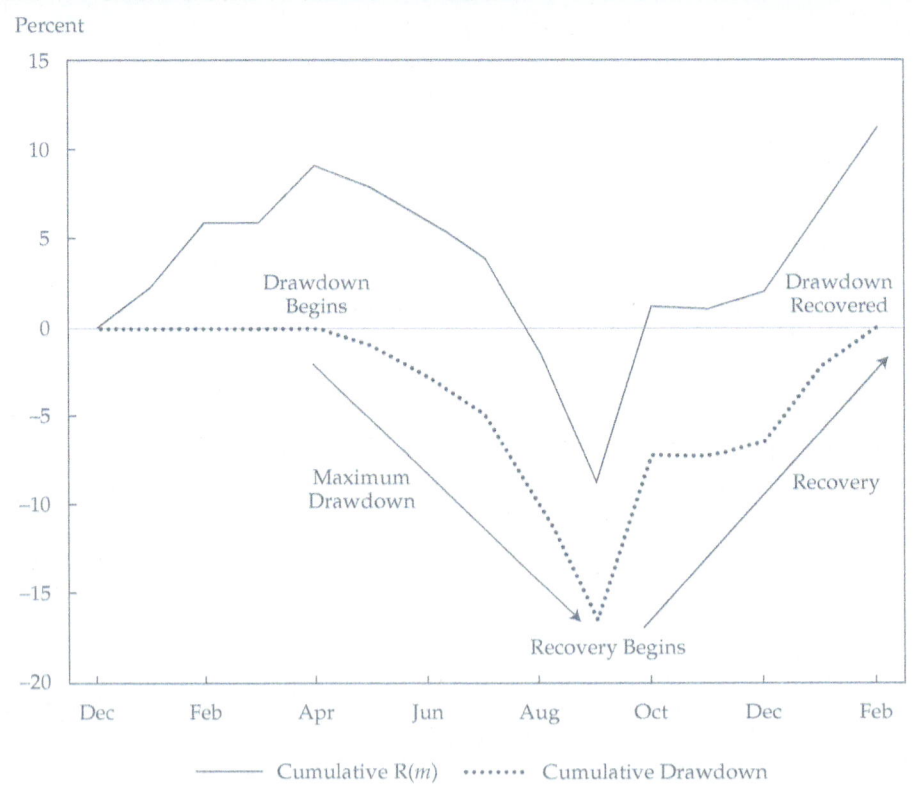

An asymmetrical return profile or avoiding large drawdowns, particularly during periods when the market is not trending strongly upward, can result in higher risk-adjusted returns. The reason is the all-too-familiar reality for investors that it takes proportionally larger gains to recover from increasingly large losses. This asymmetry arises from basis drift, from the change in the denominator when calculating returns, or from the practical problem of recovering from a smaller asset base after a large loss. For example, a portfolio decline of 50% must be followed by a gain of 100% to return to its previous value. Exhibit 22 illustrates this relationship.

## Exhibit 22: Percentage Gain Necessary to Offset a Given Loss

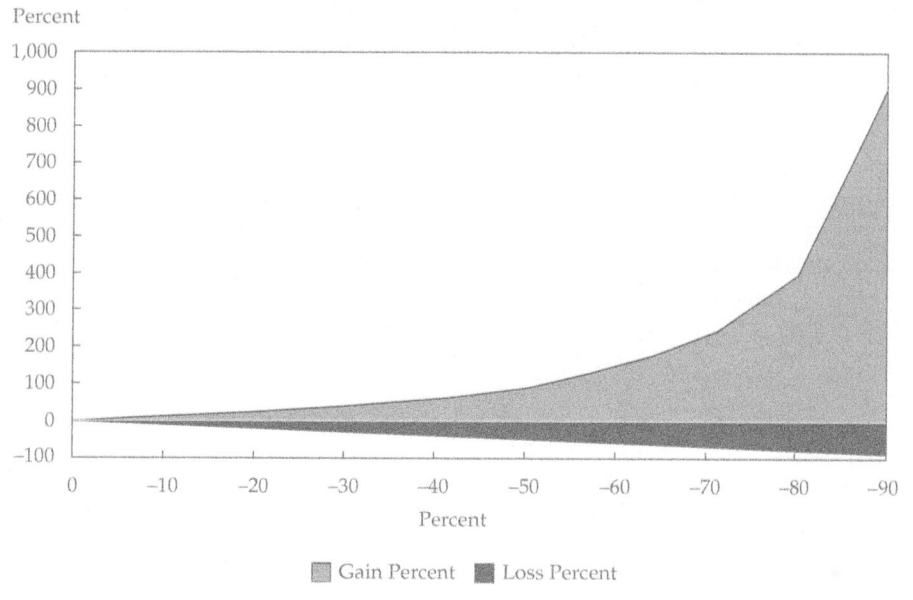

To further illustrate, consider the four return profiles with different upside and downside capture ratios shown in Exhibit 23.

## Exhibit 23: Return Profile Summary

| Profile | Upside Capture | Downside Capture | Ratio |
|---|---|---|---|
| Long only | 100% | 100% | 1.0 |
| Positive asymmetry | 75% | 25% | 3.0 |
| Low beta | 50% | 50% | 1.0 |
| Negative asymmetry | 25% | 75% | 0.3 |

We designed these four trading strategies to illustrate the potential effects of the capture ratio and drawdown on return performance and to highlight why understanding the capture ratio and drawdown is important for manager selection.[8] Each strategy's allocation to the S&P 500 Total Return (TR) Index and to 90-day T-bills (assuming monthly rebalancing to simplify the calculations) is based on the realized monthly return from January 2000 to December 2013. (We chose this time period to illustrate the need to examine the asymmetry in a strategy's returns specifically because it encompasses the extreme drawdown of 2008–2009.)

- The long-only profile is 100% allocated to the S&P 500 throughout the period.

- The low-beta profile is allocated 50% to the S&P 500 throughout the period.

- The positive asymmetry profile is allocated 75% to the S&P 500 for months when the S&P 500 return is positive and 25% when the S&P 500 return is negative.

---

8 If the market return is known beforehand, the correct strategy is to allocate 100% to the S&P 500 Total Return (TR) Index in up months and 100% to 90-day T-bills in down months (or –100% S&P 500 TR Index if shorting is allowed).

- The negative asymmetry profile is allocated 25% to the S&P 500 for months when the S&P 500 return is positive and 75% when the S&P 500 return is negative.

The remainder for all profiles is allocated to 90-day T-bills. Exhibit 24 shows each profile's cumulative monthly return for the period.

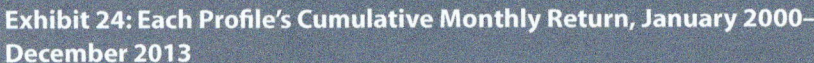

**Exhibit 24: Each Profile's Cumulative Monthly Return, January 2000–December 2013**

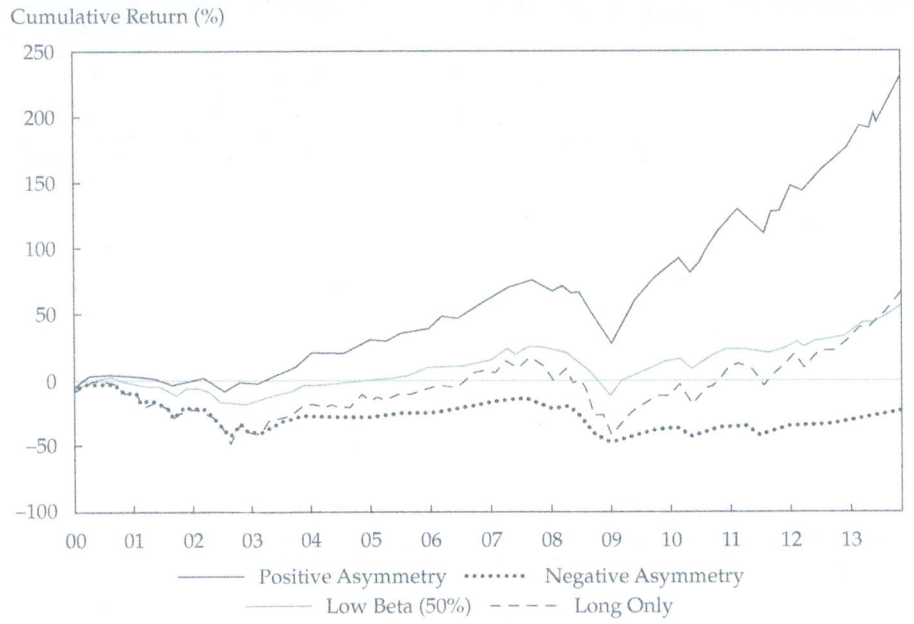

Cumulative Return (%)

Positive Asymmetry ········· Negative Asymmetry
Low Beta (50%) – – – – Long Only

Exhibit 25 provides summary statistics for each profile based on monthly returns from January 2000 to December 2013. Although the long-only profile outperformed the low-beta profile, this outperformance resulted from the strong up market of 2013. The low-beta profile outperformed the long-only profile for most of the period, with lower realized volatility and higher risk-adjusted returns during the entire period. The low-beta profile declined only 18.8%, compared with the long-only decline of 42.5%, from January 2000 to September 2002. As a result, the low-beta profile had higher cumulative performance from January 2000 to October 2007 despite markedly lagging the long-only profile (56.0% to 108.4%) from October 2002 to October 2007.

Although a low-beta approach may sacrifice performance, it shows that limiting drawdowns can result in better absolute and risk-adjusted returns in certain markets. Not surprisingly, positive asymmetry results in better performance relative to long only, low beta, and negative asymmetry. Although the positive asymmetry profile lags in up markets, this lag is more than offset by the lower participation in down markets. Not surprisingly, the negative asymmetry profile lags, with lower participation in up markets insufficient to offset the greater participation in down markets.

| Exhibit 25: Summary Statistics for Each Profile, January 2000–December 2013 | | | | |
|---|---|---|---|---|
| **Strategy** | **Long Only** | **Low Beta** | **Positive Asymmetry** | **Negative Asymmetry** |
| Cumulative return | 64.0% | 54.2% | 228.1% | −24.4% |
| Annualized return | 3.60% | 3.14% | 8.86% | −1.98% |
| Annualized standard deviation | 15.64% | 7.79% | 9.61% | 10.01% |
| Sharpe ratio | 0.10 | 0.14 | 0.71 | −0.40 |
| Beta | 1.00 | 0.50 | 0.61 | 0.64 |
| Drawdown (maximum) | −50.9% | −28.3% | −26.9% | −48.9% |

Although positive asymmetry is a desirable trait, only some strategies are convex. We need to understand the strategy and how the return profile is created, particularly whether the strategy is inherently convex or whether convexity relies on manager skill. For example, a hedging strategy implemented by rolling forward out-of-the-money put options will typically return many small losses because more options expire worthless than are compensated for by the occasional large gain during a large market downturn. This strategy will likely exhibit consistent positive asymmetry because it depends more on the nature of the strategy than on investment skill.

We should also evaluate the consistency between the stated investment process and reported investment performance. An inconsistency could indicate issues with the strategy's repeatability and implementation or more serious reporting and compliance concerns. Capture ratios can be useful in evaluating consistency issues. We also need to understand the strategy's robustness and potential risks. For example, the expected benefits of diversification—in particular, mitigating downside capture—might not be realized in a crisis if correlations converge toward 1.

Manager responses to a large drawdown provide evidence of the robustness and repeatability of the investment, portfolio construction, and risk management processes, as well as insight into the people implementing the processes. This information requires an understanding of the source of the drawdown and the potential principal–agent risk, operational risk, and business risk that it entails. Drawdowns are stress tests of the investment process and provide a natural point to evaluate and improve processes, which is particularly true of firm-specific drawdowns.

As noted, practitioners should also consider investment horizon and its relationship with risk capacity. An investor closer to retirement, with less time to recover from losses, places more emphasis on absolute measures of risk. In addition, even if the manager maintains her discipline during a large drawdown, the investor may not. This dynamic arises if the investor's perception of risk is path dependent or the drawdown changes risk tolerance. If there has been no change to investment policy and no change in the view that the manager remains suitable, the temptation to exit should be resisted to avoid exiting at an inauspicious time. Investors with shorter horizons, with lower risk capacity, or who are prone to overreact to losses may bias selection toward managers with shallower and shorter expected drawdowns.

**EXAMPLE 13**

## Capture Ratios and Drawdown

1. Do losses require proportionally greater gains to reverse or offset? Choose the best response.

   A. Yes, because in investing, it is easier to lose than to gain.

   B. No, gains should reflect losses.

   C. Yes, because we calculate percentage gains/losses on the basis of the starting amount of portfolio holdings.

**Solution:**

C is the correct response. If the denominator of the gain calculation is lower, a higher percentage gain is required to offset the loss. For example, if you lose 10% of $100, your new holding is $90. To earn back the $10 loss, you must earn 10/90, or 11%. A is not correct because the "ease" of gaining or losing is not relevant. B is not correct because proportionally higher gains are required.

| $t$ | R(m) (%) | R(B) (%) |
|---|---|---|
| 1 | −3.06 | −3.60 |
| 2 | 6.32 | 3.10 |
| 3 | 6.00 | 6.03 |
| 4 | 3.21 | 1.58 |
| 5 | −9.05 | −7.99 |
| 6 | −4.09 | −5.23 |
| 7 | 4.34 | 7.01 |
| 8 | −5.72 | −4.51 |
| 9 | 12.76 | 8.92 |
| 10 | 5.38 | 3.81 |
| 11 | 0.33 | 0.01 |
| 12 | 5.68 | 6.68 |

2. Using the return information in the table above, what is the manager's downside capture ratio?

   A. 103%

   B. 108%

   C. 115%

**Solution:**

A is the correct answer. See the table below.

| | | | Upside Return | | | | Downside Return | | | |
|---|---|---|---|---|---|---|---|---|---|---|
| $t$ | R(m) | R(B) | R(m) | R(B) | Cum R(m) | Cum R(B) | R(m) | R(B) | Cum R(m) | Cum R(B) |
| 1 | −3.06% | −3.60% | | | 0.00% | 0.00% | −3.06% | −3.60% | −3.06% | −3.60% |
| 2 | 6.32% | 3.10% | 6.32% | 3.10% | 6.32% | 3.10% | | | −3.06% | −3.60% |
| 3 | 6.00% | 6.03% | 6.00% | 6.03% | 12.70% | 9.32% | | | −3.06% | −3.60% |

| t | R(m) | R(B) | Upside Return | | | | Downside Return | | | |
|---|---|---|---|---|---|---|---|---|---|---|
| | | | R(m) | R(B) | Cum R(m) | Cum R(B) | R(m) | R(B) | Cum R(m) | Cum R(B) |
| 4 | 3.21% | 1.58% | 3.21% | 1.58% | 16.32% | 11.04% | | | −3.06% | −3.60% |
| 5 | −9.05% | −7.99% | | | 16.32% | 11.04% | −9.05% | −7.99% | −11.83% | −11.30% |
| 6 | −4.09% | −5.23% | | | 16.32% | 11.04% | −4.09% | −5.23% | −15.44% | −15.94% |
| 7 | 4.34% | 7.01% | 4.34% | 7.01% | 21.36% | 18.83% | | | −15.44% | −15.94% |
| 8 | −5.72% | −4.51% | | | 21.36% | 18.83% | −5.72% | −4.51% | −20.28% | −19.73% |
| 9 | 12.76% | 8.92% | 12.76% | 8.92% | 36.85% | 29.43% | | | −20.28% | −19.73% |
| 10 | 5.38% | 3.81% | 5.38% | 3.81% | 44.21% | 34.36% | | | −20.28% | −19.73% |
| 11 | 0.33% | 0.01% | 0.33% | 0.01% | 44.69% | 34.37% | | | −20.28% | −19.73% |
| 12 | 5.68% | 6.68% | 5.68% | 6.68% | 52.91% | 43.35% | | | −20.28% | −19.73% |
| Geometric average | | | 5.45% | 4.60% | | | −5.51% | −5.35% | | |
| Upside capture | | | 5.45%/4.60% = 118% | | | | **Downside capture** | | **−5.51%/−5.35% = 103%** | |
| Capture ratio | | | 118%/103% = 115% | | | | | | | |

# EVALUATION OF INVESTMENT MANAGER SKILL

**12**

☐ | evaluate the skill of an investment manager

Using the tools and principles of performance evaluation presented in this reading, this section presents a specific case to use those tools in an evaluation of manager skill.

For this section, we will consider the case of Manager A, benchmarked against the MSCI Pacific Index. Drawing from the previous sections in this reading, we compiled sample data to evaluate the skill of Manager A. For simplicity of analysis and presentation, we exclude the impact from currency.

Over a five-year period, Manager A's performance is 9.42%, versus the benchmark performance of 9.25%. So, we know that the manager added 17 bps (9.42 – 9.25) of outperformance. But did the manager earn the 17 bps through skill, or was she the beneficiary of luck?

To further evaluate the outperformance, we turn to the tools presented throughout this reading. We include a sample attribution analysis to tell us how the outperformance was achieved. We then use appraisal ratio analysis to compare Manager A's performance to other managers during the same period. Combining the analyses helps present a more balanced assessment of the manager's skill.

## Performance Attribution Analysis

Attribution analysis, as we have shown, is one of the most important tools for evaluating manager skill. Attribution will tell us how the outperformance was achieved, distinguishing the stock selection from country allocation. In the Exhibit 26, we present the sample attribution analysis (for simplicity, we have combined the interaction effect with stock selection).

### Exhibit 26: Sample Attribution Analysis

| | Manager A | | MSCI Pacific | | Attribution Effects | | |
| Market | Weight | 5-Year Return | Weight | 5-Year Return | Allocation | Selection + Interaction | Total |
|---|---|---|---|---|---|---|---|
| Japan | 51.0% | 12.40% | 60.5% | 11.48% | −0.21% | 0.47% | 0.26% |
| Australia | 30.0% | 5.12% | 25.4% | 4.10% | −0.24% | 0.31% | 0.07% |
| Hong Kong SAR | 15.0% | 8.90% | 10.0% | 10.08% | 0.04% | −0.18% | −0.14% |
| Singapore | 3.5% | 5.10% | 3.0% | 5.38% | −0.02% | −0.01% | −0.03% |
| New Zealand | 0.5% | 8.75% | 1.0% | 9.08% | 0.00% | 0.00% | 0.00% |
| Total | 100% | 9.42% | 100% | 9.25% | −0.43% | 0.59% | 0.17% |

Using this analysis, let us consider the impacts of country allocation weights versus the benchmark weights. Overall, the portfolio manager lost 43 bps of performance as a result of allocation decisions. Specifically, the manager's decision to overweight Australia (30% to 25%) lost 24 bps, because Australia underperformed the total MSCI Pacific benchmark (4.10% versus 9.25%). In addition, the decision to underweight Japan (51% to 60%) lost 21 bps, because Japan outperformed the total benchmark (12.4% versus 9.25%). With this attribution analysis, we can say the manager did not make good weighting decisions over the five-year period.

Now, let us consider the impact from the manager's stock selection decisions. Overall, the portfolio manager gained 59 bps of performance from stock selection decisions. Specifically, the manager added 47 bps through selecting Japanese stocks and 31 bps from selecting Australian stocks. Stock selection in Hong Kong SAR was not as successful, where the manager lost 18 bps.

Overall, we can conclude from the attribution analysis that the manager is a good stock picker, especially for Japanese and Australian stocks. But the manager has not been as successful in choosing the markets to allocate assets. We infer these conclusions on the basis of an analysis of the manager's performance attribution over a five-year period. To better evaluate the manager's performance, we need to understand the risk incurred to achieve that performance. For that risk assessment, we will consider Manager A relative to other managers, using a sample appraisal ratio analysis over the same five-year period.

## Appraisal Measures

As described previously, appraisal analysis uses techniques to review past periods of performance and risk. Consider the sample results presented in Exhibit 27. For the same five-year period, we have calculated a set of performance appraisal measures for Manager A, presented previously, as well as two other managers with the same benchmark over the same period, Managers B and C.

### Exhibit 27: Sample Analysis Using Various Appraisal Measures

| | Appraisal Measures | | | |
| | Manager A | Manager B | Manager C | Benchmark |
|---|---|---|---|---|
| Annualized return | 9.42 | 8.23 | 10.21 | 9.25 |
| Annualized std. dev. | 10.83 | 8.10 | 12.34 | 9.76 |

|  | Appraisal Measures | | | |
| --- | --- | --- | --- | --- |
|  | Manager A | Manager B | Manager C | Benchmark |
| Sharpe ratio | 0.68 | 0.76 | 0.66 | 0.73 |
| Treynor ratio | 0.35 | 0.32 | 0.19 | 0.57 |
| Information ratio | 0.43 | 0.41 | 0.30 | 0.00 |
| Sortino ratio (MAR = 3%) | 0.82 | 0.51 | 1.03 | 0.97 |

In considering this historical analysis, note that Manager A has a higher volatility of returns than the benchmark (manager standard deviation of 10.83 versus benchmark standard deviation of 9.76). This volatility is greater than that for Manager B (8.10) but is less than that for Manager C (12.34). In general, Manager A's return is slightly more volatile—riskier—than the benchmark's and slightly more and less volatile than that of Managers B and C, respectively.

This consistency is demonstrated in the Sharpe ratio measurement as well. Recall that the Sharpe ratio indicates the amount of performance earned over a risk-free proxy per unit of risk. In this assessment, Manager A's Sharpe ratio is less than the benchmark's Sharpe ratio (0.68 versus 0.73) and less than Manager B's Sharpe ratio (0.76). Thus, for this period, we know Manager A certainly incurred more risk than the benchmark and Manager B did for the same amount of return generated. Is the manager incurring too much risk for the return generated? To answer this question, we should consider some of the other appraisal measures as well.

Unlike the Sharpe ratio, the Treynor ratio measures the return earned per unit of *systematic* risk. The information ratio indicates how well the manager has performed relative to the benchmark, *after accounting for the differences in the volatility of the portfolio and the benchmark.* Given that Manager A has the highest Treynor and information ratios for this period, she has been able to produce a higher return relative to systematic risk. In addition, consider her Sortino ratio of 0.82, not significantly higher than the Sharpe ratio, but again indicative of an ability to generate higher returns relative to downside risk (where the target is 3%).

## Sample Evaluation of Skill

In summary, the analysis based on these appraisal measures supports the conclusion generated by the performance attribution analysis that Manager A has been able to generate excess return over the benchmark through stock selection. She has done so without incurring significant excess risk relative to the benchmark and two similar managers. Therefore, within the limits of these analyses, Manager A has exhibited some level of skill worthy of further analysis.

The analysis does not, however, help us evaluate the country allocation conclusions of our attribution analysis. We know that the manager made incorrect bets in Japan and Australia. What beliefs about country selection are embedded in her investment philosophy? Are country allocations an integral part of her investment approach, or are they a by-product of her stock selection? Answers to these questions will help us determine whether our assessment of skill should be penalized by the poor outcomes of the country selection decisions in this period.

It is important to recognize that our analysis encompasses only a small sample of the possible outcomes that are not necessarily indicative of future outcomes. A long track record is necessary to have any statistical certainty in a conclusion of skill or no skill. Practitioners will want to conduct additional analyses to increase their confidence in their conclusions. These additional studies could include some of the other tools presented in this reading, such as risk attribution or *ex ante* analyses. In addition, practitioners will want to include qualitative analyses of the manager (e.g., direct interviews with management to assess abilities), assessment of investment goals and management fees, and so on. In the end, we must understand and acknowledge the limits of all tools, being careful to qualify any conclusions regarding investment skill with the appropriate level of prudence.

---

### EXAMPLE 14

## Investment Manager Skill

Use the examples in Exhibit 26 and Exhibit 27 to help answer the following questions.

1. Which statement *best* describes Manager A's performance during this five-year period?

   **A.** On an absolute basis, Manager A performed better than either Manager B or Manager C.

   **B.** Relative to systematic risk, Manager A performed better than either Manager B or Manager C.

   **C.** Manager C incurred the least risk.

### Solution:

B is correct. The Treynor ratio measures performance relative to systematic risk. Manager A's Treynor ratio was better than that of both Manager B and Manager C for the period. A is not correct because Manager A's return for the period was less than Manager C's return. C is not correct because Manager C's annualized standard deviation (volatility) was highest.

---

2. Which of the following *best* provides evidence of manager skill?

   **A.** Security selection attribution effect of 47 bps

   **B.** Annualized performance equal to 9.42%

   **C.** Annualized standard deviation equal to 12.34%

### Solution:

A is correct. Performance attribution can be indicative of manager skill, especially over longer historical time periods. Neither B nor C is correct because neither performance nor standard deviation, on their own, is necessarily indicative of manager skill.

---

3. How can a practitioner *best* distinguish manager skill from luck?

   **A.** Run thousands of analyses of the same manager over an extended period.

   **B.** Avoid making broad-based judgments without statistical evidence.

   **C.** Use multiple analysis tools to jointly infer conclusions, sensitive to the limits of those tools.

### Solution:

C is correct. Practitioners should use multiple analyses with different tools to find multiple sources that agree on evidence of skill. A is not correct, because thousands of analyses, especially the same types of analyses, may not necessarily lead to more conclusive results. B is not correct because it states best practice but not necessarily techniques to distinguish skill from luck.

# SUMMARY

Performance evaluation is an essential tool for understanding the quality of the investment process. Practitioners must take care, however, to understand how performance results are generated. They need a good understanding of the performance methods used, the data inputs, and the limitations of those methods. They particularly need to be careful not to infer results beyond the capabilities of the methods or the accuracy of the data. In this reading, we have discussed the following:

- Performance measurement provides an overall indication of the portfolio's performance.

- Performance attribution builds on performance measurement to explain how the performance was achieved.

- Performance appraisal leverages both returns and attribution to infer the quality of the investment process.

- An effective attribution process must reconcile to the total portfolio return/ risk, reflect the investment decision-making process, quantify the active portfolio management decisions, and provide a complete understanding of the excess return/risk of the portfolio.

- Return attribution analyzes the impact of investment decisions on the returns, whereas risk attribution analyzes the risk consequences of the investment decisions.

- Macro attribution considers the decisions of the fund sponsor, whereas micro attribution considers the decisions of the individual portfolio manager.

- Returns-based attribution uses returns to identify the factors that have generated those returns.

- Holdings-based attribution uses the holdings over time to evaluate the decisions that contributed to the returns.

- Transactions-based attribution uses both holdings and transactions to fully explain the performance over the evaluation period.

- There are various techniques for interpreting the sources of portfolio returns using a specified attribution approach.

- Fixed-income attribution considers the unique factors that drive bond returns, including interest rate risk and default risk.

- When selecting a risk attribution approach, practitioners should consider the investment decision-making process and the type of attribution analysis.

- Attribution is used to calculate and interpret the contribution to portfolio return and volatility from the asset allocation and within-asset-class active/ passive decisions.

- Liability-based benchmarks focus on the cash flows that the assets are required to generate.

- Asset-based benchmarks contain a collection of assets to compare against the portfolio's assets.

- Valid benchmarks should be unambiguous, investable, measurable, appropriate, reflective of current investment opinions, specified in advance, and accountable.

- Benchmark misspecification creates subsequent incorrect performance measurement and invalidates the attribution and appraisal analyses.

- Alternative investments are difficult to benchmark because they are typically less liquid, have fewer available market benchmarks, and often lack transparency.

- Investment performance appraisal ratios—including the Sortino ratio, upside/downside capture ratios, maximum drawdown, and drawdown duration—measure investment skill.

- Appraisal ratios must be used with care, noting the assumptions of each ratio and affording the appropriateness to the measured investment process, risk tolerance, and investor time horizon.

- Although appraisal ratios help identify manager skill (as opposed to luck), they often are based on investment return data, which are often limited and subject to error.

- Evaluation of investment manager skill requires the use of a broad range of analysis tools, with fundamental understanding of how the tools work, how they complement each other, and their specific limitations.

# REFERENCES

Bailey, Jeffery V. and David E. Tierney. 1998. Controlling Misfit Risk in Multiple-Manager Investment Programs. Charlottesville, VA: Research Foundation of CFA Institute.

Bailey, Jeffery V., Thomas M. Richards, and David Tierney. 2007. "Evaluating Portfolio Performance." In Managing Investment Portfolios: A Dynamic Process. 3rd ed., ed. Maginn, John, Donald Tuttle, Dennis McLeavey, Jerald Pinto. Hoboken, NJ: John Wiley & Sons.

Brinson, Gary and Nimrod Fachler. 1985. "Measuring Non-US Equity Portfolio Performance." *Journal of Portfolio Management* 11 (5): 73–76. 10.3905/jpm.1985.409005

Brinson, Gary, Randolph Hood, and Gilbert Beebower. 1986. "Determinants of Portfolio Performance." *Financial Analysts Journal* 42 (4): 39–44. 10.2469/faj.v42.n4.39

Brown, Stephen and William Goetzmann. 1997. "Mutual Fund Styles." *Journal of Financial Economics* 43 (3): 373–99. 10.1016/S0304-405X(96)00898-7

Carhart, M. M. 1997. "On Persistence in Mutual Fund Performance." *Journal of Finance* 52 (1): 57–82. 10.1111/j.1540-6261.1997.tb03808.x

Cariño, David. 1999. "Combining Attribution Effects over Time." *Journal of Performance Measurement* (Summer).

Giguère, C. 2005. "Thinking through Fixed Income Attribution—Reflections from a Group of French Practitioners." *Journal of Performance Measurement* (Summer): 46–65.

Menchero, Jose. 2000. "An Optimized Approach to Linking Attribution Effects over Time." *Journal of Performance Measurement* (Fall).

Murira, Bernard and Hector Sierra. 2006. "Fixed Income Attribution: A United Framework—Part 1." *Journal of Performance Measurement* 11 (1): 23–35.

Treynor, J. 1965. "How to Rate Management of Investment Funds." *Harvard Business Review* 43 (1): 63–75.

Treynor, J. and F. Black. 1973. "How to Use Security Analysis to Improve Portfolio Selection." *Journal of Business* 46 (1): 66–86. 10.1086/295508

## PRACTICE PROBLEMS

# The following information relates to questions 1-5

Alexandra Jones, a senior adviser at Federalist Investors (FI), meets with Erin Bragg, a junior analyst. Bragg just completed a monthly performance evaluation for an FI fixed-income manager. Bragg's report addresses the three primary components of performance evaluation: measurement, attribution, and appraisal. Jones asks Bragg to describe an effective attribution process. Bragg responds as follows:

Response 1:          Performance attribution draws conclusions regarding the quality of a portfolio manager's investment decisions.

Response 2:          Performance attribution should help explain how performance was achieved by breaking apart the return or risk into different explanatory components.

Bragg notes that the fixed-income portfolio manager has strong views about the effects of macroeconomic factors on credit markets and follows a top-down investment process.

Jones reviews the monthly performance attribution and asks Bragg whether any risk-adjusted historical performance indicators are available. Bragg produces the following data:

### Exhibit 1: 10-Year Trailing Risk-Adjusted Performance

| | |
|---|---|
| Average annual return | 8.20% |
| Minimum acceptable return (MAR) | 5.00% |
| Sharpe ratio | 0.95 |
| Sortino ratio | 0.87 |
| Upside capture | 0.66 |
| Downside capture | 0.50 |
| Maximum drawdown | −24.00% |
| Drawdown duration | 4 months |

1. Which of Bragg's responses regarding effective performance attribution is correct?

   A. Only Response 1

   B. Only Response 2

   C. Both Response 1 and Response 2

2. The *most appropriate* risk attribution approach for the fixed-income manager is to:

   A. decompose historical returns into a top-down factor framework.

    **B.** evaluate the marginal contribution to total risk for each position.

    **C.** attribute tracking risk to relative allocation and selection decisions.

3. Based on Exhibit 1, the target semideviation for the portfolio is *closest to:*

    **A.** 2.78%.

    **B.** 3.68%.

    **C.** 4.35%.

4. Based on Exhibit 1, the capture ratios of the portfolio indicate:

    **A.** a concave return profile.

    **B.** positive asymmetry of returns.

    **C.** that the portfolio generates higher returns than the benchmark during all market conditions.

5. The maximum drawdown and drawdown duration in Exhibit 1 indicate that:

    **A.** the portfolio recovered quickly from its maximum loss.

    **B.** over the 10-year period, the average maximum loss was −24.00%.

    **C.** a significant loss once persisted for four months before the portfolio began to recover.

# The following information relates to questions 6-14

Stephanie Tolmach is a consultant hired to create a performance attribution report on three funds held by a defined benefit pension plan (the Plan). Fund 1 is a domestic equity strategy, Fund 2 is a global equity strategy, and Fund 3 is a domestic fixed-income strategy.

Tolmach uses three approaches to attribution analysis: the return-based, holdings-based, and transaction-based approaches. The Plan's investment committee asks Tolmach to (1) apply the attribution method that uses only each fund's total portfolio returns over the last 12 months to identify return-generating components of the investment process and (2) include the impact of specific active investment decisions and the attribution effects of allocation and security selection in the report.

Tolmach first evaluates the performance of Fund 1 by constructing a Carhart factor model; the results are presented in Exhibit 1.

## Exhibit 1: Fund 1 Factor Model Attribution

| | Factor Sensitivity | | | | Contribution to Active Return | |
|---|---|---|---|---|---|---|
| Factor* | Portfo-lio (1) | Bench-mark (2) | Difference (3) | Factor Return (4) | Absolute (3) × (4) | Proportion of Active Return |
| RMRF | 1.22 | 0.91 | 0.31 | 16.32% | 5.06% | −126.80% |
| SMB | 0.59 | 0.68 | −0.09 | −3.25% | 0.29% | −7.33% |
| HML | −0.17 | 0.04 | −0.21 | −9.60% | 2.02% | −50.53% |
| WML | −0.05 | 0.07 | −0.12 | 3.38% | −0.41% | 10.17% |
| | | | A. Factor Tilt Return: | | 6.96% | −174.49% |
| | | | B. Security Selection: | | −10.95% | 274.49% |
| | | | C. Active Return (A + B): | | −3.99% | 100.00% |

*\* RMRF is the return on a value-weighted equity index in excess of the one-month T-bill rate, SMB is the small minus big market capitalization factor, HML is the high minus low factor, and WML is the winners minus losers factor.*

Tolmach turns her attention to Fund 2, constructing a region-based, Brinson–Fachler micro attribution analysis to evaluate the active decisions of the portfolio manager. The results are presented in Exhibit 2.

## Exhibit 2: Fund 2 Performance—Allocation by Region

| Return Attribution (Region Level) | Portfolio Weight | Benchmark Weight | Portfolio Return | Benchmark Return |
|---|---|---|---|---|
| North America | 10.84% | 7.67% | 16.50% | 16.47% |
| Greater Europe | 38.92% | 42.35% | 23.16% | 25.43% |
| Developed Asia and Australasia | 29.86% | 31.16% | 11.33% | 12.85% |
| South America | 20.38% | 18.82% | 20.00% | 35.26% |
| Total | 100.00% | 100.00% | 18.26% | 22.67% |

Next, Tolmach evaluates Fund 3 and the appropriateness of its benchmark. The benchmark is a cap-weighted bond index with daily reported performance; the index is rebalanced frequently, making it difficult to replicate. The benchmark has a meaningful investment in foreign bonds, whereas Fund 3 invests only in domestic bonds.

In the final section of the report, Tolmach reviews the entire Plan's characteristics, asset allocation, and benchmark. Tolmach observes that the Plan's benefits are no longer indexed to inflation and that the workforce is, on average, younger than it was when the current fund allocations were approved. Tolmach recommends a change in the Plan's asset allocation policy.

6. Of the three attribution approaches referenced by Tolmach, the method requested by the committee:

A. is the least accurate.

B. uses the underlying holdings of the actual portfolio.

    **C.** is the most difficult and time consuming to implement.

7. Based on Exhibit 1 and relative to the benchmark, the manager of Fund 1 *most likely* used a:

    **A.** growth tilt.

    **B.** greater tilt toward small cap.

    **C.** momentum-based investing approach.

8. Based on Exhibit 1, which of the following factors contributed the *least* to active return?

    **A.** HML

    **B.** SMB

    **C.** RMRF

9. Based on Exhibit 1, the manager could have delivered more value to the portfolio during the investment period by weighting more toward:

    **A.** value stocks.

    **B.** small-cap stocks.

    **C.** momentum stocks.

10. Based on Exhibit 2, the allocation effect for South America is *closest* to:

    **A.** −0.04%.

    **B.** 0.03%.

    **C.** 0.20%.

11. Based on Exhibit 2, the decision to overweight or underweight which of the following regions contributed positively to performance at the overall fund level?

    **A.** North America

    **B.** Greater Europe

    **C.** Developed Asia and Australasia

12. Based on Exhibit 2, the underperformance at the overall fund level is predominantly the result of poor security selection decisions in:

    **A.** South America.

    **B.** greater Europe.

    **C.** developed Asia and Australasia.

13. The benchmark for Fund 3 has which of the following characteristics of a valid benchmark?

    **A.** Investable

    **B.** Measurable

   **C.** Appropriate

14. Based on the final section of Tolmach's report, the Plan should use:

   **A.** a liability-based benchmark.

   **B.** an absolute return benchmark.

   **C.** a manager universe benchmark.

# SOLUTIONS

1. B is correct. Performance attribution helps explain how performance was achieved; it breaks apart the return or risk into different explanatory components. Effective performance attribution must account for all of the portfolio's return or risk exposure, reflect the investment decision-making process, quantify the active decisions of the portfolio manager, and provide a complete understanding of the excess return/risk of the portfolio.

2. C is correct. The portfolio is managed against a benchmark, which indicates a relative-risk type of risk attribution analysis. For a top-down investment approach, the analysis should attribute tracking risk to allocation and selection decisions relative to the benchmark.

3. B is correct. The target semi-standard deviation or target semideviation is the denominator of the Sortino ratio. The numerator of the Sortino ratio is the average portfolio return minus the target rate of return (minimum acceptable return, or MAR).

$$\text{Sortino ratio} = \frac{(\text{Average portfolio return} - \text{MAR})}{\text{Target semideviation}}$$

Substituting the values provided in Exhibit 3, the target semideviation is as follows:

$$\text{Target semideviation} = \frac{8.20\% - 5.00\%}{0.87}$$
$$= 3.678\% = 3.68\%$$

4. B is correct. The upside/downside capture, or simply the capture ratio (CR), is the upside capture ratio divided by the downside capture ratio.

(Upside capture)/(Downside capture) = 0.66/0.50 = 1.32.

A capture ratio greater than 1 indicates positive asymmetry of returns, or a convex return profile.

5. A is correct. Maximum drawdown is the cumulative peak-to-trough loss during a continuous period. Drawdown duration is the total time from the start of the drawdown until the cumulative drawdown recovers to zero, which can be segmented into the drawdown phase (start to trough) and the recovery phase (trough to zero cumulative return). The maximum drawdown was –24.00%, with a drawdown period of four months. Given the 10-year time frame, the portfolio recovered quickly from its maximum loss.

6. A is correct. The committee described a return-based attribution, which is the least accurate of the three approaches (the return-based, holdings-based, transaction-based approaches). Return-based attribution uses only the total portfolio returns over a period to identify the components of the investment process that have generated the returns.

7. A is correct. Based on the factor sensitivities in column 1 (negative sensitivity of –0.17 to HML) and the differences relative to the benchmark shown in column 3, the manager likely had a growth tilt.

8. B is correct. With an absolute return of 0.29% and with 7.33% of the contribution to return, SMB contributed far less than HML (2.02% and 50.53%, respectively) and RMRF (5.06% and 126.80%, respectively).

9.  C is correct. Had the manager weighted more toward momentum stocks during the period, the momentum factor (WML) return of 3.38% would have contributed positively to the portfolio.

    A is incorrect because the HML factor return was –9.60%; thus, weighting more toward value stocks would have detracted from portfolio returns.

    B is incorrect because the SMB factor return was –3.25%; thus, weighting more toward small-cap stocks would have detracted from portfolio returns.

10. C is correct. The allocation effect for South America is 0.20%.

$$\text{Allocation} = (w_i - W_i)(B_i - B)$$

$$= (20.38\% - 18.82\%)(35.26 - 22.67\%)$$

$$= 0.1964\% = 0.20\%$$

11. C is correct. The decision to underweight developed Asia and Australasia was a good one because the benchmark for this region underperformed the total benchmark (12.85% versus 22.67%). Alternatively, the question can be answered by calculating the allocation effects for the three regions, as follows:

$$\text{Allocation} = (w_i - W_i)(B_i - B)$$

$$\text{North America} = (10.84\% - 7.67\%)(16.47\% - 22.67\%)$$

$$= -0.20\%$$

$$\text{Greater Europe} = (38.92\% - 42.35\%)(25.43\% - 22.67\%)$$

$$= -0.09\%$$

$$\text{Developed Asia and Australasia} = (29.86\% - 31.16\%)(12.85\% - 22.67\%)$$

$$= 0.13\%$$

Developed Asia and Australasia is the only region of the three that had a positive allocation effect.

12. A is correct. The total –441 bps of underperformance from security selection and interaction at the overall fund level is predominantly the result of poor South American security selection decisions (–311 bps = 3.11%).

| Return Attribution (Segment Level) | Allocation | Selection + Interaction | Total |
|---|---|---|---|
| North America | –0.1966% | 0.0033% | –0.1934% |
| Greater Europe | –0.0946% | –0.8835% | –0.9781% |
| Developed Asia and Australasia | 0.1277% | –0.4539% | –0.3262% |

| Return Attribution (Segment Level) | Allocation | Selection + Interaction | Total |
|---|---|---|---|
| South America | 0.1964% | −3.1100% | −2.9136% |
| Total | 0.0329% | −4.4441% | −4.4112% |

$$\text{Allocation} = (w_i - W_i)(B_i - B)$$

$$\text{North America} = (10.84\% - 7.67\%)(16.47\% - 22.67\%)$$

$$= -0.20\%$$

$$\text{Greater Europe} = (38.92\% - 42.35\%)(25.43\% - 22.67\%)$$

$$= -0.09\%$$

$$\text{Developed Asia and Australasia} = (29.86\% - 31.16\%)(12.85\% - 22.67\%)$$

$$= 0.13\%$$

$$\text{South America} = (20.38\% - 18.82\%)(35.26\% - 22.67\%)$$

$$= 0.20\%$$

$$\text{Selection + Interaction} = W_i(R_i - B_i) + (w_i - W_i)(R_i - B_i)$$

$$\text{North America} = 7.67\%(16.50\% - 16.47\%) + (10.84\% - 7.67\%)(16.50\% - 16.47\%)$$

$$= 0.00\%$$

$$\text{Greater Europe} = 42.35\%(23.16\% - 25.43\%) + (38.92\% - 42.35\%)(23.16\% - 25.43\%)$$

$$= -0.88\%$$

$$\text{Developed Asia and Australasia} = 31.16\%(11.33\% - 12.85\%) + (29.86\% - 31.16\%)(11.33\% - 12.85\%)$$

$$= -0.45\%$$

$$\text{South America} = 18.82\%(20.00\% - 35.26\%) + (20.38\% - 18.82\%)(20.00\% - 35.26\%)$$

$$= -3.11\%$$

13. B is correct. Daily reported performance is available for the benchmark; thus, it is possible to measure the benchmark's return on a reasonably frequent and timely basis.

A is incorrect because the benchmark is a cap-weighted bond index that is rebalanced frequently, making it difficult to replicate. For a benchmark to be investable, it must be possible to replicate and hold the benchmark to earn its return (at least gross of expenses). The sponsor should have the option of moving assets from active management to a passive benchmark. If the benchmark is not investable, it is not a viable investment alternative. Bond indexes are often not investable and are rebalanced frequently over time.

C is incorrect because the index has a meaningful investment in foreign bonds, whereas Fund 3 invests only in domestic bonds, making the benchmark inappropriate. The benchmark must be consistent with the manager's investment style or area of expertise.

14. A is correct. Based on the Plan's type (defined benefit) and its characteristics as detailed in the final section of Tolmach's report, a liability-based benchmark is most appropriate. Liability-based benchmarks are used most frequently when assets are required to pay a specific future liability, as in a defined benefit pension plan.

# 2

# Investment Manager Selection

by Jeffrey C. Heisler, PhD, CFA, and Donald W. Lindsey, CFA.

*Jeffrey C. Heisler, PhD, CFA, is at TwinFocus Capital Partners (USA). Donald W. Lindsey, CFA (USA).*

## LEARNING OUTCOMES

| Mastery | The candidate should be able to: |
|---|---|
| ☐ | describe the components of a manager selection process, including due diligence |
| ☐ | contrast Type I and Type II errors in manager hiring and continuation decisions |
| ☐ | describe uses of returns-based and holdings-based style analysis in investment manager selection |
| ☐ | describe uses of the upside capture ratio, downside capture ratio, maximum drawdown, drawdown duration, and up/down capture in evaluating managers |
| ☐ | evaluate a manager's investment philosophy and investment decision-making process |
| ☐ | discuss how behavioral factors affect investment team decision making, and recommend techniques for mitigating their effects |
| ☐ | evaluate the costs and benefits of pooled investment vehicles and separate accounts |
| ☐ | compare types of investment manager contracts, including their major provisions and advantages and disadvantages |
| ☐ | describe the three basic forms of performance-based fees |
| ☐ | analyze and interpret a sample performance-based fee schedule |

## INTRODUCTION

**1**

Most investors do not hold securities directly but rather invest using intermediaries. Whether the intermediary is a separately managed account or a pooled investment vehicle, such as a UCITS (undertakings for collective investment in transferable securities) fund, a hedge fund, a private equity fund, or an exchange-traded fund (ETF), a professional investment manager is entrusted with helping investors achieve their investment objectives. In all these cases, the selection of appropriate investment managers is a challenge with important financial consequences.

Evaluating an investment manager is a complex and detailed process that encompasses a great deal more than analyzing investment returns. The investigation and analysis in support of an investment action, decision, or recommendation is called **due diligence**. In conducting investment manager due diligence, the focus is on understanding how the investment results were achieved and on assessing the likelihood that the investment process that generated these returns will produce superior or at least satisfactory investment results going forward. Due diligence also entails an evaluation of a firm's integrity, operations, and personnel. As such, due diligence involves both quantitative and qualitative analysis.

This learning module provides a framework that introduces and describes the important elements of the manager selection process. Although it is important to have a well-defined methodology, this learning module is not intended to be a rigid checklist, a step-by-step guide, or an in-depth analysis but rather to present a structure from which the reader can develop their own approach.

We assume that the investment policy statement (IPS) has been drafted, the asset allocation determined, and the decision to use an outside adviser has been made. As a result, the focus is on determining which manager offers the "best" means to implement or express those decisions. The discussion has three broad topics:

- Outlining a framework for identifying, evaluating, and ultimately selecting investment managers.
- Quantitative considerations in manager selection.
- Qualitative considerations in manager selection.

The learning module concludes with a summary of selected important points.

## 2    A FRAMEWORK FOR INVESTMENT MANAGER SEARCH AND SELECTION

☐ | describe the components of a manager selection process, including due diligence

An underlying assumption of investment manager due diligence is that a consistent, robust investment process will generate a similar return distribution relative to risk factors through time, assuming the underlying dynamics of the market have not dramatically changed. One important goal of manager due diligence is to understand whether the manager's investment process, people, and portfolio construction satisfy this assumption—that is, will the investment process generate the expected return from the expected sources? The manager search and selection process has three broad components: the universe, a quantitative analysis of the manager's performance track record, and a qualitative analysis of the manager's investment process. The qualitative analysis consists of investment due diligence, which evaluates the manager's investment process, and operational due diligence, which evaluates the manager's infrastructure and firm. Exhibit 1 details these components.

## Exhibit 1: Manager Selection Process Overview

| Key aspects | Key Question |
| --- | --- |
| **Universe** | |
| Defining the universe | What is the feasible set of managers that fit the portfolio need? |
| ▪ Suitability | Which managers are suitable for the IPS? |
| ▪ Style | Which have the appropriate style? |
| ▪ Active vs. passive | Which fit the active versus passive decision? |
| **Quantitative Analysis** | |
| Investment due diligence | Which manager "best" fits the portfolio need? |
| Quantitative | What has been the manager's return distribution? |
| ▪ Attribution and Appraisal | Has the manager displayed skill? |
| ▪ Capture ratio | How does the manager perform in "up" markets versus "down" markets? |
| ▪ Drawdown | Does the return distribution exhibit large drawdowns? |
| **Qualitative Analysis** | |
| Investment due diligence | Which manager "best" fits the portfolio need? |
| Qualitative | Is the manager expected to continue to generate this return distribution? |
| ▪ Philosophy | What market inefficiency does the manager seek to exploit? |
| ▪ Process | Is the investment process capable of exploiting this inefficiency? |
| ▪ People | Do the investment personnel possess the expertise and experience necessary to effectively implement the investment process? |
| ▪ Portfolio | Is portfolio construction consistent with the stated investment philosophy and process? |
| Operational due diligence | Is the manager's track record accurate, and does it fully reflect risks? |
| ▪ Process and procedure | Is the back office strong, safeguarding assets and able to issue accurate reports in a timely manner? |
| ▪ Firm | Is the firm profitable, with a healthy culture, and likely to remain in business? Is the firm committed to delivering performance over gathering assets? |
| ▪ Investment vehicle | Is the vehicle suitable for the portfolio need? |
| ▪ Terms | Are the terms acceptable and appropriate for the strategy and vehicle? |
| ▪ Monitoring | Does the manager continue to be the "best" fit for the portfolio need? |

## EXAMPLE 1

## Components of the Manager Selection Process

1. Qualitative analysis of the manager selection process includes:

    A. attribution.

**B.**   setting ESG objectives.

**C.**   investment and operational due diligence.

**Solution**

C is correct. Qualitative analysis consists of investment due diligence, which evaluates the manager's investment process, and operational due diligence, which evaluates the manager's infrastructure and firm.

2. Which of the following is considered a key aspect of operational due diligence?

**A.**   People

**B.**   Philosophy

**C.**   Procedures

**Solution**

C is correct. Process and procedures are key aspects of operational due diligence, whereas people and philosophy are key aspects of investment due diligence.

## Defining the Manager Universe

The manager selection process begins by defining the universe of feasible managers, those managers that potentially satisfy the identified portfolio need. The objective is to reduce the manager universe to a manageable size relative to the resources and time available to evaluate it. This process also involves balancing the risks of too narrow a search, which potentially excludes interesting managers, and too broad a search, which leads to little gain in reducing the list of potential managers. Like many interesting problems, this step is a combination of art and science. In the initial screening process, the search parameters can be narrowed and widened to determine which managers enter and exit and to evaluate whether these additions or deletions improve the universe.

The IPS and the reason for the manager search largely determine the universe of managers considered and the benchmark against which they are compared. A new search based on a strategic or tactical view, such as adding a new strategy or risk exposure, will examine a broad universe of comparable managers and look to select the best within the universe. Adding a manager to increase capacity or diversification within a strategy already held will look for a complement to current holdings. Replacing a single manager in a particular strategy will look for the best manager within the strategy universe. The IPS in part determines what the relative terms "best," "complement," and "cost/benefit" mean.

Typically, a search starts with a benchmark that represents the manager's role within the portfolio. The benchmark also provides a reference for performance attribution and appraisal. There are several approaches to assigning a manager to a benchmark:

- *Third-party categorization.* Database or software providers and consultants typically assign managers to a strategy sector. This categorization provides an easy and efficient way to define the universe. The risk is that the provider's definition may differ from the desired portfolio role. As such, it is important to understand the criteria used by the provider.

- *Returns-based style analysis.* The risk exposures derived from the manager's actual return series has the advantage of being objective. The disadvantage is additional computational effort and the limitations of returns-based analysis.

- *Holdings-based style analysis.* This approach allows for the estimation of current factor exposures but adds to computational effort and depends on timing and amount of transparency.
- *Manager experience.* The assignment can be based on an evaluation of the manager and observations of portfolios and returns over time.

Not surprisingly, a hybrid strategy that combines elements of each approach is recommended. Using third-party categorizations is an efficient way to build an initial universe that can then be complemented and refined with quantitative methods and experience. The screening should avoid using performance at this point. The focus should be on understanding the manager's risk profile and identifying candidates to fill the desired role in the portfolio. Lastly, the universe of potential managers is not static—it will evolve through time not only as manager strategies evolve but also as a result of the entry and exit of managers.

## TYPE I AND TYPE II ERRORS IN MANAGER SELECTION

**3**

☐ | contrast Type I and Type II errors in manager hiring and continuation decisions

Certain concepts from hypothesis testing, discussed earlier in the curriculum, can be relevant to the decision to hire an investment manager or to retain or dismiss a manager previously hired.

The determination of whether a manager is skillful typically starts with the null hypothesis (the hypothesis assumed to be true until demonstrated otherwise) that the manager is not skillful. As a result, there are two types of potential error (see Exhibit 2):

- Type I: Hiring or retaining a manager who subsequently underperforms expectations. Rejecting the null hypothesis of no skill when it is correct; a false positive.
- Type II: Not hiring or firing a manager who subsequently outperforms, or performs in line with, expectations. Not rejecting the null hypothesis when it is incorrect; a false negative.

**Exhibit 2: Type I and Type II Errors**

| | | Realization | |
|---|---|---|---|
| | | Below expectations (no skill) | At or above expectations (skill) |
| Decision | Hire/Retain | Type I | Correct |
| | Not Hire/Fire | Correct | Type II |

Type I and Type II errors can occur anytime a decision is made regarding the hiring or firing of a manager. The decision maker must determine which error is preferred based on the expected benefits and costs of changing managers.

## Qualitative Considerations in Type I and Type II Errors

Decision makers appear predisposed to worry more about Type I errors than Type II errors. Potential reasons for this focus on Type I errors are as follows:

- Psychologically, people seek to avoid feelings of regret. Type I errors are mistaken rejections, whereas Type II errors are failures to detect a true relationship. As a result, Type I errors create explicit costs, whereas Type II errors create opportunity costs. Because individuals appear to put less weight on opportunity costs, Type I errors are psychologically more painful than Type II errors.

- Type I errors are relatively straightforward to measure and are often directly linked to the decision maker's compensation. Portfolio holdings are regularly monitored, and managers' out- and underperformance expectations are clearly identified. Type II errors are less likely to be measured—what is the performance impact of not having selected a particular manager? As such, the link between compensation and Type II errors is less clear.

- Similarly, Type I errors are more transparent to investors, so they entail not only the regret of an incorrect decision but the pain of having to explain this decision to the investor. Type II errors, firing (or not hiring) a manager with skill, are less transparent to investors, unless the investor tracks fired managers or evaluates the universe themselves.

Although Type I errors are likely more familiar and more of a concern to most decision makers, a consistent pattern of Type II errors can highlight weaknesses in the manager selection process. One approach to examine this issue is to monitor not only managers currently held but also managers that were evaluated and not hired as well as managers that were fired. The goal of monitoring is to determine the following:

- Are there identifiable factors that differentiate managers hired and managers not hired?

- Are these factors consistent with the investment philosophy and process of the decision maker?

- Are there identifiable factors driving the decision to retain or fire managers?

- Are these factors consistent with the investment philosophy and process of the decision maker?

- What is the added value of the decision to retain or fire managers?

The objective is to avoid making decisions based on short-term performance (trend following) and to identify any evidence of behavioral biases (regret, loss aversion) in the evaluation of managers during the selection process.

## Performance Implications of Type I and Type II Errors

The cost of Type I errors is holding a manager without skill, as opposed to the cost of Type II errors, which is not holding managers with skill. The cost is driven by the size, shape, mean, and dispersion of the return distributions of the skilled and unskilled managers within the universe. The smaller the difference in sample size and distribution mean and the wider the dispersion of the distributions, the smaller the expected cost of the Type I or Type II error. More efficient markets are likely to exhibit smaller differences in the distributions of skilled and unskilled managers, indicating a lower opportunity cost of retaining and the lower the cost of hiring an unskilled manager.

The extent to which a strategy is mean-reverting also has a bearing on the cost of Type I and Type II errors. If a strategy's performance is mean reverting, firing a poor performer (or hiring a strong performer) only to see a reversion in performance results is a Type I error. A Type II error would be trimming or not hiring strong performers and hiring managers with weaker track records. There is evidence that individual investors significantly underperform the average mutual fund because of poor timing and fund selection decisions. A study of institutional plan sponsor allocation decisions found that investment products receiving contributions subsequently underperformed products experiencing withdrawals. The study estimated that more than $170 billion was lost during the period examined (Stewart, Neumann, Knittel, and Heisler 2009).

---

**EXAMPLE 2**

## Type I and Type II Errors

1. A Type I error is:

   **A.** hiring or retaining a manager that subsequently underperforms expectations.

   **B.** hiring or retaining a manager that subsequently outperforms, or performs in line with, expectations.

   **C.** not hiring or firing a manager who subsequently outperforms, or performs in line with, expectations.

   **Solution**

   A is correct. The error consists of rejecting the null hypothesis (no skill) when it is correct.

2. A Type II error is:

   **A.** hiring or retaining a manager that subsequently underperforms expectations.

   **B.** hiring or retaining a manager that subsequently outperforms, or performs in line with, expectations.

   **C.** not hiring or firing a manager who subsequently outperforms, or performs in line with, expectations.

   **Solution**

   C is correct. The error consists of not rejecting the null hypothesis (no skill) when it is incorrect.

3. The difference in expected cost between Type I and Type II errors is *most likely*:

   **A.** higher the smaller the perceived difference between the distribution of skilled and unskilled managers.

   **B.** lower the smaller the perceived difference between the distribution of skilled and unskilled managers.

   **C.** zero.

   **Solution**

   B is correct. The less distinct the distribution of skilled managers from unskilled managers, the lower the opportunity cost of retaining and cost of hiring an unskilled manager. That is, the smaller the perceived difference between the distribution of skilled and unskilled managers, the lower the cost and incentive to fire a manager.

# 4    QUANTITATIVE ELEMENTS OF MANAGER SEARCH AND SELECTION

    describe uses of returns-based and holdings-based style analysis in investment manager selection

Performance appraisal captures most aspects of quantitative analysis, evaluating a manager's strengths and weaknesses as measured by that manager's ability to add value to a stated benchmark. Although the determination of whether the manager possesses skill is important, it is equally important to understand the manager's risk profile. The manager has likely been selected to fill a particular role in the portfolio. As such, although it is important to select a skillful manager, the "best" manager may be one that delivers the desired exposures and is suitable for the investor's assumptions, expectations, and biases.

## Style Analysis

An important component of performance appraisal and manager selection is understanding the manager's risk exposures relative to the benchmark and how they evolve over time. This understanding helps define the universe of potential managers and the monitoring of selected managers. The process is referred to as style analysis.

A manager's self-reported risk exposures, such as portfolio concentration, industry exposure, capitalization exposure, and other quantitative measures, are the starting point in style analysis. They provide a means to classify managers by style for defining the selection process, a point of reference for evaluating the returns-based and holdings-based style analysis, and an interesting operational check on the manager.

The results of the returns-based style analysis (RBSA) and the holdings-based style analysis (HBSA) should be consistent with the manager's philosophy and the investment process. If not, the process might not be repeatable or might be implemented inconsistently. It is essential to look at all portfolio construction and risk management issues.

The results of the returns-based style analysis and the holdings-based style analysis should be tracked over time in order to ascertain if the risk trends or exposures are out of line with expectations or the manager's stated style. Deviations may signal that issues, such as style drift, are developing.

Returns-based and holdings-based style analyses provide a means to determine the risks and sources of return for a particular strategy. To be useful, style analysis must be:

- *Meaningful.* The risks reported must represent the important sources of performance return and risk.
- *Accurate.* The reported values must reflect the manager's actual risk exposures.
- *Consistent.* The methodology must allow for comparison over time and across multiple managers.
- *Timely.* The report must be available in a timely manner so that it is useful for making informed investment decisions.

Style analysis is most useful with strategies that hold publicly traded securities where pricing is frequent. It can be applied to other strategies (hedge funds and private equity, for example), but the insights drawn from a style analysis of such strategies are more likely to be used for designing additional lines of inquiry in the course of due diligence rather than for confirmation of the investment process.

**Returns-based style analysis** (RBSA) is a top-down approach that involves estimating a portfolio's sensitivities to security market indexes representing a range of distinct factors. Although RBSA adds the additional analytical step of estimating the risk factors, as opposed to using a third-party or self-reported style categorization, the analysis is straightforward and typically does not require a large amount of additional, or difficult to acquire, data. RBSA should identify the important drivers of return and risk factors for the period analyzed and can be estimated even for complicated strategies. In addition, the process is comparable across managers and through time, and the use of returns data provides an objective style check that is not subject to window dressing. The analysis can be run immediately after the data are available, particularly in the case of publicly traded securities. As such, RBSA has many of the attributes of effective risk reporting.

The disadvantage is that RBSA is an imprecise tool. Although the additional computational effort required is not onerous, accuracy may be compromised, because RBSA effectively attributes performance to an unchanging average portfolio during the period. This attribution limits the ability to identify the impact of dynamic investment decisions and may distort the decomposition across sources of added value. Furthermore, the portfolio being analyzed might not reflect the current or future portfolio exposures. If the portfolio contains illiquid securities, stale prices may understate the risk exposure of the strategy. This is a particular problem for private equity (PE) and venture capital (VC) managers that hold illiquid or non-traded securities. VC and PE firms report performance based on the internal rate of return of cash distributions and appraisals of ongoing projects. As a result, reported performance can understate the volatility of return for shorter horizons or time periods with limited liquidity events. Longer periods generally provide more-accurate estimates of the manager's underlying standard deviation of return. The timeliness of any analysis depends on the securities that take the longest to price, which can be challenging for illiquid or non-traded securities.

**Holdings-based style analysis** (HBSA) is a bottom-up approach that estimates the risk exposures from the actual securities held in the portfolio at a point in time. This approach allows for estimation of current risk factors and offers several advantages. Similar to RBSA, HBSA should identify all important drivers of return and risk factors; be comparable across managers and through time; provide an accurate view of the manager's risk exposures, although potentially subject to window dressing; and be estimated immediately after the data become available.

Exhibit 3 presents a typical holdings-based style map. The manager being evaluated, along with the other managers in the universe, is placed along the size ($y$-axis) and style ($x$-axis) dimensions. The portfolio holdings of the manager being evaluated exhibit a large-cap value bias in what is otherwise a rather diverse universe.

**Exhibit 3: Example of Holdings-Based Style Analysis**

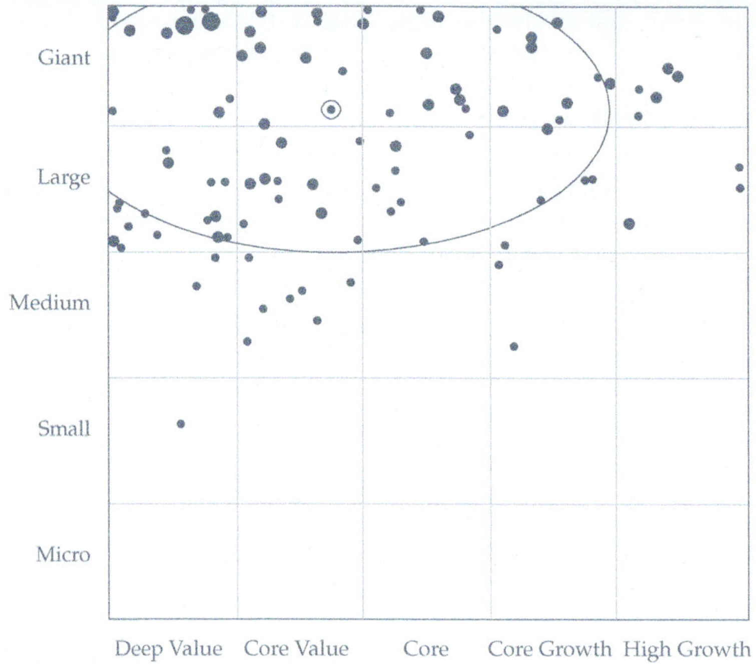

Giant
Large
Medium
Small
Micro

Deep Value    Core Value    Core    Core Growth    High Growth

*Source*: Morningstar Direct, The Mutual Fund Research Center.

---

As with RBSA, HBSA has some disadvantages. The computational effort increases with the complexity of the strategy and depends on the timing and degree of the transparency provided by the manager. This extra effort can be challenging for hedge fund, private equity, and venture capital managers that may be averse to or unable to provide position-level pricing. Even with mutual funds, the necessary transparency may come with a time lag. The usefulness of the analysis may be compromised because the portfolio reflects a snapshot in time and might not reflect the portfolio going forward, particularly for high-turnover strategies. Some factors may be difficult to estimate if the strategy is complex because HBSA requires an understanding of the underlying strategy. In general, HBSA is typically easier with equity strategies, particularly for ETFs because holdings are published daily. If the portfolio has illiquid securities, stale pricing may underestimate the risk exposure of the strategy. The report's timeliness depends on the securities that take the longest to price, which can be challenging for illiquid or non-traded securities.

**EXAMPLE 3**

## Style Analysis

1. Which of the following is an advantage of RBSA?

    **A.** It is a more precise tool than HBSA.

    **B.** It does not require potentially difficult to acquire data.

**C.** It is more accurate than HBSA when the portfolio contains illiquid securities.

**Solution**

B is correct. The data needed for RBSA are usually easier to obtain than the data required for HBSA. RBSA is not a precise tool, and it is not more accurate than HBSA when the portfolio holds illiquid securities.

---

2. Which of the following is an advantage of HBSA?

**A.** It works well for high-turnover strategies.

**B.** It can identify important drivers of return and risk factors and is comparable across managers and through time.

**C.** It effectively attributes performance to a snapshot of the portfolio at a particular time and thus is not subject to window dressing.

**Solution**

B is correct. Although HBSA allows for estimation of current risk factors and is comparable across managers and through time, the necessary computational effort increases with the strategy's complexity and depends on the timing and degree of the transparency provided by the manager. Some factors may be difficult to estimate if the strategy is complex because this approach requires an understanding of the underlying strategy. In general, HBSA is typically easier for equity strategies. If the portfolio has illiquid securities, stale pricing may underestimate the risk exposure of the strategy. Window dressing and high turnover can compromise the results because the results are attributed to a snapshot of the portfolio.

---

# CAPTURE RATIOS AND DRAWDOWNS IN MANAGER EVALUATION

**5**

☐ | describe uses of the upside capture ratio, downside capture ratio, maximum drawdown, drawdown duration, and up/down capture in evaluating managers

Because large losses require proportionally greater gains to reverse or offset, drawdowns and capture ratios can be important factors in investment manager evaluation. A manager that experiences larger drawdowns may be less suitable for an investor closer to the end of their investment horizon. The capture ratio helps assess manager suitability relative to the investor's IPS, especially in relation to the investor's time horizon and risk tolerance.

Recall the following: (1) Upside capture (UC) measures capture when the benchmark return is positive. UC greater than 100% suggests out-performance relative to the benchmark. (2) Downside capture (DC) measures capture when the benchmark return is negative. DC less than 100% generally suggests out-performance relative to the benchmark. (3) The **capture ratio** (CR)—upside capture divided by downside capture—measures the asymmetry of return. (4) **Drawdown** is the cumulative peak-to-trough loss during a particular continuous period and **drawdown duration** is the total time from the start of the drawdown until the cumulative drawdown recovers to zero.

Let's illustrate the use of capture ratios in the analysis of manager returns. Consider the four stylized return profiles in Exhibit 4.

### Exhibit 4: Return Profile Summary

| Profile | Upside Capture | Downside Capture | Ratio |
|---|---|---|---|
| Long only | 100% | 100% | 1.0 |
| Positive asymmetry | 75% | 25% | 3.0 |
| Low beta | 50% | 50% | 1.0 |
| Negative asymmetry | 25% | 75% | 0.3 |

Each strategy's allocation to the S&P 500 Total Return (TR) Index and to 90-day T-bills (assuming monthly rebalancing to simplify the calculations) is based on the realized monthly return from January 2000 to December 2013. (This time period encompasses two significant drawdowns: the "tech bubble burst" of the early 2000s and the extreme drawdown of the Global Financial Crisis in 2008–2009.)

- The long-only profile is 100% allocated to the S&P 500 throughout the period.
- The low-beta profile is allocated 50% to the S&P 500 throughout the period.
- The positive asymmetry profile is allocated 75% to the S&P 500 for months when the S&P 500 return is positive and 25% when the S&P 500 return is negative.
- The negative asymmetry profile is allocated 25% to the S&P 500 for months when the S&P 500 return is positive and 75% when the S&P 500 return is negative.

The remainder for all profiles is allocated to 90-day T-bills. Exhibit 5 shows each profile's cumulative monthly return for the period.

**Exhibit 5: Each Profile's Cumulative Monthly Return, January 2000–December 2013**

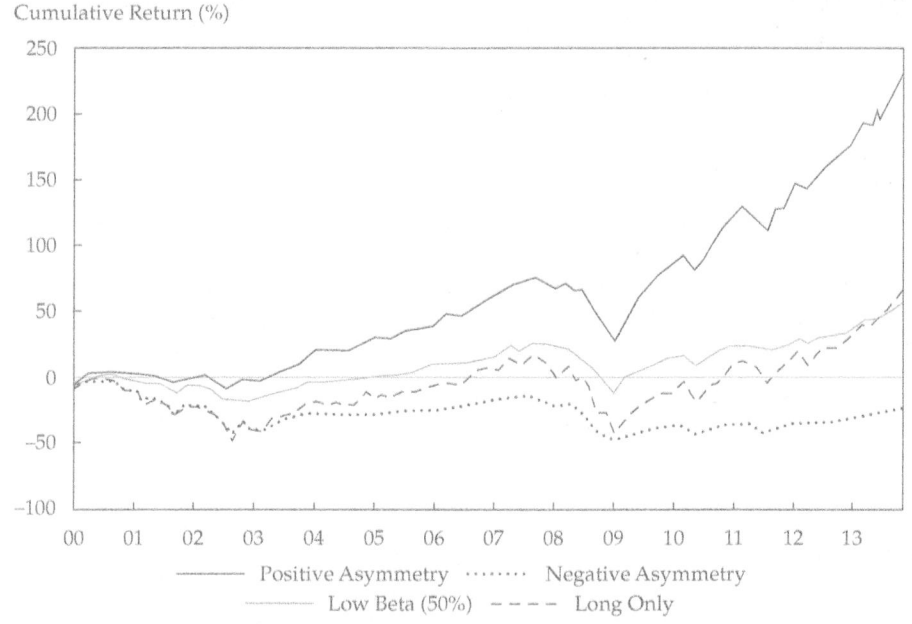

Cumulative Return (%)

—————— Positive Asymmetry ·········· Negative Asymmetry
————— Low Beta (50%) – – – – Long Only

Exhibit 6 provides summary statistics for each profile based on monthly returns from January 2000 to December 2013. Although the long-only profile outperformed the low-beta profile over the full period, this outperformance resulted from the strong up market of 2013—the long-only profile lagged the low-beta profile for most of the period. The low beta profile achieved higher risk-adjusted returns and only half the volatility for the full period. The low-beta profile declined only 18.8% from January 2000 to September 2002, compared with the long-only decline of 42.5%. As a result, the low-beta profile had higher cumulative performance from January 2000 to October 2007 despite markedly lagging the long-only profile (56.0% to 108.4%) from October 2002 to October 2007.

Although a low-beta approach may sacrifice performance, it shows that limiting drawdowns can result in better absolute and risk-adjusted returns in certain markets.

Not surprisingly, positive asymmetry results in better performance relative to long only, low beta, and negative asymmetry. Although the positive asymmetry profile lags in up markets, this lag is more than offset by the lower participation in down markets. Not surprisingly, the negative asymmetry profile lags.

**Exhibit 6: Summary Statistics for Each Profile, January 2000–December 2013**

| Strategy | Long Only | Low Beta | Positive Asymmetry | Negative Asymmetry |
|---|---|---|---|---|
| Cumulative return | 64.0% | 54.2% | 228.1% | −24.4% |
| Annualized return | 3.60% | 3.14% | 8.86% | −1.98% |
| Annualized standard deviation | 15.64% | 7.79% | 9.61% | 10.01% |
| Sharpe ratio | 0.10 | 0.14 | 0.71 | −0.40 |

| Strategy | Long Only | Low Beta | Positive Asymmetry | Negative Asymmetry |
|---|---|---|---|---|
| Beta | 1.00 | 0.50 | 0.61 | 0.64 |
| Drawdown (maximum) | −50.9% | −28.3% | −26.9% | −48.9% |

We've shown that positive asymmetry is a desirable trait. When evaluating a manager that exhibits positive asymmetry in its returns, we need to understand whether the strategy is inherently convex or whether the profile is a result of manager skill. For example, a hedging strategy implemented by rolling forward out-of-the-money put options will typically return many small losses because more options expire worthless than are compensated for by the occasional large gain during a large market downturn. A manager employing this strategy will likely exhibit consistent positive asymmetry in his returns, but the positive asymmetry is likely due to the nature of the strategy rather than investment skill.

Let's consider now the use of drawdowns in the analysis of manager returns. Drawdowns are stress tests of the investment process and can expose potentially flawed or inconsistently implemented investment processes, inadequate risk controls, or operational issues. Did the manager implement the stated investment process consistently? If yes, what lessons were learned and how might the investment process have been adapted as a result? If the drawdown resulted from a deviation from the stated investment process, why? During a large or long drawdown, a manager could start to worry more about business risk than investment risk and act in their own best interest rather than that of their investors. How a manager responds to a large drawdown as it occurs (and what lessons are learned) provides evidence of the robustness and repeatability of the investment, portfolio construction, and risk management processes, as well as insight into the people implementing the processes.

### EVENTS OF AUGUST 2007

Starting on 7 August 2007, many quantitative equity long–short strategies began to experience large drawdowns. Many managers had never experienced such losses or market conditions and started to sell positions as stop-loss and risk management policies were triggered (Khandani and Lo 2011). This activity added to additional selling pressure, and the S&P 500 declined 13.4% by 8 August. Those managers that sold ended up locking in large losses because the underperforming stocks and market subsequently recovered, with the S&P 500 down only 5.7% for the month. In many cases, those funds that sold experienced redemptions or ended up closing.

As August 2007 demonstrated, distinguishing prudent risk management from a misalignment of interests is not always straightforward. Should a manager continue to actively trade a portfolio if the market environment no longer reflects their investment philosophy? In addition, traders will claim that it is better to cut losses because losses can signal that something has changed or that the timing of the trade is not right. Conversely, selling into a down market raises the risk of crystallizing losses and missing any subsequent reversal. The decision maker must assess whether the manager's behavior was a disciplined application of the investment process, reflected a misalignment of interests, or simply resulted from panic or overreaction by the manager.

One aspect of suitability for the IPS is the investment horizon and its relationship to risk capacity. An investor closer to retirement, with less time to recover from losses, places more emphasis on absolute measures of risk. If there has been no change to investment policy and no change in the view that the manager remains suitable, the temptation to exit should be resisted to avoid exiting at an inauspicious time. Investors with shorter horizons, with lower risk capacity, or those prone to overreacting to losses may be better served by allocating to managers with shallower and shorter expected drawdowns.

### THE CONCEPT OF ACTIVE SHARE

**Active share** measures the difference in portfolio holdings relative to the benchmark. A manager that precisely replicates the benchmark will have an active share of zero; a manager with no holdings in common with the benchmark will have an active share of one.

Given a strategy with $N$ securities ($i = 1, 2, \ldots, N$), active share is calculated as

$$\text{Active Share} = \frac{1}{2} \sum_{i=1}^{N} \left| \text{Strategy Weight}_i - \text{Benchmark Weight}_i \right|$$

Typically, managers are somewhere along the spectrum. The categorization of active share and tracking risk in Exhibit 7 has been suggested for active managers. It is clear that full replication will appear as a closet indexer. A manager that uses sampling techniques to build the portfolio may, however, appear as a diversified stock picker depending on the universe under consideration and the dispersion of active share of the constituents. Tracking risk will be low, but active share might not be because only a subset of constituents is held. One reason is that high and low are relative to the universe being examined and the category definitions used. As such, it is important to examine risk factors and portfolio construction techniques of both active and passive managers.

#### Exhibit 7: Active Share vs. Tracking Risk

| | | Active Share | |
| --- | --- | --- | --- |
| | | Low | High |
| Tracking risk | High | Sector rotation | Concentrated stock pickers |
| | Low | Closet indexer | Diversified stock pickers |

# THE MANAGER'S INVESTMENT PHILOSOPHY

**6**

- [ ] evaluate a manager's investment philosophy and investment decision-making process
- [ ] discuss how behavioral factors affect investment team decision making, and recommend techniques for mitigating their effects

The goal of manager due diligence is to weigh the potential risks that may arise from entering into an investment management relationship and entrusting assets to a firm. Although it is impossible to eliminate all potential risks, the allocator must assess how the firm will manage the broad range of risks it is likely to face in the future. This lesson outlines the general aspects of manager due diligence and the particular questions the investor needs to answer.

Investment due diligence examines and evaluates the qualitative considerations that illustrate that the manager's investment process is repeatable and consistently implemented. The objective is to understand whether the investment philosophy, process, people, and portfolio construction satisfy the assumption that past performance provides some guidance for expected future performance. In other words, are the conclusions drawn from performance measurement, attribution, and appraisal reliable selection criteria? In addition, it is important to remember that investment managers are businesses. Regardless of the strength of the investment process or historical performance, investment management firms must be operated as successful businesses to ensure sustainability. Operational due diligence examines and evaluates the firm's policies and procedures, to identify potential risks that might not be captured in historical performance and to assess the firm's sustainability.

## Investment Philosophy

The investment philosophy is the foundation of the investment process. Every investment strategy is based on a set of assumptions about the factors that drive performance and the manager's beliefs about their ability to successfully exploit these sources of return. The investment manager should have a clear and concise investment philosophy.

First, every manager makes assumptions about market efficiency, including the degree and the time frame. Index-based strategies assume markets are sufficiently efficient and that active management cannot add value after transaction costs and fees. As a result, these strategies seek to capture return through exposure to systematic **risk premiums**, such as equity risk, duration risk, or credit risk. These strategies can also look to capture alternative risk premiums such as liquidity risk, natural disaster risk (through, for example, catastrophe bonds and quota shares), volatility risk, or some combination of these premiums (e.g., distressed strategies seek to capture credit and liquidity risk premiums).

In contrast, active strategies assume markets are sufficiently inefficient that security mispricings can be identified and exploited. These opportunities typically arise when market behavior deviates from the manager's fundamental assumptions. Generally speaking, inefficiencies can be categorized as behavioral or structural.

- *Behavioral inefficiencies* are perceived mispricings created by the actions of other market participants, usually associated with biases, such as trend following or loss aversion. These inefficiencies are temporary, lasting long enough for the manager to identify and exploit them before the market price and perceived intrinsic value converge.

- *Structural inefficiencies* are perceived mispricings created by external or internal rules and regulations. These inefficiencies can be long lived and assume a continuation of the rules and regulations rather than a convergence.

Active strategies also typically make assumptions about the dynamics and structures of the market, such as the following: The correlation structure of the market is sufficiently stable over the investment horizon to make diversification useful for risk management; prices eventually converge to intrinsic value, which can be estimated by using a discounted cash flow model; or market prices are driven by predictable macroeconomic trends.

It is important to evaluate these assumptions and the role they play in the investment process to understand how the strategy will behave through time and across market environments.

- Can the manager clearly and consistently articulate their investment philosophy? It is hard to have confidence in the repeatability and efficacy of an investment process if the manager, and investment personnel, cannot explain the assumptions that underpin the process. This clarity also provides a consistency check that the investment process and personnel are appropriate for the stated philosophy.

- Are the assumptions credible and consistent? That is, does the decision maker agree with the assumptions underlying the strategy, and are these assumptions consistent with the investment process? A decision maker who believes a market is efficient would likely not find the assumptions of an active manager in that market credible. In the decision maker's judgment, the assumptions must support a repeatable and robust investment process.

- How has the philosophy developed over time? Ideally, the philosophy is unchanged through time, suggesting a repeatable process. If philosophy has evolved, it is preferred that changes are judged to be reasonable responses to changing market conditions rather than a series of ad hoc reactions to performance or investor flows. Such changes suggest a lack of repeatability and robustness.  ·

- Are the return sources linked to credible and consistent inefficiencies? The decision maker must judge whether the investment philosophy is based on an inefficiency that is based on an informational advantage, or behavioral and structural inefficiencies that suggest the investment process is repeatable.

If the source of return is linked to a credible inefficiency, there is the additional issue of capacity. Capacity has several related aspects, such as the level of assets the strategy or opportunity can absorb without a dilution of returns, the number of opportunities or securities available, and the ability to transact in a timely manner at or near the market price—that is, liquidity. Overall, capacity is the level, repeatability, and sustainability of returns that the inefficiency is expected to support in the future.

- Does the inefficiency provide a sufficient frequency of opportunity and level of return to cover transaction costs and fees? If so, does this require leverage?

- Does the inefficiency provide a repeatable source of return? That is, can the opportunity be captured by a repeatable process, or is each opportunity unique, requiring a different process of skill set to exploit?

- Is the inefficiency sustainable? That is, at what asset level would the realized return from the inefficiency be unacceptably low? Sustainability will be a function of the market's depth and liquidity, as well as how much capital is allocated, either by the manager or competitors, to the inefficiency. All else equal, the more well-known an inefficiency, the more likely it is to be arbitraged away.

### UNCOMMON WAYS OF PASSING THE INVESTMENT PHILOSOPHY TEST

1. Managers that measure the success of the steps of the process and not just the ultimate outcome.

For example, consider a bond manager that makes the claim that his or her credit research not only predicts upgrades and downgrades, but makes those predictions before the expectation of a rating change is reflected in the market price. This manager tracks every prediction to see if the market consensus (as reflected by price) and rating agencies come around to his or her view. Benefits of such an approach include (1) the manager knows their views only have value if they are not only correct but different than consensus, and (2) they track how prices eventually come to reflect, or not reflect, their views. Similarly, managers that evaluate their own performance with strategy benchmarks designed to replicate their selection universe demonstrate they understand the importance of attempting to differentiate alpha from noise (see Kuenzi 2003).

2.  Managers that recognize that every strategy they come up with is potentially subject to being arbitraged away.

    For example, consider a quantitative equity manager that that plays many themes at once. Each theme is viewed as having a finite life, and the performance of each theme is isolated and monitored so as to observe the decay in the value of the theme. The manager considers his or her competitive advantage to be in the identification of new themes, and in the technology for measuring the contribution of each theme to performance. A similar idea is presented in the adaptive market hypothesis of Lo (2004), where the market is always tending toward efficiency, but the types of trades needed to move it towards efficiency rotate and evolve over time.

3.  Managers that claim they exploit inefficiencies, and identify the specific inefficiency they are exploiting with every position they take.

    Most managers that say they exploit inefficiencies use this claim as a broad justification for their investment process, but are unable to identify the specific inefficiency they are exploiting in any given decision they make. Those that routinely specify how their information or point of view differs from that reflected in price are much more credible.

4.  Managers that know their companies so well that they are quicker to interpret change, even though they have no explicit alpha thesis.

    There is always an exception to the rule. Sometimes a manager is simply talented and cannot articulate an alpha thesis.

Despite examples such as these, it remains frustratingly difficult to distinguish between true alpha-generators and alpha-pretenders. Investors should insist that alpha-generators explain their source of advantage.

*This excerpt is from John R. Minahan, CFA, "The Role of Investment Philosophy in Evaluating Investment Managers: A Consultant's Perspective on Distinguishing Alpha from Noise," Journal of Investing 15 (May 2006): 6–11. Copyright © 2006 by Institutional Investor Journals. Reprinted with permission.*

> **EXAMPLE 4**
>
> ## Investment Philosophy
>
> 1. Which of the following is *not* an important consideration when evaluating a manager's investment philosophy?
>
>    **A.** What are the compensation arrangements of key employees?
>
>    **B.** Are the investment philosophy assumptions credible and consistent?
>
>    **C.** Can the manager clearly and consistently articulate their investment philosophy?
>
>    **Solution**
>
>    A is correct. Employee compensation is a legal and compliance issue considered as part of operational due diligence.
>
> 2. Generally speaking, inefficiencies can be *most usefully* categorized as:
>
>    **A.** large and small.
>
>    **B.** internal and external.
>
>    **C.** structural and behavioral.
>
>    **Solution**
>
>    C is correct. Behavioral inefficiencies are created by the actions of other participants in the market. These inefficiencies are temporary, lasting long enough for the manager to identify and exploit them before the market price and perceived intrinsic value converge. Structural inefficiencies are created by external or internal rules and regulations. These inefficiencies can be long lived and assume a continuation of the rules and regulations rather than a convergence.
>
> 3. Which of the following is *not* an important consideration when evaluating the capacity of an inefficiency?
>
>    **A.** Does the strategy rely on unique information?
>
>    **B.** Does the inefficiency provide a repeatable source of return?
>
>    **C.** Does the inefficiency provide a sufficient frequency of opportunity and level of return to cover transaction costs and fees?
>
>    **Solution**
>
>    A is correct. The uniqueness of information used by the manager is a consideration when evaluating the assumptions of the investment process.

## Investment Personnel

An investment process can only be as good as the people who create and implement it, and even the best process can be compromised by poor execution by the people involved. This view is not a question of liking the manager or team but of trusting that they possess the expertise and experience to effectively implement the strategy.

- Does the investment team have sufficient expertise and experience to effectively execute the investment process? The need for expertise is self-evident. The greater the experience, particularly managing the current strategy across market environments, the greater the confidence in the manager's ability to effectively execute the investment process. As noted with drawdowns, it is especially instructive to see how the manager responded to stressed markets and poor performance.

- Does the investment team have sufficient depth to effectively execute the investment process? A strategy that focuses on a small universe of publicly traded stocks might not require a large investment team. A global macro or multi-strategy fund, which holds positions across numerous global markets, likely requires a large team with expertise and experience supporting the manager.

- What is the level of **key person risk**? A strategy that is overly dependent on the judgment or particular skills of an individual or small team of people faces key person risk, an overreliance on an individual or individuals whose departure would negatively affect the strategy's performance.

- What kinds of agreements (e.g., non-compete) and incentives (ownership, bonus, pay) exist to retain and attract key employees to join and stay at the firm?

- What has been the turnover of firm personnel? High personnel turnover risks the loss of institutional knowledge and experience within the team.

## Behavioral Biases among Investment Teams

Investment decisions are often made by teams rather than individuals. In 2021, team-managed mutual funds accounted for 64% of all US active mutual funds (Karagiannidis and Booth 2022). The primary motivation for team management is the idea that "two heads are better than one." More formally, the application to a task of a number of individuals, each with different skills and experiences, can provide for more effective decision making. A secondary motivation for team investment management is to mitigate key person risk.

While teams can mitigate some individual behavioral biases, such as overconfidence in forecasting, teams also introduce new biases or exacerbate others. Indeed, research on the performance of team-managed versus individual-managed mutual funds is mixed. Several studies have found that team-managed funds underperform individual-managed funds (Chen, Harrison, Ming, and Kubik 2004; Baer, Kempf, and Ruenzi 2005; Bär, Ciccotello, and Ruenzi 2010; Goldman, Sun, and Zhou 2016). Several other studies have found the opposite (Patel and Sarkissian 2017; Karagiannidis 2010). And some studies have found there is no difference in performance between the two (Bliss, Potter, and Schwarz 2008; Wang 2016; Sargis and Chang 2017). The mixed performance record suggests that there is nothing magical about a team, so managers should focus on creating an effective structure and culture.

Three common behavioral biases that can adversely affect investment teams' performance are groupthink, authority bias, and aversion to complexity.

**Groupthink** occurs when a team minimizes conflict and dissent in reaching and maintaining a consensus. The pursuit of harmony overrides individual expression and may even encourage individuals to withhold information and their perspectives from the team. Common symptoms of groupthink are closed-mindedness and confirmation bias, where fresh sources of information, different interpretations, and dissent are ignored or minimized. A portfolio management team may become convinced that a recession is imminent based on an inverted yield curve and falling commodity prices and thus seek to position the portfolio defensively by decreasing exposure to cyclicals. While this may ultimately be the right decision, the team must remain open to the possibility that it isn't. For example, other leading economic indicators may suggest a different conclusion, and it may behoove the team to speak with an analyst who has made a different call. The team should also investigate its own historical track record of recession calls, as well as the reliability of calls made based on an inverted yield curve and falling commodity prices.

**Authority bias** involves groups deferring to a group member that is a subject matter expert or in a position of authority (e.g., the senior-most group member). For example, a research analyst may recommend a semiconductor equipment stock to a team of three portfolio managers. One of the portfolio managers is a former technology research analyst and votes to not buy the stock. The other two members vote the same way, deferring to the subject matter expertise of the other manager. While this may be the right call, it undermines the reason for a team in the first place: a synthesis of diverse perspectives and skills.

**Aversion to complexity** is a well-known phenomenon of groups in many professional contexts, in which disproportionate attention is given to trivial issues at the expense of important but harder-to-grasp or contested topics. This phenomenon is also known as Parkinson's law of triviality or, colloquially, "bike-shedding," named after C. Northcote Parkinson's 1957 memorable story of a hypothetical committee organized to approve plans for a nuclear power plant that spent more time discussing the design of a bicycle storage shed outside the plant than the design of the nuclear reactor.

Aversion to complexity can surface in numerous ways. For example, a portfolio management team may spend far more time scrutinizing a position in a consumer staples company that they have personal experience with but comparatively little time on a position in a semiconductor or biotechnology company, even if the latter position is larger in the portfolio.

Investment team meetings can also be sidetracked by immaterial business issues that are best left to other venues or personnel. A survey of more than 120 investment committees asked committee members to rank their tasks from most to least important and then asked the members to keep track of how they actually allocated their time. The survey revealed that the committees spent a great deal of time on issues they rated as unimportant, at the expense of important and more difficult issues, such as asset allocation, capital market expectations, and manager selection (Payne and Wood 2002).

Similar to how investment due diligence should inquire about a manager's personnel, it can also be useful to inquire about whether the manager has built team structures and processes to mitigate behavioral biases. Such an inquiry may include the following:

- How large is the investment decision-making team? Research suggests that a team size between three and five is optimal, with larger teams introducing too many coordination issues (Patel and Sarkissian 2017) and increasing the odds of groupthink.

- How are decisions made? While it may be awkward, using a secret ballot may be preferable to open deliberation because it reduces groupthink and authority bias.

- How are meetings conducted? What makes it on the agenda? To avoid complexity aversion, as well as availability bias, meeting agendas should be agreed on in advance, with the most important topics covered first and allotted the longest time for discussion.

- Is the investment team diverse? Research suggests that team diversity—in terms of social and cognitive categories—can reduce groupthink and errors (analogous to how combinations of uncorrelated assets reduce portfolio volatility) and that members of diverse teams may devote more effort to tasks because they are less concerned with socially "fitting in" and conflict avoidance, which is common in homogeneous groups. For these reasons and others, CFA Institute has long advocated for diversity, equity, and inclusion

(DEI) in the investment industry. For more information on DEI and the CFA Institute DEI Code, visit https://rpc.cfainstitute.org/en/codes-and -standards/diversity-equity-inclusion-codes.

## 7  THE MANAGER'S INVESTMENT DECISION-MAKING PROCESS

☐ | evaluate a manager's investment philosophy and investment decision-making process

The investment decision-making process has four elements: signal creation, signal capture, portfolio construction, and portfolio monitoring.

### Signal Creation (Idea Generation)

An investment signal is a data point or fact that can be observed early enough to implement as an investment position. The basic question is, how are investment ideas generated? The efficient market hypothesis posits that the key to exploiting inefficiencies is to have information that is all of the following:

- *Unique.* Does the strategy rely on unique information? If so, how is this information collected, and how is the manager able to retain an informational edge, particularly in a regulatory environment that seeks to reduce informational asymmetries?

- *Timely.* Does the strategy possess an information timing advantage? If so, how is this information collected, and how is the manager able to retain a timing edge, particularly in a regulatory environment that seeks to reduce informational asymmetries?

- *Interpreted differently.* Interpretation is typically how managers seek to differentiate themselves. Does the manager possess a unique way of interpreting information? Or does the manager claim their strategy possesses a "secret sauce" component or that its team is simply smarter than other managers?

### Signal Capture (Idea Implementation)

The second step is signal capture, translating the generated investment idea into an investment position.

- What is the process for translating investment ideas into investment positions?

- Is this process repeatable and consistent with the strategy assumptions?

- What is the process, and who is ultimately responsible for approving an investment position?

## Portfolio Construction

The third element is portfolio construction; how investment positions are implemented within the portfolio. This element begins to capture the manager's risk management methodology. Good investment ideas need to be implemented properly to exploit opportunities and capture desired risk premiums. It is also important that portfolio construction is consistent with the investment philosophy and process as well as the expertise of the investment personnel.

- How are portfolio allocations set and adjusted? The allocation process should be consistent with investment philosophy and process. For example, if the portfolio is actively managed, its turnover should agree with the frequency of signals, the payoff horizon of the signals, and the securities' liquidity. The allocation process should be well defined and consistently applied, supporting the repeatability of the investment process. For example, are allocations made quantitatively or qualitatively?

- Do portfolio allocations incorporate the manager's conviction (besides just the securities' risks and correlations with other securities in the portfolio)?

- How have the portfolio characteristics changed with asset growth? Has the number and/or characteristics of the positions held changed to accommodate a larger amount of AUM?

- Does the portfolio use stop-losses to manage risk? If so, are they hard (positions are automatically sold when the loss threshold is reached) or soft (positions are evaluated when the loss threshold is reached)? Although stop-losses represent a clear risk management approach, the goal of protecting against large losses must be balanced with the risk of closing positions too frequently.

- What types of securities are used? Does the manager use derivatives to express investment ideas? What experience does the manager have investing in these securities? The manager should be sufficiently well-versed and experienced with the securities used to understand how they will behave in different market environments.

- How are hedges implemented? What security types are used? How are hedge ratios set? Consider a manager that focuses on stock selection to generate alpha and hedges to reduce or remove market risk. The hedges must be sized correctly, or they can be ineffective (underhedged) or they can overwhelm stock selection (overhedged), with performance driven more by beta than by alpha.

- How are long and short ideas expressed? A manager might target a certain long/short exposure that may or may not vary according to market conditions. If long and short positions are fully offset, with the idea of minimizing market risk but capturing alpha, the positions must be well matched and sized correctly. A manager can implement this by taking positions that are local-currency neutral (i.e., dollar neutral) and have an equal value of securities on both sides. However, to fully minimize any remaining market risk, the manager should also aim to be beta neutral so that aggregate long and short exposures net to zero.

Alternatively, a manager can pursue a pairs strategy to construct long and short exposures. Pairs trading is a relative value strategy where a manager selects two or more securities with similar characteristics that are correlated and whose price relationship is out of historical trading range. The manager generally establishes a short position in the overvalued securities and an equal-sized long position in the undervalued securities based on a view that their price relationship will converge to historical norms.

An important risk is liquidity. Strategies that are not intending to capture a liquidity risk premium must be aware of portfolio liquidity in terms of adapting to changing information, changing market conditions, and changing investor liquidity demands. An existing portfolio consisting of illiquid securities will be more costly to change, not only to take advantage of new opportunities but also to trade because of higher transaction costs. There is the additional cost of having to sell positions at inopportune times as a result of market events or investor liquidity demands. When assessing security liquidity, it is important to consider all of the assets under management for that particular manager and investment process.

- What percentage of the portfolio can be liquidated in five business days or less? What percentage requires more than 10 business days to liquidate? The less liquid the portfolio, the higher the transaction costs if the manager is forced to sell one or more positions. A more liquid portfolio offers flexibility if the manager faces unexpected investor liquidity demands or rapidly changing market conditions.

- What is the average daily volume weighted by portfolio position size?

- Have any of the portfolio holdings been suspended from trading? If so, what is the name of the company, and what are the circumstances pertaining to the suspension?

- Are there any holdings in which ownership by the firm across all portfolios collectively accounts for more than 5% of the market capitalization or float of the security?

- What is the firm's trading strategy? Does the investment manager tend to provide liquidity or demand it? Has the trading strategy changed in response to asset growth?

## Monitoring the Portfolio

The investment decision-making process is a feedback loop that consists of ongoing monitoring of the portfolio in light of new information and analysis. This monitoring includes an assessment of both external and internal considerations. External considerations include the economic and financial market environments. Has anything meaningful occurred that might affect the manager's ability to exploit the market inefficiency that is the strategy's focus? Internal considerations include the portfolio's performance, risk profile, and construction. Has anything changed that might signal potential style drift or other deviations from the investment process? Ongoing monitoring and performance attribution help to ensure that the manager remains appropriate for the clients' mandates.

---

## 8    OPERATIONAL DUE DILIGENCE

☐    evaluate the costs and benefits of pooled investment vehicles and separate accounts

☐    compare types of investment manager contracts, including their major provisions and advantages and disadvantages

Performance appraisal assumes that reported returns are accurate and fully reflect the manager's risk profile. Unfortunately, as we have seen, this assumption is not always true. Although investment due diligence is one step toward understanding these risks, one must remember that investment management firms are *businesses*, and in many cases, they are small businesses with a high degree of business risk. Regardless of the strength of the investment process or the historical investment results, investment management firms must be operated as a successful business in order to ensure their sustainability. This requirement creates the potential for a misalignment of interests between the manager and the investor. Operational due diligence analyzes the integrity of the business and seeks to understand and evaluate these risks by examining and evaluating the firm's policies and procedures.

Weaknesses in the firm's infrastructure represent latent risks to the investor. A strong back office (support staff) is critical for safeguarding assets and ensuring that accurate reports are issued in a timely manner. The manager should have a robust trading process that seeks to avoid human error. A repeatable process requires consistent implementation. The allocator needs to understand the following:

- What is the firm's trading policy?
- Does the firm use soft dollar commissions? If so, is there a rigorous process for ensuring compliance?
- What is the process for protecting against unauthorized trading?
- How are fees calculated and collected?
- How are securities allocated across investor accounts, including both pooled and separately managed accounts? The allocation method should be objective (e.g., based on invested capital) to avoid the potential to benefit some investors at the expense of others.
- How many different strategies does the firm manage, and are any new strategies being contemplated? Is the firm's infrastructure capable of efficiently and accurately implementing the different strategies?
- What information technology offsite backup facilities are in place?
- Does the firm have processes, software, and hardware in place to handle cybersecurity issues?

An important constituent of the infrastructure is third-party service providers, including the firm's prime broker, administrator, auditor, and legal counsel. They provide an important independent verification of the firm's performance and reporting.

- Are the firm's third-party service providers known and respected?
- Has there been any change in third-party providers? If so, when and why? This information is particularly important with regard to the firm's auditor. Frequent changes of the auditor are a red flag and may mean the manager is trying to hide something.

The risk management function should be viewed as an integral part of the investment firm and not considered a peripheral function. The extent to which integration exists provides insight into the firm's culture and the alignment of interests between the manager and the investor. The manager should have a risk manual that is readily available for review:

- Does the portfolio have any hard/soft investment guidelines?
- How are these guidelines monitored?
- What is the procedure for curing breaches?
- Who is responsible for risk management?
- Is there an independent risk officer?

## Firm

An investment management firm must operate as a successful business to ensure sustainability. A manager that goes out of business does not have a repeatable investment process. An important aspect of manager selection is assessing the level of business risk.

- What is the ownership structure of the firm?
- What are the total firm AUM and AUM by investment strategy?
- What is the firm's breakeven AUM (the asset base needed to generate enough fee revenue to cover total firm expenses)?
- Are any of the firm's strategies closed to new capital?
- How much capital would the firm like to raise?

A firm that is independently owned may have greater autonomy and flexibility than a firm owned by a larger organization, but it may have a higher cost structure and lack financial support during market events, raising potential business risks. Outside ownership could create a situation in which the outside owner has objectives that conflict with the investment strategy. For instance, the outside owner might want to increase the asset base to generate higher fee revenue, but this action could prevent the portfolio from holding lower-capitalization stocks. Ideally, ownership should be spread across as many employees as is feasible and practical. A firm managing a smaller asset base may be more nimble and less prone to dilution of returns but will likely have lower revenues to support infrastructure and compensate employees. At a minimum, the asset base needs to be sufficient to support the firm's current expenditures.

Last, and by no means least important, are legal and compliance issues. It is critical that the firm's interests are aligned with those of the investor.

- What are the compensation arrangements for key employees? For example, are any people compensated with stock in the firm, and if so, what happens to this stock when they leave the firm?
- Do employees invest personal assets in the firm's strategies? Investing their own money in the same products in which the firm's clients invest creates an alignment of interests, but too large a proportion of their own assets invested in this one product may create personal/business risk for the manager that overrides the alignment of interests.
- Does the firm foster a culture of compliance?
- What is covered in the compliance manual?
- Has the firm or any of its employees been involved with an investigation by any financial market regulator or self-regulatory organization?
- Has the firm been involved in any lawsuits?
- Are any of the firm's employees involved in legal actions or personal litigation that might affect their ability to continue to fulfill their fiduciary responsibilities?

Hiring a manager requires trust. A firm's culture as expressed by its compliance policies and procedures should provide a level of confidence that the manager's and investor's interests are aligned.

### THE INVESTMENT PROCESS

Bernard "Bernie" L. Madoff ran one of the biggest frauds in Wall Street history. One of the first indications that something was amiss at Bernard L. Madoff Investment Securities arose when Harry Markopolos was unable to reconcile the return track record with the investment process. In addition to observing the unrealistically consistent nature of the claimed returns, Markopolos concluded that there was no way to generate the returns using the claimed investment process. Further analysis convinced him that Madoff's returns resulted not from front running—that is, taking positions to exploit knowledge of investor trade flows—but rather from fraud.

In hindsight, there were many red flags over the years that indicated there was something wrong with Madoff's investment management process. The firm claimed to generate steady returns in every market environment. Mr. Madoff was known to dismiss questions about his strategy, arguing that his business was too complicated for outsiders to understand. He also operated as a broker/dealer with an asset management division, profiting from trading commissions rather than the investment management fees that hedge funds charged. The structure seemed odd to other investment professionals, raising concerns about the firm's legitimacy. Another red flag was raised when it became known that the firm used a small, unknown auditor with only three employees. If, as Mr. Madoff claimed, the strategy was so complex that no one could understand it, a small, three-person audit firm would be unlikely to be able to effectively audit the financial statements (Zuckerman 2008).

## SELF-REPORTED RISK FACTORS

Requesting and obtaining self-reported risk factors not only is important for understanding the manager's investment process but also provides an interesting operational check. A manager should readily comply with all requests for risk reporting. If not, it suggests a lack of transparency that may become challenging for monitoring the manager and strategy in the future. Additionally, it might indicate an inability to generate essential reports, which raises questions about the firm's policies and procedures.

All risk reporting should be meaningful, consistent, accurate, and timely. A lack of meaningful reporting indicates that the reports are not useful in monitoring the manager and that there is a lack of transparency. In the worst case, the manager does not understand the risk exposures or does not want to disclose them.

A lack of consistent reporting also reduces the usefulness of the reporting. Inconsistent reports preclude the ability to track levels and trends of important risk factors. The manager may be choosing to selectively report particular risks that they deem important or interesting. In the worst case, it may mean that the manager is selectively reporting in order to hide risks created by deviations from the stated investment process.

A lack of accuracy suggests that the manager cannot properly measure portfolio risks or is intentionally misreporting results. A lack of timeliness reduces the reports' usefulness and suggests either inefficient procedures or attempts to manipulate the flow of information. In all of these cases, poor risk reporting, at a minimum, suggests a reevaluation of the manager and, if issues are identified, potential termination.

## Investment Vehicle

There are two broad options for implementing investment strategies: individual separate accounts and pooled (or commingled) vehicles. An additional operational consideration is the evaluation of the investment vehicle—its appropriateness to the investment strategy and its suitability for the investor. Separate accounts offer additional control, customization, tax efficiency, reporting, and transparency advantages, but these come at a higher cost.

In a pooled or commingled vehicle, the money from multiple investors is held as a single portfolio and managed without potential customization for any investor. Such vehicles include open-end funds, closed-end funds, exchange-traded funds, exchange-traded notes, and hedge funds.

## Separately Managed Accounts

As the name implies, a separately managed account (SMA) vehicle holds assets in an investor's name separate from other investors. The assets are managed to a particular mandate with the potential to customize the strategy for each investor. The advantages of SMA vehicles include the following:

- *Ownership.* In an SMA, the investor owns the individual securities directly. This approach provides additional safety should a liquidity event occur. Although the manager continues to make investment decisions, these decisions will not be influenced by the redemption or liquidity demand of *other* investors in the strategy. An SMA also provides clear legal ownership for the recovery of assets resulting from unforeseen events, such as bankruptcy or mismanagement.

- *Customization.* SMAs allow the investor to potentially express individual constraints or preferences within the portfolio. SMAs can thus more closely address the investor's particular investment objectives.

- *Tax efficiency.* SMAs offer potentially improved tax efficiency—for example, in such jurisdictions as the United States, where investors pay taxes only on realized capital gains.

- *Transparency.* SMAs offer real-time, position-level detail to the investor, providing complete transparency and accurate attribution to the investor. Even if a pooled vehicle provides position-level detail, such information will likely be presented with a delay.

If the SMA is customized, additional investment due diligence may be required to account for differences in security selection or portfolio construction. In addition, there are operational due diligence considerations.

- *Cost.* Separate accounts represent an additional operational burden on the manager, which translates into potentially higher costs for the investor. SMAs do not scale as easily as pooled vehicles. Once a pooled investment is established and the fixed costs paid, the cost of each new investor is largely the incremental costs of custody, trading larger positions, and generating an additional report. With an SMA, a new account must be established for each investor. In addition, SMAs are likely to face higher transaction costs to the degree that trades cannot be aggregated to reduce trade volumes. These costs are a function of the extent to which the strategy is customized or traded differently to accommodate different investor needs.

- *Tracking risk.* Customization of the strategy creates tracking risk relative to the benchmark, which can confuse attribution because performance will reflect investor constraints rather than manager decisions.

- *Investor behavior.* Transparency, combined with control and customization, allows for potential micromanagement by the investor—that is, the investor attempting to manage the portfolio. Such an effort not only negates the benefit of hiring a manager but is particularly problematic if these changes decrease the portfolio's value. Potential investor behaviors include performance chasing, familiarity bias (being overly averse to unfamiliar holdings), and loss aversion (a tendency to disaggregate the portfolio and not appreciate the value of hedging).

The allocator's goal is to evaluate the costs and benefits of the vehicle used and judge its suitability for the IPS:

- Is the vehicle structure consistent with the investment process?
- Does the manager have the operational infrastructure necessary to manage the SMA?
- Is there a benefit to holding the securities in a separate account? If so, are these benefits sufficient to compensate for additional costs?
- Is tax efficiency an important objective of the IPS?
- Are there concerns that the available transparency and ability to customize will result in decisions by the investor that do not add value?

---

**EXAMPLE 5**

## Pooled Investments and Separate Accounts

1. Which of the following are advantages of separately managed accounts compared with pooled investments?

    **A.** Typically lower cost

    **B.** Potential management of the portfolio by the investor

    **C.** Ability to take close account of individual client constraints or preferences

    **Solution**

    C is correct. With SMAs, the investor owns the individual securities directly and can potentially express individual constraints or preferences within the portfolio. In particular, SMAs offer potentially improved tax efficiency in some jurisdictions, such as the United States because the investor pays taxes only on the capital gains realized and allows the implementation of tax-efficient investing and trading strategies.

---

## Evaluation of the Investment's Terms

An additional and important aspect of manager selection is understanding the terms of the investment as presented in the prospectus, private placement memorandum, and/or limited partnership agreement. These documents are, in essence, the contract between the investor and the manager, outlining each party's rights and responsibilities. Although these documents cover numerous topics, this lesson focuses on liquidity and fees. The objective of the decision maker is to determine whether the liquidity and fee structure make the manager suitable for the investor's needs and the "best" manager for expressing a particular portfolio need.

### Liquidity

Different vehicles provide different degrees of liquidity. Liquidity is defined as the timeliness with which a security or asset can be sold at or near the current price. The same criteria can be applied to managers.

The most liquid vehicles are closed-end funds and ETFs. As listed securities, they can be bought and sold intra-day, and the price received will depend on the trading volume and depth of the fund. The obvious advantage of these funds is ease of trading, although there can be some price uncertainty for less liquid funds, particularly when trying to buy or sell a large number of shares. Open-end funds are slightly less liquid, providing daily liquidity but also price certainty; shares are bought and sold at the end-of-day NAV.

Unlike open-end funds, ETFs, or closed-end funds, limited partnerships, such as hedge funds, venture capital funds, and private equity funds, typically require investors to invest their money for longer periods. Hedge fund liquidity has four basic features: redemption frequency, notification period, lockup, and gates. Redemption frequency indicates how often an investor can withdraw capital from the fund, and the notification period indicates how far in advance of the redemption investors must tell the fund of their intention to redeem. A lockup is the initial period, after making an investment, during which investors cannot redeem their holding. Lockups have two types: a hard lock, which allows for no redemptions, and a soft lock, which charges a fee, paid into the fund, for redemptions. A mutual fund redemption fee is equivalent to a hedge fund soft lock. Gates limit the amount of fund assets, or investor assets that can be redeemed at one redemption date.

Private equity and venture capital funds provide the least liquidity. Investors are contractually obligated to contribute specific amounts (capital calls) during the investment phase and then receive distributions and capital as investments are harvested during the remaining term of the fund. A typical investment phase is 5 years. The typical life of a fund is 10 years, with the option to extend the term for two 1-year periods.

The obvious disadvantage of partnership liquidity terms is the reduced flexibility to adjust portfolio allocations in light of changing market conditions or investor circumstances, as well as the reduced ability to meet unexpected liquidity needs. The advantage of such terms is that they do lock up capital for longer horizons, allowing funds to take long-term views and hold less liquid securities—such as start-up companies, buyouts, turnarounds, real estate, or natural resources—with reduced risk of having to sell portfolio holdings at inopportune times in response to redemption requests. An additional advantage, which was apparent during the 2008 financial crisis, is that limited liquidity imposes this long horizon view on investors, reducing or removing their ability to overreact.

Because SMA assets are held in the investor's name, the securities in the portfolio can be sold at any time. As a result, an SMA's liquidity will depend on the liquidity of the securities held. An SMA holding listed large-cap stocks will likely be highly liquid, whereas an investor in an SMA that holds unlisted or illiquid securities will have to accept a discount when selling.

## 9    MANAGEMENT FEES

☐     describe the three basic forms of performance-based fees

☐     analyze and interpret a sample performance-based fee schedule

Investors seek strong performance net of fees. Managers charge fees to cover operating costs and earn a return on their capital—primarily human capital. A manager's fixed costs are relatively small and primarily cover the costs of technology and the long-term lease of office space. Variable costs, which consist largely of payroll and marketing costs, dominate the income statements of asset management companies. Because a considerable portion of employee compensation comes in the form of bonuses, senior management can reduce bonus payouts as fee revenue declines in order to smooth a company's profitability.[1]

Investors are increasingly sensitive to management fees. Average asset-weighted expense ratios (management fees and fund expenses) incurred by mutual fund investors have fallen substantially. In 2000, equity mutual fund investors incurred expense ratios of 0.99%, on average, or 99 cents for every $100 invested. By 2021, that average had fallen to 0.47%, a decline of 53%. Hybrid and bond mutual fund expense ratios also have declined. The average hybrid mutual fund expense ratio fell from 0.89% in 2000 to 0.57% in 2021, a reduction of 36%. The average bond mutual fund expense ratio fell from 0.76% in 2000 to 0.39% in 2021, a decline of 49%. The decline is a function of several factors: the allocation of the fixed portion of expenses over a larger asset base, increasing investor preference for no-load share classes, and the increasing allocations to lower-cost index funds. Aside from these structural factors lowering average expense ratios, there has been more generalized downward pressure on fees—the average expense ratio of actively managed equity mutual funds declined from 1.06% in 2000 to 0.68% in 2021. Likewise, the average expense ratio of actively managed bond mutual funds declined from 0.77% in 2000 to 0.46% in 2021. Average expense ratios for index-based equity and bond funds declined from 27 bps and 21 bps in 2000, respectively, to 6 bps each in 2021.[2]

Investment firms charge fees in several different ways. In general, mutual fund managers charge fees based on a fund's assets under management.[3] Some classes of mutual funds, including those with reduced fees, require minimum balances. In contrast, institutional managers frequently offer declining percentage fees on increasing account sizes for separate or commingled pool accounts. Institutional accounts frequently specify minimum account sizes or minimum dollar fees. Fixed-percentage fees facilitate managers' and investors' planning for future cash flows, whereas dollar fees are subject to the variability of asset values.

Fee structures can influence which managers will be willing to accept a particular investment mandate. They can also strongly affect manager behavior. Economic theory suggests that the principal–agent problem is complicated by the fact that an agent's skills and actions are not fully visible to the principal. Although principals control asset availability, agents control both their expenditure of effort and portfolio risk. Moreover, the agent and principal may have different preferences; each might care about different time horizons and agents might not view losses the same way that principals do.[4] Finally, total performance is, to some extent, beyond the control of either party. As a result of these factors, the principal's and agent's interests may not be fully aligned. In reality, managers are motivated to work hard even without incentive fees because they want to retain current clients and expand their client base and pricing power. Incentives are useful, however, to help ensure that managers routinely act in their clients' best interest.

1 This lesson is based on Chapter 6 in *Essays on Manager Selection*, by Scott D. Stewart, PhD, CFA, Research Foundation of CFA Institute. © 2013 CFA Institute. All rights reserved.

2 ICI Investment Company Fact Book (2022).

3 Although mutual funds may offer a declining management fee as fund assets increase, the individual investor does not benefit from investing more money unless the extra money qualifies the investor for a lower-fee fund class.

4 For a summary of theoretical research on investment compensation, see Stracca (2006).

## Assets under Management Fees

Assets under management fees, also called "ad valorem fees" (from the Latin for "according to value"), result from applying stated percentage rates to assets under management. These fees reward managers who attract and retain assets, generate added value, and experience benefits from rising markets. Managers primarily grow their assets through skillful investing, hard work, and effective marketing. A manager's success, however, also results partly from luck, especially in the short term. Managers benefit from rising portfolio values, which are attributable to the combination of alpha and beta decisions, but are also, at least for long-only managers, greatly affected by market cycles beyond the manager's control. A decline in ad valorem percentages as assets grow helps reduce the fee impact on investors from rising markets, but does not eliminate it.

Once a manager's assets are large, he or she might not want to risk losing them. Assets are typically "sticky"—that is, once investors allocate their assets to a manager, the manager often does not need to generate the same level of returns to retain the assets as he or she did to attract them. Empirical evidence suggests this stickiness is the case, to some extent, for mutual fund assets. To motivate such managers to work harder or discourage them from closet indexing, an incentive fee determined by future performance may be useful.

## Performance-Based Fees

Performance-based fees, common for hedge funds and less common for long-only strategies, are determined by portfolio returns and are designed to reward managers with a share of return for their skill in creating value. Performance can be calculated by using either total or relative return, and the return shared can be a percentage of total performance or performance net of a base or fixed fee. Performance-based fees are structured in one of three basic ways:

1. a symmetrical structure in which the manager is fully exposed to both the downside and upside (Computed fee = Base + Sharing of performance);

2. a bonus structure in which the manager is not fully exposed to the downside but is fully exposed to the upside (Computed fee = Higher of either [1] Base or [2] Base plus sharing of positive performance); or

3. a bonus structure in which the manager is not fully exposed to either the downside or the upside (Computed fee = Higher of [1] Base or [2] Base plus sharing of performance, to a limit).

Performance fees are paid annually or, in some cases, less frequently. These fees may include maximum and high-water mark (or clawback) features that protect investors from situations such as paying for current positive performance before the negative effects of prior underperformance have been offset. Private equity, hedge fund, and real estate partnerships commonly earn performance fees on total returns and typically do not limit the amount of the performance fee. Hedge funds commonly include high-water mark features.

Consider the example of private equity partnerships, in which base fees are commonly applied to committed (not just invested) capital. Performance fees are earned as profits are realized, and invested capital is returned to investors. A common provision that helps protect private equity limited partners (the investors) is a requirement that the limited partners receive their principal and share of profits before performance fees are distributed to the general partner (the manager).

Specific performance-based fee structures are designed by both clients and managers. A formula is agreed upon based on the anticipated distribution of returns and the perceived attractiveness of the investment strategy. Managers who can command attractive terms, such as real estate managers that are in high demand and have limited capacity, have the power to stipulate the highest base fees and profit sharing in their fee agreements. Fee schedules are typically designed by fund managers, included in marketing materials, and set forth in partnership agreements. Large investors may influence the terms of fee schedules or negotiate side letters for special treatment.

A simple performance-based fee, as illustrated in Exhibit 8, specifies a base fee below which the computed fee can never fall. In this case, the manager is protected against sharing for performance below 25 bps. To make the result symmetrical around the commonplace 50 bps fee, the manager does not share in active performance beyond 2.75%.

### Exhibit 8: Sample Performance-Based Fee Schedule

**Panel A. Sample Fee Structure**

| | |
|---|---|
| Standard fee | 0.50% |
| Base fee | 0.25% |
| Sharing* | 20% |
| Breakeven active return | 1.50% |
| Maximum annual fee | 0.75% |

**Panel B. Numerical Examples for Annual Periods**

| | Active Return | | | | |
|---|---|---|---|---|---|
| | ≤ 0.25% | 1.00% | 1.50% | 2.00% | ≥ 2.75% |
| Billed fee | 0.25% | 0.40% | 0.50% | 0.60% | 0.75% |
| Net active return | ≤ 0.00% | 0.60% | 1.00% | 1.40% | ≥ 2.00% |

*On active return, beyond base fee.*

If investment outcomes result from a mix of skill and luck (i.e., a probability distribution around a positive mean alpha), then performance fees constitute risk sharing. Fee structures must be designed carefully to avoid favoring one party over the other. Performance-based fees work to align the interests of managers and investors because both parties share in investment results. Investors benefit by paying performance-based fees, rather than standard fees, when active returns are low. Managers may work harder to earn performance-based fees, inspiring the term "incentive based." Empirical evidence suggests a correlation between performance-based fees and higher alphas (also, lower fees) for mutual funds and higher risk-adjusted returns for hedge funds.[5] Asset managers may consider performance-based fees attractive because such fees provide an opportunity to enhance profits on the upside and ensure guaranteed, although perhaps minimal, streams of revenue from base fees when performance is poor.

Performance-based fees can also create tensions between investors and managers. Investors must pay base fees even when managers underperform. Management firm revenues decline when cash is needed to invest in operations or retain talent. In fact, the failure rate for poor-performing and even zero-alpha managers may tend to be higher when performance-based rather than standard fees are used.[6]

Performance-based fee structures may also lead to misestimates of portfolio risk. Such fee structures convert symmetrical gross active return distributions into asymmetrical net active return distributions, reducing variability on the upside but not the

---

5 See Elton, Gruber, and Blake (2003) and Ackermann, McEnally, and Ravenscraft (1999).
6 See Grinold and Rudd (1987).

downside. As a result, a single standard deviation calculated on a return series that incorporates active returns, above and below the base fee, can lead to the underestimation of downside risk.[7]

Investors and managers may have different incentives when performance-based fees are used. For example, according to a utility maximization model, fully symmetric fees, in which the manager is fully exposed to the downside, tend to yield closer alignment in risk and effort than bonus-style fees.[8] Understandably, symmetrical fee structures are unpopular with managers because of their impact on bankruptcy risk.

Bonus-style fees are the close equivalent of a manager's call option on a share of active return, for which the base fee is the strike price. Consider Exhibit 9, which shows a familiar-looking option payoff pattern using the fee parameters defined in Exhibit 8. In this case, the option payoff is modified by a maximum fee feature. The graph illustrates three fee components: a 25 bps base fee, plus a long call option on active return with a strike price equal to the minimum (base) fee, minus another (less valuable) call option with a strike price equal to the maximum fee.

### Exhibit 9: Payoff Line of Sample Performance-Based Fee Schedule

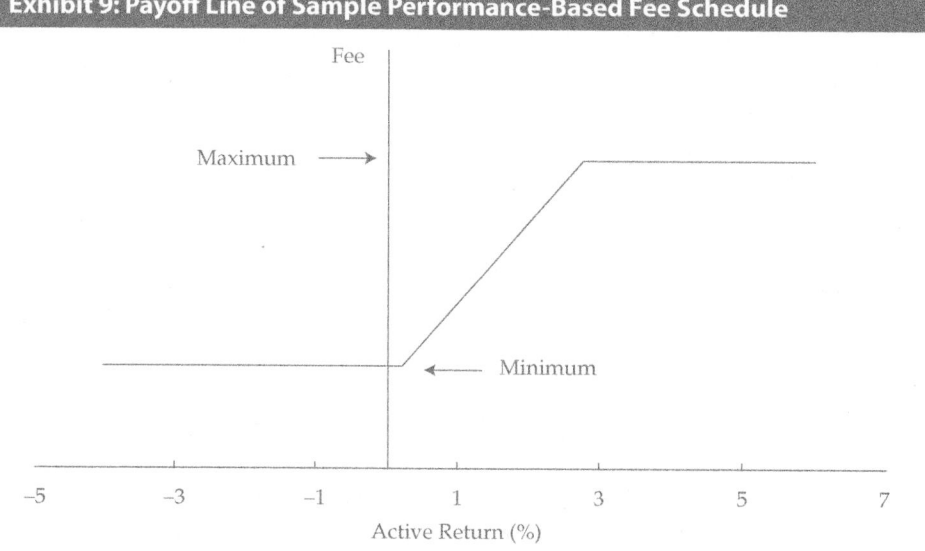

Managers must retain clients year to year, avoid poor performance, and not violate management guidelines. But managers also tend to have an interest in increasing risk, which may conflict with these goals. Based on option pricing theory,[9] higher volatility leads to higher option value, which encourages managers to assume higher portfolio risk. This behavior has been observed in the marketplace.[10] As a result, investors, when possible, should carefully select benchmarks and monitor risk in their portfolios.[11]

---

7  See Kritzman (2012).

8  See Starks (1987).

9  Margrabe (1978) notes that an incentive fee (without a maximum) consists of a call option on the portfolio and a put on the benchmark. As a result, the value depends on the volatility of the portfolio and the benchmark and the correlation between the two—in other words, the active risk.

10  See Elton et al. (2003).

11  Starks (1987) notes that an investor can simply set a fee schedule incorporating penalties for observed risk to align interests regarding risk levels.

Senior management at investment firms should also ensure that their compensation systems penalize portfolio managers for assuming excessive risk as well as reward them for earning superior returns.[12]

> **REAL STORY: THE CLIENT'S FREE OPTION IN A PERFORMANCE FEE AGREEMENT**
>
> Consider the case of an equity manager in the early 1990s offering a performance-based fee that consisted of a 10 bp base fee and a 20% share of active return in excess of the benchmark index (net of the 10 bps). The fee structure also included a maximum annual fee provision that reserved excess fees for subsequent years. Because there was no penalty for cancelling the fee agreement, clients could opt out of the performance-based fee in exchange for a standard flat fee when performance was particularly strong. This arrangement allowed them to avoid paying the manager's accrued, fully earned share, and is precisely what many clients did in the mid-1990s following a period of high active returns.

Other problems exist with performance-based fees. When managers have clients with varying fee structures, it is in their (short-term) interest to favor customers that have performance-based fees. Although doing so may be unethical or potentially illegal, managers can direct trades or deals (including initial public offerings) to performance-fee clients to their benefit and to the detriment of others. It may be difficult for clients to monitor this activity. Fortunately, most managers recognize that such actions, once discovered, could destroy their careers or lead to criminal charges. Here again, due diligence, including the review of internal compliance systems, will help limit an investor's exposure to unscrupulous managers.

When managers can control the timing of profit realization, as is often the case with private equity partnerships, they may have an incentive to hold on to assets until a profit can be realized. Managers may do so even when clients would benefit from selling assets at a loss and investing the proceeds outside of the partnership. In contrast, hedge fund managers have an incentive to return assets in poor-performing partnerships when the high-water mark is substantially above current value (i.e., the performance-fee option is considerably out of the money). This action results in the investor missing the opportunity to recoup previously paid fees based on future strong performance.

Funds of funds (FoFs) commonly charge fees in addition to the fees charged by the underlying funds.[13] These fees pay for the investor's access to the underlying funds and for the FoFs' due diligence, portfolio construction, and monitoring. In addition to these two sets of fees, investors are required to share the profits from well-performing underlying funds but incur the full loss from poorly performing funds.[14] To protect investors from paying overly high fees, hedge fund consortiums have recently begun to offer fee structures based on the total portfolio value of underlying funds, rather than the sum of fees computed at the individual fund level.

---

12 Although it adds a layer of complexity to the evaluation process, an active-risk-adjusted bonus formula can be specified.

13 When funds of funds were popular in the 2000s, it was common for them to charge a performance-based fee.

14 Kritzman (2012) calls this result an "asymmetry penalty."

## THE IMPACT OF FEE STRUCTURE ON NET RETURNS

Consider four fee structures applied to the same 12-month return series gross of fees:

- 0.50% management fee, 0% performance fee
- 0.50% management fee, 15% performance fee
- 1.50% management fee, 0% performance fee
- 1.50% management fee, 15% performance fee

The fees are accrued at the end of each month. This example is a simplification but illustrates the important effects of fee level and structure on net performance. As Exhibit 10 shows, the average monthly gross return is 0.72% with a 1.37% monthly standard deviation. Not surprisingly, charging a management fee (MF) lowers the level of realized return without affecting the standard deviation of the series. The management fee is a constant shift in the level and thus does not affect volatility. The addition of a performance fee (PF) also lowers the level of realized returns but has the added effect of lowering the realized standard deviation. This dynamic occurs because in up months, the performance fee is accrued, and in down months, it is subtracted from the accrual balance to reflect the appropriate fee for the cumulative performance. This accounting has the effect of adjusting the monthly returns toward zero and lowering the measured volatility. The larger the performance fee, the more pronounced this effect. Exhibit 11 shows a graph of the cumulative returns for each fee structure.

### Exhibit 10: Effects of Expense on Portfolio Performance

| | Monthly Gross Return | | | | |
| | MF = 0% | MF = 0.5% | | MF = 1.5% | |
| Month | PF = 0% | PF = 0% | PF = 15% | PF = 0% | PF = 15% |
|---|---|---|---|---|---|
| 1 | 2.00% | 1.96% | 1.66% | 1.88% | 1.59% |
| 2 | 3.00% | 2.96% | 2.51% | 2.88% | 2.44% |
| 3 | −0.20% | −0.24% | −0.21% | −0.32% | −0.28% |
| 4 | −0.50% | −0.54% | −0.46% | −0.62% | −0.53% |
| 5 | 0.50% | 0.46% | 0.39% | 0.37% | 0.32% |
| 6 | 0.90% | 0.86% | 0.73% | 0.77% | 0.66% |
| 7 | 1.00% | 0.96% | 0.81% | 0.88% | 0.74% |
| 8 | −2.00% | −2.04% | −1.74% | −2.12% | −1.81% |
| 9 | 1.50% | 1.46% | 1.24% | 1.37% | 1.17% |
| 10 | 2.00% | 1.96% | 1.66% | 1.88% | 1.59% |
| 11 | −0.50% | −0.54% | −0.46% | −0.62% | −0.53% |
| 12 | 1.00% | 0.96% | 0.81% | 0.88% | 0.74% |
| Average Return | 0.72% | 0.67% | 0.57% | 0.59% | 0.50% |
| S.D. | 1.37% | 1.37% | 1.16% | 1.37% | 1.16% |

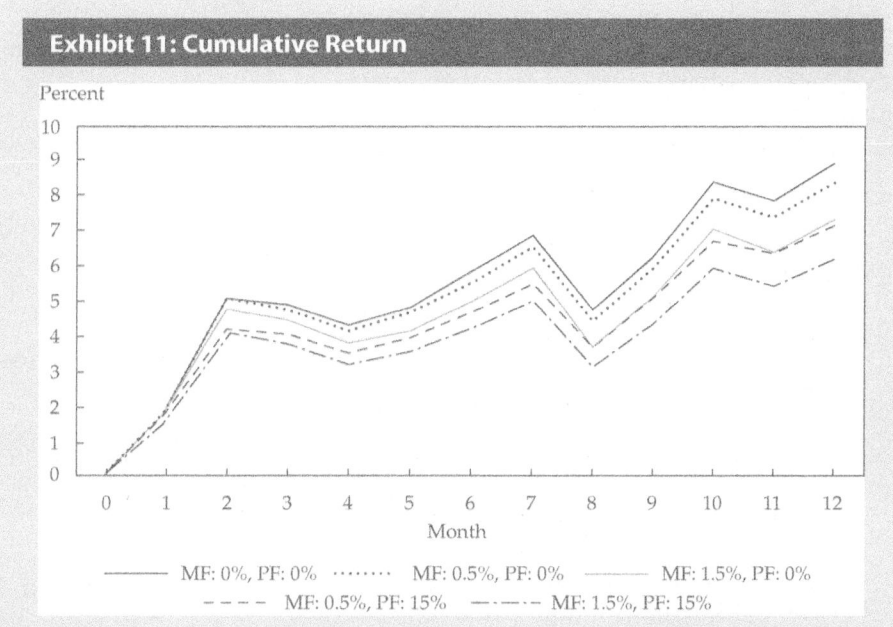

**Exhibit 11: Cumulative Return**

Given the potentially significant effect of expenses, a clear distinction must be drawn between performance analysis based on gross returns and net of expenses returns.

An additional consideration is the different degree of uncertainty between expenses and the potential added value of the active portfolio manager. Expenses are paid for certain, whereas the added value of the active strategy compared with the passive strategy is uncertain. For example, suppose an active strategy is expected to generate a gross return that is 2% greater than the passive strategy, but the cost of the active strategy is 2% greater than the passive strategy. A risk-averse investor would likely prefer the passive strategy; although the expected net return of the strategies is the same, the uncertainty of the outperformance would be unappealing. The riskier the active strategy, the greater the return volatility and the greater the volatility of the added value relative to the passive strategy. The significance is, the added value of the active strategy has to be sufficiently large and certain to justify the higher cost of the strategy.

In sum, the presence of positive significant average excess return is evidence for manager skill. This excess return, however, must be net of fees and expenses for the benefit of this skill to accrue to the investor.[15] The preference is for more linear compensation to the manager to reduce the incentives to change the portfolio's risk profile at inflection points.

## SUMMARY

Evaluating an investment manager is a complex and detailed process. It encompasses a great deal more than analyzing investment returns. In conducting investment manager due diligence, the focus is on understanding how the investment results were achieved and assessing the likelihood that the manager will continue to follow the same investment process that generated these returns. This process also entails operational

---

15 Ultimately, the net return to the investor accounts not only for fees and expenses but also for taxes. This more complex issue is beyond the scope of this learning module.

due diligence, including an evaluation of the integrity of the firm, its operations, and personnel, as well as evaluating the vehicle structure and terms. As such, due diligence involves both quantitative and qualitative analysis.

This learning module provides a framework that introduces and describes the important elements of the manager selection process:

- Investment manager selection involves a broad set of qualitative and quantitative considerations to determine whether a manager displays skill and the likelihood that the manager will continue to display skill in the future.

- The qualitative analysis consists of investment due diligence, which evaluates the manager's investment process, investment personnel, and portfolio construction; and operational due diligence, which evaluates the manager's infrastructure.

- A Type I error is hiring or retaining a manager who subsequently underperforms expectations—that is, rejecting the null hypothesis of no skill when it is correct. A Type II error is not hiring or firing a manager who subsequently outperforms, or performs in line with, expectations—that is, not rejecting the null hypothesis when it is incorrect.

- The manager search and selection process has three broad components: the universe, a quantitative analysis of the manager's performance track record, and a qualitative analysis of the manager's investment process. The qualitative analysis includes both investment due diligence and operational due diligence.

- Capture ratio measures the asymmetry of returns, and a ratio greater than 1 indicates greater participation in rising versus falling markets. Drawdown is the loss incurred in any continuous period of negative returns.

- The investment philosophy is the foundation of the investment process. The philosophy outlines the set of assumptions about the factors that drive performance and the manager's beliefs about their ability to successfully exploit these sources of return. The investment manager should have a clear and concise investment philosophy. It is important to evaluate these assumptions and the role they play in the investment process to understand how the strategy will behave over time and across market environments. The investment process has to be consistent and appropriate for the philosophy, and the investment personnel need to possess sufficient expertise and experience to effectively execute the investment process.

- Investment teams, rather than individual investors, often have the responsibility for making investment decisions and are subject to behavioral biases. It is important for investment teams to implement procedures to alleviate the effect of behavioral biases and improve decision making. An investment due diligence process should inquire about an investment manager's team size, structure, and decision-making processes.

- Style analysis, understanding the manager's risk exposures relative to the benchmark, is an important component of performance appraisal and manager selection, helping to define the universe of suitable managers.

- Returns-based style analysis is a top-down approach that involves estimating the risk exposures from an actual return series for a given period. Although RBSA adds an additional analytical step, the analysis is straightforward and should identify the important drivers of return and risk factors for the period analyzed. It can be estimated even for complicated strategies and is comparable across managers and through time. The disadvantage is that RBSA is an imprecise tool, attributing performance to an unchanging average portfolio during the period that might not reflect the current or future portfolio exposures.

- Holdings-based style analysis is a bottom-up approach that estimates the risk exposures from the actual securities held in the portfolio at a point in time. HBSA allows for the estimation of current risk factors and should identify all important drivers of return and risk factors, be comparable across managers and through time, and provide an accurate view of the manager's risk exposures. The disadvantages are the additional computational effort, dependence on the degree of transparency provided by the manager, and the possibility that accuracy may be compromised by stale pricing and window dressing.

- The prospectus, private placement memorandum, and/or limited partnership agreement are, in essence, the contract between the investor and the manager, outlining each party's rights and responsibilities. The provisions are liquidity terms and fees. Limited liquidity reduces the investor's flexibility to adjust portfolio allocations in light of changing market conditions or investor circumstances. On the other hand, limited liquidity allows the funds to take long-term views and hold less liquid securities with reduced risk of having to divest assets at inopportune times in response to redemption requests. A management fee lowers the level of realized return without affecting the standard deviation, whereas a performance fee has the added effect of lowering the realized standard deviation. The preference is for more linear compensation to reduce the incentives to change the portfolio's risk profile at inflection points.

- The choice between individual separate accounts and pooled (or commingled) vehicles is dependent upon the consistency with the investment process, the suitability for the investor IPS, and whether the benefits outweigh the additional costs.

- Investment management fees take one of two forms: a fixed percentage fee based on assets under management or a performance-based fee which charges a percentage of the portfolio's total return or excess return over a benchmark or hurdle rate. Performance-based fees work to align the interests of managers and investors because both parties share in investment results. Most managers that charge a performance fee also charge some level of fixed percentage fee to aid business continuity efforts. Fee structures must be designed carefully to avoid favoring one party over the other.

# REFERENCES

Ackermann, Carl, Richard McEnally, and David Ravenscraft. 1999. "The Performance of Hedge Funds: Risk, Return and Incentives." *Journal of Finance* 54 (3): 833–74. 10.1111/0022-1082.00129

Bär, M., C. S. Ciccotello, and S. Ruenzi. 2010. "Risk Management and Team-Managed Mutual Funds." *Journal of Risk Management and Financial Institutions* 4 (1): 57–73.

Baer, M., A. Kempf, and S. Ruenzi. 2005. "Team Management and Mutual Funds." Working paper, Centre for Financial Research. 10.2139/ssrn.809484

Bliss, R. T., M. E. Potter, and C. Schwarz. 2008. "Performance Characteristics of Individual-Managed versus Team-Managed Funds." *Journal of Portfolio Management* 34 (3): 110–19. 10.3905/jpm.2008.706248

Chen, J., H. Harrison, H. Ming, and J. Kubik. 2004. "Does Fund Size Erode Mutual Fund Performance: The Role of Liquidity and Organization." *American Economic Review* 94 (5): 1276–302. 10.1257/0002828043052277

Elton, Edwin, Martin Gruber, Christopher Blake. 2003. "Incentive Fees and Mutual Funds." *Journal of Finance* 58 (2): 779–804. 10.1111/1540-6261.00545

Goldman, E., Z. Sun. and X. (T.) Zhou. 2016. "The Effect of Management Design on the Portfolio Concentration and Performance of Mutual Funds." *Financial Analysts Journal* 72 (4): 49–61. 10.2469/faj.v72.n4.9

Grinold, Richard and Andrew Rudd. 1987. "Incentive Fees: Who Wins? Who Loses?" *Financial Analysts Journal* 43 (1): 27–38. 10.2469/faj.v43.n1.27

Karagiannidis, I. 2010. "Management Team Structure and Mutual Fund Performance." *Journal of Financial Markets, Institutions and Money* 20 (2): 197–211. 10.1016/j.intfin.2009.10.003

Karagiannidis, Iordanis and G. Geoffrey Booth. 2022. "The Influence of Management Design on Mutual Fund Performance." *Multinational Finance Journal* 26 (1/2): 1–26.

Khandani, Amir E. and Andrew W. Lo. 2011. "What Happened to the Quants in August 2007? Evidence from Factors and Transactions Data." *Journal of Financial Markets* 14 (1): 1–46. 10.1016/j.finmar.2010.07.005

Kritzman, Mark. 2012. "Two Things about Performance Fees." *Journal of Portfolio Management* 38 (2): 4–5. 10.3905/jpm.2012.38.2.004

Kuenzi, David E. 2003. "Strategy Benchmarks." *Journal of Portfolio Management* 29 (2): 46–56. 10.3905/jpm.2003.319872

Lo, Andrew W. 2004. "The Adaptive Markets Hypothesis: Market Efficiency from an Evolutionary Perspective." *Journal of Portfolio Management* 30 (5): 15–29. 10.3905/jpm.2004.442611

Margrabe, William. 1978. "The Value of an Option to Exchange One Asset for Another." *Journal of Finance* 33 (1): 177–86. 10.1111/j.1540-6261.1978.tb03397.x

Patel, S. and S. Sarkissian. 2017. "To Group or Not to Group? Evidence from Mutual Fund Databases." *Journal of Financial and Quantitative Analysis* 52 (5): 1989–2021. 10.1017/S0022109017000655

Payne, John and Arnold Wood. 2002. "Individual Decision Making and Group Decision Processes." *Journal of Psychology and Financial Markets* 3 (2): 94–101. 10.1207/S15327760JPFM0302_04

Sargis, M. and K. Chang. 2017. The Aftermath of Fund Management Change. Morningstar.

Starks, Laura. 1987. "Performance Incentive Fees: An Agency Theoretic Approach." *Journal of Financial and Quantitative Analysis* 22 (1): 17–32. 10.2307/2330867

Stewart, Scott D., John J. Neumann, Christopher R. Knittel, and Jeffrey Heisler. 2009. "Absence of Value: An Analysis of Investment Allocation Decisions by Institutional Plan Sponsors." *Financial Analysts Journal* 65 (6): 34–51. 10.2469/faj.v65.n6.4

Stracca, Livio. 2006. "Delegated Portfolio Management: A Survey of the Theoretical Literature." *Journal of Economic Surveys* 20 (5): 823–48. 10.1111/j.1467-6419.2006.00271.x

Wang, D. 2016. "What Does It Mean to Be a Team? Evidence from U.S. Mutual Fund Managers." 29th Australasian Finance and Banking Conference, Sydney, Australia. 10.2139/ssrn.2825534

Zuckerman, Gregory. 2008. "Fees, Even Returns and Auditor All Raised Red Flags." *Wall Street Journal* (13 December).

## PRACTICE PROBLEMS

1. Which of the following qualitative considerations is *most* associated with determining whether investment manager selection will result in superior repeatable performance?

    A. Transparency

    B. Investment process

    C. Operational process

2. The manager selection process begins by defining the universe of feasible managers. When defining this manager universe, the selection process should avoid:

    A. excluding managers based on historical risk-adjusted returns.

    B. identifying the benchmark against which managers will be evaluated.

    C. using third-party categorizations of managers to find those that might fill the desired role in the portfolio.

## The following information relates to questions 3-5

John Connell inherited $700,000 at the beginning of the year and has been developing related investment goals and policies with a financial adviser. The adviser has identified three potential investment funds for consideration. All three have earned similar returns over the last five years and are expected to earn similar returns going forward. Publishing their investment results on a timely and routine basis, they include the following asset classes:

- US equities
- Global equities
- Venture capital
- Corporate bonds
- Government bonds
- Cash reserves

Exhibit 1 presents information about the funds.

### Exhibit 1: Fund Characteristics

| Characteristic | Zeta | Eta | Theta |
| --- | --- | --- | --- |
| Organization | Independent investment fund | Part of a medium-sized investment firm with multiple funds | Part of a large investment firm that rotates investment professionals among funds |
| Team Size | Small | Small | Small |
| Staff Turnover | High | Medium | Low |

| Characteristic | Zeta | Eta | Theta |
|---|---|---|---|
| Incentive Compensation | Salary adjustment when returns exceed benchmark | Annual salary adjustment | Annual salary adjustment and performance-based bonus |
| Key People | Founder directs all trades and investment decisions | Fund manager and assistant fund manager make investment decisions | Fund manager and assistant fund manager lead team in selecting investments |
| Longevity/Experience | Founder in the investment business for > 25 years | Fund manager in the investment business for > 15 years; assistant fund manager for > 12 years | Fund manager in the investment business for > 20 years; assistant fund manager for > 10 years. Fund family is more than 50 years old. |

3. Based on the Exhibit 1 data, which fund is *most appropriate* for Connell's needs. Justify your selection with *two* reasons.

4. Connell elects to defer fund selection and places his inheritance in a short-term money market account. A year later, Connell reviews the one-year performance results of the three funds compared to the benchmark, as shown in Exhibit 2.

### Exhibit 2: Fund Performance Compared to Benchmark*

| Fund | Underperforms | In Line | Outperforms |
|---|---|---|---|
| Zeta | | X | |
| Eta | X | | |
| Theta | | | X |

*Assume performance is mean reverting within this period.*

Connell believes he now has two main alternatives for fund investment:

Alternative 1   Keep his inheritance in the money market account to avoid the Eta fund.

Alternative 2   Place his inheritance in the Theta fund.

Identify the type of error Connell is at risk of committing and its associated cost for *each* alternative. Justify your selection.

5. Connell asks the adviser about the conditions under which any form of style analysis would be useful for understanding the funds he is considering.
Identify the conditions under which the adviser would find style analysis *most* useful.

## The following information relates to questions 6-7

Donna Grimmett is working with a financial adviser to establish her investment goals for €850,000, which she recently earned as a bonus. She asks the adviser about how to best select a manager for her funds.

The adviser responds that both qualitative and quantitative components are involved in outlining a framework for identifying, evaluating, and ultimately selecting a manager.

6. Describe *two* considerations for *each* type of component recommended to Grimmett for her manager selection process.

7. Grimmett asks the adviser if any other preparatory steps should be taken before choosing the best investment manager(s). The adviser produces a checklist related to manager selection in response to Grimmett's question.

---

8. A decision-making investor is *most likely* to worry more about making a Type I error than a Type II error because:

   A. Type II errors are errors of mistaken rejection.

   B. Type I errors are more easily measured.

   C. Type II errors are more likely to have to be explained as to why a skilled manager was fired.

9. An investor is considering hiring three managers who have the following skill levels:

   | Manager | Large-cap skill level | Small-cap skill level |
   |---------|----------------------|----------------------|
   | 1 | Skilled | Unskilled |
   | 2 | Skilled | Skilled |
   | 3 | Unskilled | Unskilled |

   Type I and Type II errors both occur when the investor is:

   A. hiring Manager 1 for large-cap stocks and not hiring Manager 3 for small-cap stocks.

   B. hiring Manager 3 for large-cap stocks and not hiring Manager 2 for small-cap stocks.

   C. hiring Manager 3 for large-cap stocks and not hiring Manager 1 for small-cap stocks.

10. A return distribution of skilled managers that is highly distinct from the return distribution of unskilled managers, *most likely* implies a:

    A. highly efficient market.

    B. low opportunity cost of not hiring a skilled manager.

    C. high opportunity cost of not hiring a skilled manager.

11. Boinic Corporation introduced an employee pension plan and set aside $20 million to fund the plan. Assessing five investment management firms, A through E, and expecting all to perform in line with their benchmarks, Boinic selected three firms (A, D, and E) to manage part of the pension plan assets. Exhibit 1 shows the managers' performance compared to their benchmark in the one year after being

selected.

**Exhibit 1: Year 1 Investment Firm Performance versus Benchmark**

|                                      | Firm A | Firm B | Firm C | Firm D | Firm E |
|--------------------------------------|--------|--------|--------|--------|--------|
| Year 1 performance versus benchmark  | Above  | Above  | Below  | Below  | Above  |

On analyzing these results, Boinic determines that it has made both a Type I and Type II error.

Identify the firm associated with Boinic's Type I and Type II error. Justify your selection for *each* error type, discussing the psychological effects of its Year 1 performance on Boinic.

12. Suppose that the results of a style analysis for an investment manager are not consistent with the stated philosophy of the manager and the manager's stated investment process. These facts suggest the:

    A. absence of style drift.

    B. investment process may not be repeatable.

    C. manager should be included in the universe of potential managers.

13. Compared with holdings-based style analysis (HBSA), a returns-based style analysis (RBSA):

    A. is subject to window dressing.

    B. requires less effort to acquire data.

    C. is more accurate when illiquid securities are present.

14. A manager has a mandate to be fully invested with a benchmark that is a blend of large-cap stocks and investment-grade bonds. Which of the following is *not* an indication that style drift has occurred? The manager:

    A. initiates an allocation to small-cap stocks.

    B. decreases investments in investment-grade corporate bonds.

    C. increases allocation to cash in anticipation of a market decline.

15. An advantage of a returns-based style analysis is that such analysis:

    A. is comparable across managers.

    B. is suitable for portfolios that contain illiquid securities.

    C. can effectively profile a manager's risk exposures using a short return series.

16. Which of the following types of style analysis use(s) a bottom-up approach to estimate the risk exposures in a portfolio?

    A. Returns-based style analysis only

    B. Holdings-based style analysis only

    **C.**  Both return-based and holdings-based style analysis

17. A manager whose relative performance is worse during market downturns *most likely* has a capture ratio that is:

    **A.**  less than one.

    **B.**  equal to one.

    **C.**  greater than one.

18. In a quarter, an investment manager's upside capture is 75% and downside capture is 125%. We can conclude that the manager underperforms the benchmark:

    **A.**  only when the benchmark return is positive.

    **B.**  only when the benchmark return is negative.

    **C.**  when the benchmark return is either positive or negative.

## The following information relates to questions 19-20

Cassandra Yang, age 59, is a manager at a large US manufacturing firm. Yang is single, owns a home, is debt free, and saves 20% of her pre-tax income in a company retirement plan and 15% of her after-tax income in a short-term money market account. Her accounts are self-directed; Yang makes all related decisions independently.

While Yang hates to suffer investment losses, she now seeks higher returns on 80% of the funds in her money market account. To help achieve her goal of retiring within three years, she is considering the actively managed investment funds listed in Exhibit 1.

#### Exhibit 1: Return Profile Summary

| Fund | Upside Capture | Downside Capture | Most Recent Drawdown Loss | Most Recent Drawdown Duration |
|------|---------|---------|---------|---------|
| Alpha | 80 | 20 | 57% | 21 months |
| Beta | 55 | 45 | 38% | 15 months |
| Gamma | 50 | 50 | 28% | 12 months |

19. Select the *best* fund for Yang, using only the information provided. Justify your selection.

20. Yang is also considering Aspen Investments (Aspen) for a portion of her money market funds. Aspen's investment philosophy states: "We pursue a passive investment strategy, which seeks to identify and exploit structural inefficiencies through identifying mispricings created by loss aversion. Our strategy and philosophy have evolved over time in response to fund and market performance."

Determine whether Yang is likely to judge that Aspen follows a consistent investment philosophy, using only the information provided. Justify your response with *two* reasons.

21. Which of the following is consistent with the expectation that exploiting a structural inefficiency is repeatable?

   A. The inefficiency is a unique event that occurs infrequently.

   B. The level of gross return is equal to the amount of transaction costs and expenses.

   C. The aggregate value of all assets affected by the inefficiency is larger than the AUM of the manager and its competitors.

22. Susan Patnode, age 66, was recently widowed and received £2,000,000 from a spousal life insurance policy. Patnode would like to invest the proceeds to generate predictable income to cover her ongoing living expenses.

   Patnode is considering three investment managers, Laurbær Partners, Alcanfor Limited, and Mylesten Management, to manage the insurance policy proceeds. All three take an active investment approach. Further information regarding each of the investment manager's investment philosophy and approach is provided in Exhibit 1.

| Exhibit 1: Information on Investment Manager Philosophy/Approach | |
| --- | --- |
| **Investment Manager** | **Investment Philosophy/Approach** |
| Laurbær Partners | Seeks to produce returns through investing in new investment themes and emphasizes measuring the contribution of each to performance. |
| Alcanfor Limited | Seeks to produce returns through investing in securities that appear to be mispriced in their industry sectors and tracks their ultimate performance against market benchmarks. |
| Mylesten Management | Seeks to produce returns through investing with maximum flexibility to the most popular investor sentiments worldwide |

   Identify which investment manager is *most* suitable for Patnode. Justify your response based solely on *each* manager's investment philosophy and approach.

23. Which of the following statements is consistent with the manager adhering to a stated investment philosophy and investment decision-making process?

   A. Senior investment team members have left to form their own firm.

   B. A senior employee has been cited by the SEC for violating insider trading regulations.

   C. A large drawdown occurs because of an unforeseen political event in a foreign country.

# The following information relates to questions 24-25

Frances Lute is an investment manager for a large institutional investment management firm in London. His client, Parade University (Parade), has an endowment worth approximately GBP1.6 billion. Lute is considering three active investment managers in order to add one new style. Parade's investment policy statement (IPS) highlights the endowment's preference for low turnover and trading costs.

Lute is particularly concerned about portfolio construction and the prospective implementation of investments within the portfolio. All else equal, Lute has identified these distinguishing characteristics for the processes affecting portfolio construction by the three managers.

- Manager A uses hard-stop losses to manage risk.
- Manager B's portfolio can be liquidated within five business days or less.
- Manager C's portfolio turnover is greater than the frequency of signals generated.

24. Identify which manager is *most* appropriate for Parade. Justify your response.

25. Upon choosing a manager, Lute must allocate the funds either to a separately managed account (SMA) customized for Parade or a pooled vehicle called Diversified. In addition to low turnover and trading costs, Parade's IPS also prioritizes the following characteristics for its investment: transparency, investor behavior, cost, liquidity, and tracking risk. While each type of investment vehicle offers distinct advantages, Parade is unclear as to which advantage is applicable by type.

    Identify which investment vehicle *best* addresses *each* characteristic highlighted in Parade's IPS. Justify your response.

---

26. Brickridge Investment Consultants meets weekly to review the positives and negatives of investment managers being considered for client portfolios. In the latest meeting, analyst Brad Moore discusses investment manager Lyon Management (Lyon). His in-depth analysis of one of Lyon's investment strategies includes the following summary details:

    detail 1   Long and short positions are paired.

    detail 2   Investment strategy relies on unique information.

    detail 3   AUM connected with the strategy have grown substantially, while the number and characteristics of positions have stayed the same.

    Asked about Lyon's regulatory context, Moore states, "The regulatory environment is strong and seeks to decrease information symmetries."

    Identify whether each detail from Moore's summary is *most likely* a benefit or a drawback of the strategy. Justify your selection.

27. Which of the following is *most likely* a key consideration in investment due diligence?

    A. Suitability of the investment vehicle

    B. Back office processes and procedures

    C. Depth of expertise and experience of investment personnel

28. Which of the following is *not* a reason that an investor might favor a separately managed account rather than a pooled vehicle? The investor:

    A.  is tax exempt.

    B.  requires real-time details on investment positions.

    C.  has expressed certain constraints and preferences for the portfolio.

29. Which of the following investment vehicles provide investors with the highest degree of liquidity?

    A.  Open-end funds

    B.  Private equity funds

    C.  Limited partnerships

30. An investor should prefer a pooled investment vehicle to a separately managed account when she:

    A.  is cost sensitive.

    B.  focuses on tax efficiency.

    C.  requires clear legal ownership of assets.

31. Which of the following investment types is the most liquid?

    A.  ETFs

    B.  Hedge funds

    C.  Private equity funds

# The following information relates to questions 32-34

Jack Porter and Melissa Smith are co-managers for the Circue Library Foundation (Circue) in Canada. Within the next six months, Porter and Smith will be replacing one of Circue's underperforming active managers. This choice will rely on the terms of investment management contracts—specifically, liquidity and management fee structure. Circue's IPS indicates some tolerance for lower liquidity, a moderate sensitivity to management fees, and a heightened sensitivity to closet indexing.

Circue is considering the following three investment vehicles with distinct fee structures:

- Hedge funds with a soft lock
- Open-end funds with an incentive fee
- Closed-end funds with no incentive fee

32. Determine which of the three investment vehicles is *most* appropriate for Circue's IPS. Justify your response.

33. Porter and Smith next consider how the performance-based fee structures of the

prospective managers may affect portfolio risk.

Porter states: "I've noticed more managers are applying a bonus structure in which the manager is not fully exposed to the downside but is fully exposed to the upside."

Smith states: "Circue's current market view is that there are increasing risks to the downside."

Discuss how Smith's stated expectation would be reflected in estimated portfolio risk under the fee structure identified by Porter.

34. After narrowing their choice to three managers with different fee structures, Porter and Smith analyze the effect of the performance-based fee structure for each manager. Exhibit 1 provides applicable data for one of the managers.

### Exhibit 1: Selected Performance-Based Fee Data for a Prospective Manager

| Fee Structure | Fee (%) |
| --- | --- |
| Standard Fee | 0.35 |
| Base Fee | 0.20 |
| Sharing* | 0.25 |
| Breakeven Active Return | 1.25 |
| Maximum Annual Fee | 0.90 |

*On active return, beyond base fee.

To understand the effect each fee structure has on its respective portfolio, Porter and Smith must estimate the net active return for several possible gross active returns, including less than or equal to 0.20%, 0.75%, 1.25%, and 1.75%.

Calculate the net active return based on each possible gross active return provided using the selected data in Exhibit 1. Show your calculations.

35. Institutional investment consultant Wilsot Consultants (Wilsot) is reviewing multiple investment managers within a prospective client's portfolio. Two of the managers, Vaudreuil Capital Management (Vaudreuil) and Pourtir Investments (Pourtir), have similar strategies that show comparable performance on a net-of-fees basis. Assessing the portfolio effects of management fees, a Wilsot analyst reviews both manager contracts to determine their advantages and disadvantages to the client. Checking client fee structures, the analyst notes Vaudreuil's fees are AUM-based while Pourtir's are performance-based.

Discuss *one* advantage and *one* disadvantage to the client of *each* manager's contracted fee structure.

36. Which of the following fee structures *most likely* decreases the volatility of a portfolio's net returns?

A. Incentive fees only

B. Management fees only

C. Neither incentive fees nor management fees

# The following information relates to questions 37-42

The Tree Fallers Endowment plans to allocate part of its portfolio to alternative investment funds. The endowment has hired Kurt Summer, a consultant at Summer Brothers Consultants, to identify suitable alternative investment funds for its portfolio.

Summer has identified three funds for potential investment and will present the performance of these investments to the endowment's board of directors at their next quarterly meeting.

Summer is reviewing each of the fund's fee schedules and is concerned about the manager's incentive to take on excess risk in an attempt to generate a higher fee. Exhibit 1 presents the fee schedules of the three funds.

## Exhibit 1: Fee Schedules

| Fund | Computed Fee | Base Fee | Sharing | Maximum Annual Fee |
|------|-------------|----------|---------|--------------------|
| Red Grass Fund | Higher of either (1) base or (2) base plus sharing of positive performance; sharing is based on return net of the base fee. | 1.00% | 20% | na |
| Blue Water Fund | Higher of either (1) base or (2) base plus sharing of positive performance, up to a maximum annual fee of 2.50%; sharing is based on active return. | 0.50% | 20% | 2.50% |
| Yellow Wood Fund | Base plus sharing of both positive and negative performance; sharing is based on return net of the base fee. | 1.50% | 20% | na |

Exhibit 2 presents the annual gross returns for each fund and its respective benchmark for the period of 2016–2018. All funds have an inception date of 1 January 2016. Summer intends to include in his report an explanation of the impact of the fee structures of the three funds on returns.

## Exhibit 2: Fund and Benchmark Returns

| | 2016 | | 2017 | | 2018 | |
|------|------|------|------|------|------|------|
| Fund | Gross Return (%) | Benchmark Return (%) | Gross Return (%) | Benchmark Return (%) | Gross Return (%) | Benchmark Return (%) |
| Red Grass Fund | 8.00 | 8.00 | −2.00 | −10.00 | 5.00 | 4.50 |
| Blue Water Fund | 10.00 | 9.00 | −4.00 | −1.50 | 14.00 | 2.00 |
| Yellow Wood Fund | 15.00 | 14.00 | −5.00 | −6.50 | 7.00 | 9.50 |

The board of directors of the Tree Fallers Endowment asks Summer to recalculate the fees of the Red Grass Fund assuming a high-water mark feature whereby a sharing percentage could only be charged to the extent any losses had been recouped.

37. Based on Exhibit 1, which fund has a symmetrical fee structure?

    A. Red Grass

    B. Blue Water

    C. Yellow Wood

38. Based on the fee schedules in Exhibit 1, the portfolio manager of which fund has the greatest incentive to assume additional risk to earn a higher investment management fee?

    A. Red Grass

    B. Blue Water

    C. Yellow Wood

39. Based on Exhibit 1 and Exhibit 2, the Yellow Wood Fund's 2016 investment management fee is:

    A. 3.00%.

    B. 4.20%.

    C. 4.50%.

40. Based on Exhibit 1 and Exhibit 2, the Red Grass Fund's 2017 investment management fee is:

    A. 0.40%.

    B. 1.00%.

    C. 2.60%.

41. Based on Exhibit 1 and Exhibit 2, the Blue Water Fund's 2018 investment management fee is:

    A. 2.40%

    B. 2.50%.

    C. 2.90%

42. In which year would the Red Grass Fund's investment management fee be affected by Summer's recalculation using the high-water mark?

    A. 2016

    B. 2017

    C. 2018

43. At a meeting for the local municipal pension fund, a group of beneficiaries expressed concern about current investment management fees. The beneficia-

ries asked the Investment Committee for a fee summary of each manager in the portfolio.

The next day, a pension fund staff member briefed the Committee on the managers' full contracted fee schedules. The Committee was surprised to hear that the managers work under numerous different fee structures and rates. A sample of these fee schedules for two managers is provided in Exhibit 1:

### Exhibit 1: Fee Schedules for Selected Managers: Hidden Lake and Carpenter Management

| Fee Type | Hidden Lake | Carpenter Management |
|---|---|---|
| Base Fee | 0.30% | 0.18%* |
| Sharing** | 15% | 20% |
| Maximum Annual Fee | N/A | 0.80% |

*Minimum fee.
**On active return, beyond base fee.

In explaining the differences, the staff member said that fee structures may lead to misestimates of portfolio risk. She also noted that performance-based fees sometimes are a close equivalent to a manager's call option on active return.

Identify which manager's fee structure is *most* similar to a call option on a share of active return. Justify your selection.

## SOLUTIONS

1. B is correct. A critical element of manager selection is to assess if the investment process is superior, repeatable, and can be consistently applied.

2. A is correct. The focus of the initial screening process is on building a universe of managers that could potentially satisfy the identified portfolio need and should not focus on historical performance. Identifying a benchmark is a key component of defining the manager's role in the portfolio, and third-party categorizations are an efficient way to build an initial universe which can then be further refined.

3. The Theta fund, which is managed by an investment team rather than a single manager (as at Zeta) or by two managers (as at Eta), has lower key person risk. If the single manager at Zeta leaves or either manager at Eta leaves, the fund's performance could suffer.

   The Theta fund has the lowest level of staff turnover among the three funds. This higher level of personnel continuity limits the risk of the loss of institutional knowledge and experience within the investment team.

   The Theta fund offers a more attractive compensation package than Eta or Zeta. This incentivizes its investment professionals to stay at Theta, leading to greater longevity and experience over time. Additionally, Theta's package, unlike those of the other funds, will directly increase the rewards to its managers when performance exceeds benchmarks. This better aligns their interests with those of Connell.

4. *Alternative 1*

   If Connell avoids the Eta fund because of its recent underperformance, with performance reverting to the mean, he is at risk of making a Type II error (by not retaining managers with skill). A Type II error is an error of failing to detect a true relationship, or in this case, the opportunity cost associated with not hiring Eta and seeing its performance improve.

   *Alternative 2*

   If Connell selects the Theta fund because of its recent superior performance, with performance reverting to the mean, he is at risk of making a Type I error. A Type I error occurs when hiring or retaining a manager who subsequently underperforms expectations. The cost of a Type I error is explicit and relatively straightforward to measure.

   In deciding which fund to hire, the goal is to avoid making decisions based on short-term performance (trend following) and to identify evidence of behavioral biases in the evaluation of managers during the selection process.

5. The adviser would find style analysis most useful, whether it be returns-based (RBSA) or holdings-based (HBSA), when applied to strategies that hold publicly-traded securities where pricing is frequent. It can be applied to other strategies (hedge funds and private equity, for example), but the insights drawn from a style analysis of such strategies are more likely to be used for designing additional lines of inquiry in the course of due diligence rather than for confirmation of the investment process.

   In addition, style analysis, whether returns-based or holdings-based, must be meaningful, accurate, consistent, and timely in order to be useful. Accordingly, style analysis would be most useful to Connell in understanding most of the asset classes in the funds he is considering, including the equities and bonds. However, it would be less meaningful for evaluating the venture capital assets since they are not traded and are thus illiquid.

6. *Qualitative*

   Process and people: Evaluating the manager's investment process, including the manager's philosophy, process, people, and portfolio. This consideration is broadly described as part of "investment due diligence."

   Operational due diligence: Evaluating the manager's infrastructure and firm, including the accuracy of the manager's track record and whether the record fully reflects risks; the back office processes and procedures; the terms and if they are acceptable and appropriate for the strategy and vehicle; and the firm's profitability, its culture, and if it's likely to remain in business. This and the following bulleted considerations as a whole are broadly described as part of "operational due diligence":

   • Investment vehicle: Is the investment vehicle suitable for the portfolio need?

   • Terms: Are the terms acceptable and appropriate for the strategy and vehicle?

   • Monitoring: Does the manager continue to be the "best" fit for the portfolio need?

   *Quantitative:*

   Attribution and appraisal: To assess if the manager has displayed skill in investing.

   The capture ratio: How has the manager performed in "up" versus "down" markets?

   Drawdown: Does the return distribution exhibit large drawdowns?

7. Grimmett, with her adviser, would ensure the following tasks were performed prior to manager selection:

   • Decide that outside support is necessary.

   • Complete an investment policy statement (IPS).

   • Determine the appropriate asset allocation.

   Short of these key actions, Grimmett will be unable to identify the managers who fit her needs, confirm that the managers are suitable for her IPS, and be confident that they will act upon the appropriate asset allocation.

8. B is correct. Type I errors are more easily measured than Type II errors. In addition, Type I errors may be linked to the compensation of the decision maker. Type I errors are errors of mistaken rejection, whereas Type II are errors failing to detect a true relationship. Firing a skilled manager is less transparent to the investor.

9. B is correct. Hiring unskilled Manager 3 for large-cap stocks is an error of mistaken rejection or Type I error, whereas not hiring skilled Manager 2 for small-cap stocks is an error of failing to detect a true relationship or Type II error.

10. C is correct. When the two distributions are highly distinct, the unskilled managers are expected to significantly underperform the skilled managers, implying a high opportunity cost of not hiring the skilled managers. Efficient markets are likely to exhibit smaller differences of returns between skilled and unskilled managers.

11. *Type I:*

    Hiring Firm D, which later underperformed expectations, resulted in a Type I error. A Type I error occurs when a manager is hired or retained who subsequently underperforms expectations. This situation involves rejecting the null hypothesis of no skill when it is correct.

It is most likely Boinic will find its hiring of Firm D to be psychologically troubling.

Decision makers appear predisposed to worry more about Type I errors than Type II errors. Potential reasons for this focus are as follows:

- Psychologically, people seek to avoid feelings of regret. Type I errors are errors of mistaken rejection, active decisions that turn out to be incorrect, whereas Type II errors are errors of failing to detect a true relationship. Type I errors create explicit costs, whereas Type II errors create opportunity costs. Because individuals appear to put less weight on opportunity costs, Type I errors are psychologically more painful than Type II errors.

- Type I errors are more transparent to investors, so they entail not only the regret of an incorrect decision but the pain of having to explain this decision to the investor. Type II errors, such as firing (or not hiring) a manager with skill, are less transparent to investors—unless the investor tracks fired managers or evaluates the universe themselves.

*Type II:*

Not hiring Firm B, which later outperformed expectations, resulted in a Type II error. A Type II error occurs when a manager who subsequently outperforms, or performs in line with, expectations is not hired. This situation involves not rejecting an incorrect null hypothesis. As noted previously, a Type II error is typically less psychologically troubling than a Type I error.

The other three decisions did not result in either a Type I or Type II error.

12. B is correct. The results of the returns-based style analysis and the holdings-based style analysis should be consistent with the philosophy of the manager and the investment process. If this is not the case, it may suggest that the process is not repeatable or not consistently implemented. For these results, the manager should not be included in the universe of potential managers, whereas if the results track over time, they may suggest style drift.

13. B is correct. RBSA typically does not require a large amount of additional, or difficult to acquire, data. HBSA requires data on each security in the investment portfolio. HBSA is a snapshot of the portfolio at a single point of time and thus is subject to window dressing. Both HBSA and RBSA are subject to difficulties in interpreting returns when illiquid securities are present.

14. B is correct. In the normal course of business, the manager conforms to its style by reducing exposure to some class of investment grade bonds. Increasing allocation to cash and small-cap stocks is in violation of the mandate to be fully invested with equity exposure to large-cap stocks.

15. A is correct. Returns-based style analysis on portfolios of liquid assets is generally able to identify the important drivers of return and the relevant risk factors for the period analyzed, even for complicated strategies. In addition, the process is comparable across managers and through time. If the portfolio contains illiquid securities, the lack of current prices on those positions may lead to an underestimation of the portfolio's volatility in a returns-based style analysis. Longer return series generally provide a more accurate estimate of the manager's underlying standard deviation of return.

16. B is correct. Holdings-based style analysis estimates the portfolio's risk exposures using the securities held in the portfolio (a bottom-up approach), whereas returns-based style analysis uses portfolio returns to estimate a portfolio's sensitivities to security market indexes (a top-down approach).

17. A is correct. A capture ratio less than one indicates the downside capture is greater than upside capture and reflects greater participation in falling markets than in rising markets.

18. C is correct. Upside capture of 75% suggests that the manager only gained 75% of benchmark increase when the benchmark return was positive. Downside capture of 125% suggests that the manager lost 125% as much as the benchmark when the benchmark return was negative. Therefore, the manager underperformed the benchmark in both scenarios.

19. With Yang hoping to retire in three years and not wanting to suffer investment losses, she has less time to recover from losses than someone with a longer time horizon. Yang should seek a fund with a shallower and shorter expected drawdown. The Gamma fund has the smallest drawdown and the shortest drawdown duration.

20. Passive strategies seek to earn risk premiums, which are defined as the return in excess of a minimal risk ("risk-free") rate of return that accrues to bearing a risk that is not easily diversified away—so-called systematic risk. Active strategies, in contrast, assume markets are sufficiently inefficient that security mispricings can be identified and exploited.

    So, in assessing Aspen, Yang first would find its investment philosophy to be inconsistent because it states an active strategy but labels its strategy as a passive one. Aspen is unable to clearly and consistently articulate its investment philosophy.

    Yang would also note that Aspen has altered its investment philosophy over time in response to market performance. This suggests Aspen is reacting to markets, not pursuing a consistent philosophy. With this approach, Aspen's performance results may not be repeatable.

21. C is correct. Given the amount of inefficient assets compared with the AUM of managers likely to exploit them provides some assurance that the inefficiency is repeatable. It would likely take some time for the inefficiency to converge to efficient valuation. The infrequent nature of the inefficiency and the zero marginal return suggest that the inefficiency is probably not worthwhile to pursue.

22. Given Patnode's goal of predictably covering expenses and given the choice among these three active managers to invest her insurance policy proceeds, Laurbær is most suitable. Laurbær recognizes its strategy is exposed to potentially being arbitraged away and is more likely to evolve over time to deliver the ongoing returns desired by Patnode.

    Alcanfor and Mylesten, in contrast, are making more generic claims that have a weaker foundation for long-term results. Alcanfor is making its judgments based on performance in industry sectors but is judging effectiveness based on overall market benchmarks. This is not providing evidence related to success within its selection domain but instead gauging itself against a broader market standard. Mylesten is offering a more ad hoc reaction to changing market conditions and investment flows, suggesting a lack of repeatability and robustness. So, both of them would have greater uncertainty as to the production of the income Patnode needs.

23. C is correct. A large drawdown that results from an unforeseen event is explainable as a single isolated event that does not prohibit the manager from adhering to its investment philosophy and process. The events of senior team members leaving to form their own investment firm and an insider trading investigation by the SEC call into question the ability of the firm to adhere to its philosophy and

decision-making process.

24. All else equal, Manager B is most appropriate for Parade because the portfolio is liquid. That will reduce trading costs in comparison to a portfolio consisting of illiquid securities. Investment strategies not intending to capture a liquidity risk premium must be aware of portfolio liquidity. An existing portfolio consisting of illiquid securities will be more costly to change, not only to take advantage of new opportunities but also to trade because of higher transaction costs. Manager A is not the most appropriate choice because its use of hard-stop losses can risk closing positions too frequently. That, in turn, will increase turnover as well as trading costs. Manager C is problematic because in the case of an actively managed portfolio, the portfolio turnover should agree with (not be greater than) the frequency of signals generated and the securities' liquidity.

25. Transparency: SMA. Offering real-time, position-level detail to the investor, SMAs provide complete transparency and accurate attribution. Even if Diversified offers position-level detail, it is likely available with a delay.

Investor Behavior: Diversified. Diversified is not as susceptible to investor micromanagement. Decisions are set by the manager, and portfolio value is determined by the related strategy without investor modification.

Cost: Diversified. An SMA investor owns individual securities directly, which provides additional safety should a liquidity event occur. Although the manager continues to make investment decisions, those will not be influenced by the redemption or liquidity demands of other investors in the strategy.

Liquidity: SMA. An SMA investor owns individual securities directly, which provides additional safety should a liquidity event occur. Although the manager continues to make investment decisions, those will not be influenced by the redemption or liquidity demands of other investors in the strategy.

Tracking Risk: Diversified. Diversified would have lower tracking risk compared to SMAs, whose customization increases the chances of tracking risk relative to the benchmark. This can confuse attribution because performance will reflect investor constraints rather than manager decisions.

26. Detail 1. Benefit: This is a benefit if Lyon's positions are paired with the idea of capturing alpha as prices converge while offsetting market risk and are well-matched and sized correctly.

Detail 2. Drawback: The reliance of Lyon's strategy on unique information is a drawback as it is difficult for Lyon to have an informational edge in a regulatory environment that seeks to reduce informational symmetries.

Detail 3. Drawback: This is a drawback because in a context of significant asset growth, Lyon should adjust the number and/or characteristics of the positions held to accommodate the increase in AUM.

27. C is correct. Experienced investment personnel is a key aspect of investment due diligence. A strong back office and suitable investment vehicles are key aspects of operational due diligence.

28. A is correct. The tax advantages to separately managed accounts do not accrue to a tax exempt investor. Choices B and C are considerations that reflect the investor's preferences and could be better satisfied using a separately managed account.

29. A is correct. Open-end funds provide daily liquidity; shares are bought and sold at the end-of-day NAV. Limited partnerships and private equity funds typically require investors to invest their money for longer periods.

30. A is correct. Pooled investment vehicles are typically operated at a lower cost than separately managed accounts because operational costs can be spread among multiple investors. An investor who is focused on tax efficiency would prefer a separately managed account because a separate account allows the implementation of tax-efficient investing and trading strategies, and the investor pays taxes only on capital gains realized. If the investor requires clear legal ownership, they would prefer a separately managed account in which the investor owns the individual security directly.

31. A is correct. ETFs, as listed securities that can be bought and sold intra-day, are the most liquid vehicles. Hedge fund liquidity features—such as redemption frequency, notification period, lockup, and gates—limit the liquidity of hedge funds. Private equity funds return capital and make profit distributions to investors only as investments are sold during the life of the fund, which is often 10 years and may be extended.

32. Open-end funds with an incentive fee. Open-end funds with an incentive fee are the most appropriate among the three investment vehicles being considered by Circue. Although slightly less liquid than closed-end funds, open-end funds still offer daily liquidity—with Circue indicating some tolerance for lower liquidity. An incentive fee is applicable in this case as mutual fund assets are often "sticky"; investors are reluctant to switch allocations once made and may accept lower returns. This outcome decreases manager motivation and leads to closet indexing, to which Circue has a heightened sensitivity among its active managers. Thus, the incentive fee can help motivate managers to work harder to improve performance. Closed-end funds are the most liquid of the three choices. Without an accompanying incentive fee, however, the closed-end fund manager may not have the same motivation to work harder than the open-end fund manager, who does have an incentive fee. Hedge funds are inappropriate here because they are the least liquid of the three options. A soft lock charges a redemption fee, paid into the fund, which is inconsistent with Circue's moderate sensitivity to fees.

33. Under the fee structure identified by Porter, Smith's stated expectation would be reflected in a misestimation of portfolio risk because performance-based fee structures may lead to such misestimates. Performance-based fee structures convert symmetrical gross active return distributions into asymmetrical net active return distributions, reducing variability on the upside but not the downside. As a result, a single standard deviation calculated on a return series that incorporates active returns, above and below the base fee, can lead to the underestimation of downside risk. In contrast, fully symmetric fees (fully exposing the manager to both upside and downside results) tend to yield closer alignment in risk and effort than bonus-style fees.

34. Gross Active Return ≤ 0.20%: Gross Active Return at or below the Base Fee – Base Fee = Net Active Return: 0.20 – 0.20 = 0.00, therefore Base Fee = Billed Fee (No Sharing Fee)0.20

Gross Active Return = 0.75%: Active Return − Base Fee = Return Subject to Sharing Fee: 0.75 − 0.20

= 0.55

Return Subject to Sharing Fee × Sharing Fee = Additional Fee Due to Sharing Fee: 0.55 × 0.25

= 0.1375

Base Fee + Additional Fee Due to Sharing Fee = Billed Fee: 0.20 + 0.1375

= 0.3375

Active Return − Billed Fee = Net Active Return: 0.75 − 0.3375

= 0.4125, rounded to 0.41%

Gross Active Return = 1.25% is the breakeven active return (No Sharing Fee):
Gross Active Return − Standard Fee = Net Active Return: 1.25 − 0.35

= 0.90 or 0.90%

Standard Fee = Billed Fee (No Sharing Fee)0.35

Gross Active Return = 1.75%: Gross Active Return − Base Fee = Return Subject
to Sharing Fee: 1.75 − 0.20

= 1.55

Return Subject to Sharing Fee × Sharing Fee = Additional Fee Due to Sharing
Fee: 1.55 × 0.25

= 0.3875

Base Fee + Additional Fee Due to Sharing Fee = Billed Fee: 0.2 + 0.3875

= 0.5875

Gross Active Return − Billed Fee = Net Active Return: 1.75 − 0.5875

= 1.1625, rounded to 1.16%

35. Vaudreuil. The impact of Vaudreuil's fees on the client is lower as assets grow
    in a rising market. This is a benefit to the client. The client might not achieve
    the same level of returns as would be available under a different fee structure.
    Vaudreuil might not want to risk losing assets once they are large and may not
    work to generate the same level of returns to retain assets because they tend to be
    "sticky."

    Pourtir. Performance-based fees work to align the interests of Pourtir and the
    client because both parties share in the investment results.

    The client benefits by paying lower fees when active returns are low.

    Pourtir may work harder. Tension can be created between the client and Pourtir,
    as the client must pay base fees even if Pourtir underperforms.

    Pourtir's fee structure may lead to misestimates of portfolio risk and may incen-
    tivize Pourtir to assume higher portfolio risk.

    The client and Pourtir may have different incentives when performance-based
    fees are used, specifically in the case of bonus-style fees.

    Performance-based fees may incentivize Pourtir to hold on to assets until a profit
    can be realized even if the client would benefit from selling the assets at a loss
    and investing the proceeds elsewhere.

36. A is correct. Because incentive fees are fees charged as a percentage of returns
    (reducing net gains in positive months and reducing net losses in negative
    months), its use lowers the standard deviation of realized returns. Charging a
    management fee (a fixed percentage based on assets) lowers the level of realized
    return without affecting the standard deviation of the return series.

37. C is correct. A symmetrical fee structure is one in which the fees are affected by
    both positive and negative performance. Of the three funds in Exhibit 1, only Yel-
    low Wood has a symmetrical structure. Yellow Wood's profit sharing component
    will be negative if its return is negative and positive if it is positive.

38. A is correct. Red Grass's fee arrangement allows for unlimited
    performance-based fees on the upside and no negative consequences on the

downside.

39. B is correct. The fund's fee schedule includes a base fee of 1.50% and a 20% performance-based fee. The performance-based fee is applied after the base fee is deducted. The total fee is calculated as follows:

    1.5% + [20% × (15% − 1.5%)] = 4.20%

40. B is correct. Red Grass Fund's fee schedule states that the fee will be the higher of either (1) the base fee or (2) the base fee plus the sharing of the positive performance. The 2017 return was negative and only the base fee should be applied.

41. B is correct. The fee schedule states that the fee will be the higher of either (1) the base fee or (2) the base fee plus sharing of the positive performance, with a maximum fee of 2.50%. Furthermore, it states that the performance-based fee is assessed on the active return. Without an upper limit, the fee would be 0.5% + [20% × (14% − 2%)] = 2.90%, which is greater than 2.50%; so, the 2.50% fee is assessed.

42. C is correct. The 2016 fee calculation would not be affected by the high-water mark provision because it is the first year of operation of the fund and the return is positive (no prior losses to be offset). The investment management fee in 2016 is calculated as follows:

    Investment management fee = 1.00% + [20% × (8.0% − 1.00%)] = 2.4%.

    The 2017 fee calculation would also not be affected by the high-water mark provision because the profit-sharing component of the fee is zero as a result of a negative return in that year. The investment management fee is calculated as follows:

    Investment management fee = 1.00% + 0.00% = 1.00%.

    The 2018 fee would be affected by the high-water mark provision because the sharing fee percentage would now be part of the 2018 gain and will need to offset the prior year losses, and only the remaining gains will generate a fee. The performance-based fee would be based on only the gains in excess of the high-water mark. The actual investment management fee charged (percentage and dollar value) will depend on the specific feature of the calculation, which is beyond the scope of this learning module. Note that the correct answer can be identified by observing that 2018 is the only year in which a positive return follows a negative return in the prior year.

43. Carpenter Management. Carpenter Management has a bonus-style fee with a maximum fee feature. Bonus-style fees are the close equivalent of a manager's call option on a share of active return, for which the base fee is the strike price—for example, the 18 bps base fee, plus a long call option on active return with a strike price equal to the minimum (base) fee, minus another (less valuable call option) with a strike price equal to the maximum fee. Hidden Lake has a symmetrical fee structure in which the manager is fully exposed to both the downside and upside. So, of the two firms, Carpenter Management's fee structure is most similar to a call option.

# Overview of the Global Investment Performance Standards

by Philip Lawton, PhD, CFA, CIPM.

*Philip Lawton, PhD, CFA, CIPM (USA)*

## LEARNING OUTCOMES

| Mastery | The candidate should be able to: |
|---------|----------------------------------|
| ☐ | discuss the objectives and scope of the GIPS standards and their benefits to prospective clients and investors, as well as investment managers |
| ☐ | explain the fundamentals of compliance with the GIPS standards, including the definition of the firm and the firm's definition of discretion |
| ☐ | discuss requirements of the GIPS standards with respect to return calculation methodologies, including the treatment of external cash flows, cash and cash equivalents, and expenses and fees |
| ☐ | explain the recommended valuation hierarchy of the GIPS standards |
| ☐ | explain requirements of the GIPS standards with respect to composite return calculations, including methods for asset-weighting portfolio returns |
| ☐ | explain the meaning of "discretionary" in the context of composite construction and, given a description of the relevant facts, determine whether a portfolio is likely to be considered discretionary |
| ☐ | explain the role of investment mandates, objectives, or strategies in the construction of composites |
| ☐ | explain requirements of the GIPS standards with respect to composite construction, including switching portfolios among composites, the timing of the inclusion of new portfolios in composites, and the timing of the exclusion of terminated portfolios from composites |
| ☐ | explain requirements of the GIPS standards with respect to presentation and reporting |
| ☐ | explain the conditions under which the performance of a past firm or affiliation may be linked to or used to represent the historical performance of a new or acquiring firm |
| ☐ | discuss the purpose, scope, and process of verification |

# 1    OBJECTIVE AND SCOPE OF THE GIPS STANDARDS

☐ | discuss the objectives and scope of the GIPS standards and their benefits to prospective clients and investors, as well as investment managers

This reading explains the rationale and application of certain provisions of the 2020 edition of the Global Investment Performance Standards (GIPS®) for Firms. The 2020 edition of the GIPS standards contains three chapters: the GIPS Standards for Firms, the GIPS Standards for Asset Owners, and the GIPS Standards for Verifiers, each with its own glossary. ***Candidates are responsible not only for the material contained directly in this reading but also for the sections of the GIPS Standards for Firms specifically referenced within this reading.*** The entirety of the 2020 GIPS Standards for Firms can be found here:

https://www.cfainstitute.org/en/ethics/codes/gips-standards/firms

The GIPS standards fulfill an essential role in investment management around the world. They meet the need for globally accepted standards for investment management firms in calculating and presenting their investment returns to **prospective clients** and **prospective investors**. (In the context of the GIPS Standards for Firms, a prospective *client* is any person or entity that has expressed interest in one of the firm's strategies and qualifies to invest in that strategy via a segregated account, irrespective of whether the person or entity currently invests with the firm through another strategy that the firm offers. A prospective *investor* is any person or entity that has expressed interest in one of the firm's pooled funds and qualifies to invest in the pooled fund, again irrespective of any other current investments with the firm. These and other terms bolded in this reading are defined in the glossary of the GIPS Standards for Firms. For purposes of this reading, the terms *client* and *investor* may be used interchangeably.)

The GIPS standards are based on the ideals of fair representation and full disclosure of an investment management firm's performance history. Firms that claim compliance with the GIPS standards must adhere to rules governing not only return calculations but also the way in which returns are displayed in a **GIPS Report**. (A GIPS Report is a specific type of performance presentation that must be provided to *prospective* clients and investors when a firm claims compliance with the GIPS standards.) They are further required to make certain disclosures and are encouraged to make others in a GIPS Report, thereby assisting the user in interpreting and evaluating the reported returns. Prospective and current clients can have a high degree of confidence that the information shown in a GIPS Report reflects the results of the firm's past investment decisions. They can also be confident that the returns are calculated and presented on a consistent basis and are objectively comparable for a given strategy with those reported by other firms claiming compliance with the GIPS standards.

## Objective and Scope of the GIPS Standards

The GIPS standards evolved from earlier efforts to improve the reliability of investment performance information and to standardize calculation methodologies and presentation standards. In this part of the reading, we explain the objectives and scope of the GIPS standards.

## *The Need for Global Investment Performance Standards*

To appreciate the value of industry-wide performance presentation standards, consider some of the many ways in which unscrupulous employees might attempt to gather and retain assets by misrepresenting a firm's historical record. In communicating with a prospective client or investor, they could

- present returns only for the best-performing portfolios as though those returns fully represented the firm's expertise in a given strategy or style;

- base portfolio values on their own unsubstantiated estimates of asset prices;

- inflate returns by annualizing partial-period results;

- select the most favorable measurement period, calculating returns from a low point to a high point;

- present simulated returns as though they had actually been earned;

- choose as a benchmark the particular index the selected portfolios have outperformed by the greatest margin during the preferred measurement period;

- portray the growth of assets in the style or strategy of interest so as to mask the difference between investment returns and client contributions; or

- use the marketing department's expertise in graphic design to underplay unfavorable performance data and direct the prospect's attention to the most persuasive elements of the sales presentation.

Some of the foregoing examples are admittedly egregious abuses. They are not, however, farfetched. The investment management industry is highly competitive, and people whose careers and livelihoods depend on winning new business want to communicate their firm's performance in the most favorable light. The GIPS standards are ethical criteria designed to ensure that the firm's performance history is fairly represented and adequately disclosed. Indeed, employees who are pressured to misrepresent their firm's investment results can and should cite the GIPS standards.

Without established, well-formulated, and widely adopted standards for investment performance measurement and presentation, the prospective client's or investor's ability to make sound decisions in selecting investment managers would be impaired. Individual clients, investors, and their advisors, as well as pension plan sponsors, foundation trustees, and other institutional investors with fiduciary responsibility for asset pools, need reliable information. The GIPS standards increase their confidence that the returns shown fairly represent an investment firm's historical record. The GIPS standards also enable them to make reasonable comparisons among different investment management firms before hiring one of them. Evaluating past returns is only one dimension of the manager selection process, but it is an important one in fulfilling the due diligence responsibilities expected of fiduciaries.

Global standards for performance presentation, including a requirement to show a strategy's returns alongside the returns of an appropriate **benchmark**, can lead to an informative discussion about the firm's investment decision-making process. A prospective client might ask, for instance, why the strategy outperformed the benchmark in some periods and not in others, inviting the firm's spokespersons to explain past returns and to describe how the investment product is positioned for the future. The firm's representatives should be able to explain the sources of past returns reasonably, credibly, and insightfully in light of the firm's investment philosophy and investment decision-making process as well as the then-prevailing capital market environment.

(It must be stressed in this context that reviewing properly calculated, fully disclosed historical results does not exempt the prospective client from a thorough investigation of the candidate firm's background, resources, and capabilities for the mandate under consideration. Due diligence in selecting an investment manager includes, among many other important elements, examining a firm's regulatory history, the experience and professional credentials of its decision makers, the soundness of its investment philosophy, the nature of its investment and operational risk controls, and the independence of its service providers.)

The benefits of the GIPS standards to prospective and current clients are clear. What, if any, are the benefits to the investment management firms incurring the expenses required to achieve and maintain compliance with the GIPS standards?

There is, first, an immeasurable benefit to the investment management industry as a whole. The development of well-founded, thoughtfully defined performance presentation standards is a great credit not only to the vision of certain professionals and organizations but, above all, to the leadership of the investment management firms that adopted the standards early on. The GIPS standards may reassure investors about compliant firms' integrity in the area of investment performance reporting, especially if they have been verified. **Verification**, discussed later in this reading, refers to an investment firm's voluntarily engaging an independent third party to test the firm's design and implementation of certain performance measurement policies and procedures. Verification brings additional credibility to the firm's claim of compliance with the GIPS standards.

The practical benefits to individual firms facing the initial and ongoing expenses of GIPS compliance have increased over time. In some markets, the GIPS standards are so well accepted by plan sponsors and consultants that non-compliance is a serious competitive impediment to a firm's winning new institutional business. Requests for proposals (RFPs) in manager searches routinely ask if the responding firm is in compliance with the GIPS standards and if the firm has been independently verified. In addition, the global recognition the GIPS standards have gained helps the compliant firm to compete in international markets because prospective clients and investors value the ability to equitably compare its investment performance to that of local GIPS-compliant firms. Compliance with the GIPS standards has appropriately been characterized as the investment management firm's passport to the international marketplace.

Because the GIPS standards reflect best practices in the calculation and presentation of investment performance, firms may also realize internal benefits. In the course of implementing the GIPS standards, they might identify opportunities to strengthen managerial controls. The discipline of reviewing portfolio guidelines and defining, documenting, and adhering to internal policies in support of compliance with the GIPS standards typically improves the firm's oversight of investment operations and provides management with additional comfort in the accuracy of the firm's performance reporting and the quality of the presentations provided to prospective clients and investors. Similarly, technological enhancements designed to provide valid calculation input data and presentation elements, such as dispersion statistics, may improve the quality of information available to the firm.

### The Scope of the GIPS Standards for Firms

Only investment management firms and asset owners that manage assets on a discretionary basis—and compete for business—may claim compliance with the GIPS Standards for Firms. (An asset owner that manages investments, directly and/or through the use of external managers, on behalf of participants, beneficiaries, or the organization itself—but does not compete for business—would comply with the GIPS Standards for Asset Owners.) Consultants, software houses, or third-party performance measurement providers such as custodians may not claim to be GIPS-compliant.

GIPS compliance cannot be claimed for only some of an investment firm's products, nor for specific **composites, pooled funds,** or **portfolios**; compliance can be achieved only on a firm-wide basis. A firm's claim of compliance signifies, among other things, that the firm's performance measurement data inputs, processes, and return calculation methodology conform to the prescribed guidelines; that all of the firm's fee-paying discretionary **segregated accounts** have been assigned to at least one composite; and that all **limited distribution pooled funds** meeting a **composite definition** are properly included in the appropriate composites.

---

**UNDERSTANDING KEY TERMS**

Here we pause for a brief detour to define a few terms that have very specific meaning in the context of the GIPS standards:

*Composite.* A composite is an aggregation of one or more portfolios that are managed according to a similar investment mandate, objective, or strategy.

*Segregated Account.* A segregated account is a portfolio owned by a single client, sometimes referred to in practice as a separately managed account (SMA).

*Pooled Fund.* A pooled fund is also a "portfolio," but we distinguish between a segregated account portfolio and a pooled fund portfolio in this reading because the requirements of the GIPS standards for pooled funds may differ from those that apply to segregated accounts. Pooled funds are further distinguished between limited distribution and broad distribution pooled funds. A broad distribution pooled fund is a pooled fund that is regulated under a framework that would permit the general public to purchase or hold the pooled fund's shares and is not exclusively offered in one-on-one presentations. Mutual fund and UCITs are examples of broad distribution pooled funds. A limited distribution pooled fund is any pooled fund that is not a broad distribution pooled fund. Examples of limited distribution pooled funds include many private equity or hedge funds.

---

This reading is based on the 2020 edition of the GIPS standards, which are effective as of 1 January 2020. **GIPS Reports** that include performance for periods ending on or after 31 December 2020 must be prepared in accordance with the 2020 edition of the GIPS standards.

### Overview of the GIPS Standards

The Introduction to the GIPS standards articulates the mission and objectives of the GIPS standards and provides an overview of key concepts important to understanding the objectives and scope of the GIPS standards.

The mission of the GIPS standards is "to promote ethics and integrity and instill trust through the use of the GIPS standards by achieving universal demand for compliance by asset owners, adoption by asset managers, and support from regulators for the ultimate benefit of the global investment community."

The five objectives of the GIPS standards are to:

- promote investor interests and instill investor confidence;
- ensure accurate and consistent data;
- obtain worldwide acceptance of a single standard for calculating and presenting performance;
- promote fair, global competition among investment firms; and
- promote industry self-regulation on a global basis.

Key concepts of the GIPS Standards for Firms include the following:

- *Fair representation and full disclosure of investment performance is the key principle underlying the GIPS standards.* As ethical standards, the GIPS standards are voluntary.

- *Fair representation and full disclosure likely requires adherence to both the minimum requirements and the recommendations of the GIPS standards.* When appropriate, firms have the responsibility to include information in the GIPS Reports that is not specifically addressed by the GIPS standards.

- *Firms must comply with all applicable requirements of the GIPS standards, including any Guidance Statements, interpretations, and Questions & Answers (Q&As) published by CFA Institute and the GIPS standards governing bodies.* The GIPS standards consist of requirements which must be followed in order for a firm to claim compliance. The GIPS standards also include recommendations, which are optional but should be followed because they represent best practice in performance presentation.

- *The GIPS standards do not address every aspect of performance measurement and will continue to evolve over time to address additional areas of investment performance.* The GIPS standards will continue to evolve as the industry tackles additional areas of performance measurement and recognizes the implications of new investment strategies, instruments, and technologies.

- *Composites are required for all strategies managed on behalf of or marketed to segregated account clients to prevent firms from cherry-picking the performance presented to prospective clients.* To promote fair representations of performance, the GIPS standards require firms to include *all* actual fee-paying, discretionary segregated accounts in at least one composite. Composites are defined by investment mandate, objective, or strategy. Pooled funds must also be included in any composite if the pooled fund meets the composite definition.

- *The GIPS standards rely on the integrity of input data, including the valuations of portfolio holdings and the use of certain calculation methodologies.* Because the GIPS standards are global, **prospective clients** and **prospective investors** engaged in an evaluation of competing GIPS-compliant firms' historical performance know that rates of return have been calculated in accordance with a common set of valuation principles and methodological guidelines.

The GIPS standards require that firms must meet *all* the applicable requirements set forth in the GIPS standards. There can be no exceptions. As stated in the part of the Introduction headed "Claiming Compliance and Verification," firms must take all steps necessary to ensure that they have satisfied all of the applicable requirements before claiming compliance with the GIPS standards. Moreover, firms are strongly encouraged to perform periodic internal compliance checks to confirm the validity of compliance claims. Implementing adequate internal controls during all stages of the investment performance process will instill confidence in the performance presented and in the claim of compliance. The GIPS standards recommend that firms be verified.

When the GIPS standards conflict with laws and/or regulations regarding the calculation and presentation of performance, the GIPS standards obligate firms to comply with laws and regulations and to disclose the conflict in the GIPS Report. Firms are strongly encouraged to comply with the GIPS standards in addition to applicable regulatory requirements.

In the next sections, we discuss specific requirement of the GIPS standards. The GIPS Standards for Firms are divided into eight sections:

1. Fundamentals of Compliance
2. Input Data and Calculation Methodology
3. Composite and Pooled Fund Maintenance
4. Composite Time-Weighted Return Report
5. Composite Money-Weighted Return Report
6. Pooled Fund Time-Weighted Return Report
7. Pooled Fund Money-Weighted Return Report
8. GIPS Advertising Guidelines

Sections 4, 5, 6, and 7 detail the requirements and recommendations for the various report types specified by the GIPS standards: Composite Time-Weighted Return Reports, Composite Money-Weighted Return Reports, Pooled Fund Time-Weighted Return Reports, and Pooled Fund Money-Weighted Return Reports. Section 8 focuses on the GIPS Advertising Guidelines, outlining the conditions under which a firm that claims compliance with the GIPS standards can include such a claim in its advertising. The balance of this reading focuses primarily on the remaining sections of the GIPS standards: (1) Fundamentals of Compliance, (2) Input Data and Calculation Methodology, and (3) Composite and Pooled Fund Maintenance.

Exhibit 1 contains an excerpt from the GIPS standards introducing each of these topics.

## Exhibit 1: Content of the Global Investment Performance Standards

1. **Fundamentals of Compliance:** Several core principles create the foundation for the GIPS standards, including properly defining the firm, providing GIPS Reports to all prospective clients and prospective pooled fund investors, adhering to applicable laws and regulations, and ensuring that information presented is not false or misleading. Two important issues that a firm must consider when becoming compliant with the GIPS standards are the definition of the firm and the firm's definition of discretion. The definition of the firm is the foundation for firm-wide compliance and creates defined boundaries whereby total firm assets can be determined. The firm's definition of discretion establishes criteria to judge which portfolios must be included in a composite and is based on the firm's ability to implement its investment strategies.

2. **Input Data and Calculation Methodology:** Consistency of input data used to calculate performance is critical to effective compliance with the GIPS standards and establishes the foundation for full, fair, and comparable investment performance presentations. Achieving comparability among investment management firms' performance presentations requires uniformity in methods used to calculate returns. The GIPS standards mandate the use of certain calculation methodologies to facilitate comparability.

3. **Composite and Pooled Fund Maintenance:** A composite is an aggregation of one or more portfolios managed according to a similar investment mandate, objective, or strategy. The composite return is the asset-weighted average of the performance of all portfolios in the composite. Creating meaningful composites is essential to the fair presentation, consistency, and comparability of performance over time and among firms. A composite must include all portfolios that meet the composite definition.

In the next seventeen sections, we discuss select required provisions of Fundamentals of Compliance, Input Data and Calculation Methodology, and Composite and Pooled Fund Maintenance.

## 2    FUNDAMENTALS OF COMPLIANCE

☐ | explain the fundamentals of compliance with the GIPS standards, including the definition of the firm and the firm's definition of discretion

Section 1 of the GIPS Standards for Firms, "Fundamentals of Compliance," contains 39 requirements and seven recommendations. For our purposes, we focus on selected *required* fundamentals of compliance, emphasizing the definition of the firm.

*Candidates should read all of Section 1.A of the GIPS Standards for Firms for a complete understanding of the required fundamentals of compliance.*

Although the concept of discretion, specifically the firm's definition of discretion, is not technically a part of the Fundamentals of Compliance, the concept is integral to developing an understanding of the applications of the GIPS standards and thus is covered prior to delving more deeply into the standards themselves.

### Definition of the Firm

The **firm** must be defined as an investment firm, subsidiary, or division held out to the public as a **distinct business entity**. The Glossary defines a distinct business entity as a "unit, division, department, or office that is organizationally and functionally segregated from other units, divisions, departments, or offices and that retains discretion over the assets it manages and that should have autonomy over the investment decision-making process." Possible criteria for identifying a distinct business entity are the organization being a legal entity, having a distinct market or client type, or using a separate and distinct investment process.

The way in which the investment management organization is held out to the public is a key factor in defining the firm. For example, if a unit of a larger company specializes in providing investment management services to private clients, and it is marketed as a specialist in meeting the investment needs of high-net-worth individuals and family offices, then that organizational unit might qualify as a "firm" for the purpose of compliance with the GIPS standards. Certainly, however, the unit's entitlement to be considered a firm under the GIPS standards could be justified if it additionally were incorporated as a subsidiary and had its own dedicated financial analysts, portfolio managers, and traders located in a separate building or area of the company and reporting through a separate chain of command to the parent organization's senior management.

### IMPLEMENTATION

### Defining the Firm

For small investment management boutiques, defining the firm may be a relatively easy task, but it can prove challenging for large firms.

Consider the case of a super-regional bank whose wealth management department consists of two separate and distinct divisions: the private client division and the institutional client division. The private client division, called Eastern National Bank Wealth Management Services, offers investment management to private individuals and families. The institutional client division, called Eastern Institutional Asset Advisors, serves tax-exempt non-profit organizations including pension funds and charitable foundations; it does not solicit or handle non-institutional business. Each division has its own investment management team, traders, marketing department, administrative personnel, and accounting department. After a few years of operating in this manner, the institutional investment unit decides to achieve compliance with the GIPS standards, but the private client division makes a business decision not to implement the GIPS standards. The institutional client division may nonetheless be in position to become GIPS-compliant because it holds itself out to customers as a distinct business unit, with its own autonomous investment management, research, trading, and administrative team.

Based on the information provided, the institutional client division appears to satisfy the conditions for defining itself as a firm for the purpose of compliance with the GIPS standards. Sample language might be, "The firm is defined as Eastern Institutional Asset Advisors, the institutional asset management division of Eastern National Bank."

On the other hand, if both divisions were to use the same investment process, approved security list, style models, and so on, and they merely divided assets between personal and institutional portfolios, then neither division alone could compellingly claim compliance. If the senior investment personnel of the Private Client division had authority to dictate the Institutional Client division's investment strategy or tactical asset allocations, or to mandate the investment of institutional clients' funds in specific securities, then the Institutional Client division would likely not qualify as a distinct business unit having autonomy over the investment decision-making process and discretion over the assets it manages. If the two divisions were organizationally segregated but shared the same trading desk, the Institutional Client division would have to determine whether its decision-making autonomy is compromised by the trading arrangement. If the traders merely fill the portfolio manager's orders, then the Institutional Client division arguably remains autonomous, but if the traders actively participate in the identification of misvalued securities, a greater impediment to the autonomy argument would exist.

Defining the firm in such a situation calls for the scrupulous exercise of professional judgment, with due attention to the ethical objectives of the Global Investment Performance Standards.

In view of the complexity of modern organizational structures, it may require judgment to determine if a given unit properly meets the definition of a firm. The decision has immediate and lasting practical consequences, however. Because the GIPS standards apply firm-wide, the definition of the firm will determine the extent of the initial implementation and ongoing compliance activities. It also establishes the boundaries for determining total firm assets. The phrase **total firm assets** refers to the aggregate **fair value** of all assets (whether or not discretionary or fee-paying) for which a firm has investment management responsibility. Total firm assets include assets managed by sub-advisors that the firm has authority to select but do not include **advisory-only assets** or uncalled **committed capital**.

A firm that has been defined for the purposes of the GIPS standards may very well undergo subsequent changes in its corporate structure or organizational design. Changes in a firm's organization are not permitted to lead to alteration of historical performance, however. Indeed, we may put it down as a general rule that, apart from correcting errors, historical performance is not to be altered.

## Definition of Discretion

The GIPS Standards for Firms require that all discretionary, fee-paying segregated accounts must be included in at least one composite. Discretionary, fee-paying pooled funds must also be included in at least one composite if they meet a composite definition. A key term in this requirement is "discretionary," although the GIPS standards do not define the term itself. Generally speaking, a portfolio is discretionary if the manager is able to implement the intended investment strategy. For example, the manager of a discretionary domestic mid-cap value portfolio is free to purchase any stock issued in the investor's home country that meets the pertinent market capitalization and style criteria. The firm might define mid-cap stocks as those whose market capitalization falls within a certain range. Similarly, the firm might define value stocks in terms of their price-to-earnings multiple, price-to-book ratio, dividend yield, or other characteristics intended to distinguish them from growth stocks. In line with best practice, the firm and the client will agree in advance that the portfolio's investment objective is to outperform a specified benchmark that is an appropriate measure of success in the domestic mid-cap market. For instance, the firm might construct a custom benchmark that is acceptable to the client, or the firm and the client might agree to use a commercially available index that mirrors the domestic mid-cap market.

Although both discretionary and non-discretionary portfolios are included in total firm assets, only discretionary portfolios are included in composites. If the client imposes restrictions on the manager's freedom to make investment decisions to buy, hold, and sell securities so as to carry out the investment strategy and achieve the portfolio's financial objectives, then the manager must consider whether the portfolio is in fact discretionary. In general, restrictions that impede the investment process to such an extent that the strategy cannot be implemented as intended may be presumed to render the portfolio non-discretionary, and it should not be included in a composite.

## Other Fundamentals of Compliance

Other requirements under Section 1, Fundamentals of Compliance, can be broadly characterized as relating to:

- the minimum number of years required in order to initially claim compliance with the GIPS standards;
- documenting policies and procedures related to compliance;
- complying with laws and regulations;
- avoiding false or misleading performance and performance-related information;
- the requirements concerning the distribution of GIPS Reports and lists of firm composites and pooled funds;
- the use of total return benchmarks reflective of the investment strategy;
- the requirement to correct **material errors** in a GIPS Report and the redistribution of the report to the appropriate parties;
- the maintenance of data and information necessary to support the elements of the GIPS Reports; and

- conditions under which performance may be used or linked to that of another firm.

# TIME-WEIGHTED RETURN

**3**

☐ | discuss requirements of the GIPS standards with respect to return calculation methodologies, including the treatment of external cash flows, cash and cash equivalents, and expenses and fees

Section 2.A of the GIPS Standards for Firms addresses, among other aspects, the requirements for calculating portfolio and composite returns. The GIPS standards mandate the use of a **time-weighted return** (TWR). **Money-weighted returns** (MWRs) may be used for portfolios meeting certain conditions (described later). In the following paragraphs, we address TWR, MWR, and the treatment of cash balances and fees and expenses.

**Candidates should read Section 2.A, Provisions 2.A.1 through 2.A.39 of the GIPS Standards for Firms. Candidates are not responsible for the provisions in Section 2 related to Private Market Investments, Real Estate, Carve-Outs, Wrap Fees, and Side Pockets and Subscription Lines of Credit (Provisions 2.A.40 through 2.A.50).**

## Time-Weighted Return

TWR is a method of calculating period-by-period returns that reflects the change in value and negates the effects of **external cash flows**. Except for private market investment portfolios, portfolios using TWR must be valued monthly, and the TWR must be calculated at least monthly as of the calendar month end or last business day of the month. If returns are not calculated daily and the portfolio receives an intra-month **large cash flow**, the portfolio must be valued and a sub-period return must be calculated at the time of the large cash flow. Private market investment portfolios (e.g., real estate and infrastructure, private equity, and similar investments that are illiquid, not publicly traded, and not traded on an exchange) must be valued quarterly.

What constitutes a large cash flow is defined by the firm. It is usually an external cash flow of such size that it may distort the return if the portfolio is not valued and a sub-period return is not calculated at the time of the cash flow. A large cash flow may be defined either relative to an absolute monetary threshold or as a percentage of the portfolio or composite assets.

If the portfolio is a pooled fund (a fund whose ownership interests may be held by more than one investor), and the pooled fund is not included in one of the firm's composites, the fund must be valued and returns must be calculated at least annually. Similar to the composite requirements presented above, the pooled fund must be valued at the time of any subscriptions or redemptions and a sub-period return calculated as of that date. The sub-period return is then linked with other sub-period returns.

In the simplest case, when no external cash flows (i.e., client-initiated additions to or withdrawals from invested assets) occur during the period, calculating the TWR is straightforward:

$$r_t = \frac{V_1 - V_0}{V_0} \tag{1}$$

where $r_t$ is the TWR for period $t$; $V_1$ is the ending value of the portfolio, including cash and accrued income, at the end of the period; and $V_0$ is the portfolio's beginning value, including cash and accrued income, at the beginning of the specified period. Equation 1 assumes that there are no cash inflows or cash outflows and expresses return as the ratio of the change in value during the period to the value at the start of the period. Despite its simplicity, the TWR equation produces an accurate representation of investment results in a single period with no external cash flows. As we will see, this equation is also used to calculate sub-period results under the intra-period valuation method when external cash flows occur.

Most portfolios, of course, do have external cash flows. A segregated account for an institutional investor, for example, may routinely have contributions and withdrawals based on the institution's needs. The TWR methodology removes the effect of such contributions and withdrawals from the return calculation, allowing the performance evaluator to focus on the value added by investment decisions that are controlled by the investment management firm.

If the portfolio experiences a cash flow that is not a large cash flow, the GIPS Standards for Firms do not require that the portfolio be valued as of the date of the cash flow. Instead, firms must use a method that adjusts for daily weighted cash flows, which is an approximation of a true TWR.

The most accurate way to calculate a total return while eliminating the impact of external cash flows is to value the portfolio whenever an external cash flow occurs, compute a sub-period return, and geometrically link sub-period returns expressed in relative form according to Equation 2:

$$r_{twr} = (1 + r_{t,1}) \times (1 + r_{t,2}) \times ... \times (1 + r_{t,n}) - 1 \tag{2}$$

where $r_{twr}$ is the time-weighted total return for the entire period and $r_{t,1}$ through $r_{t,n}$ are the sub-period returns. The GIPS standards require that the periodic returns be geometrically linked.

For example, consider a portfolio with a beginning value of $100,000 as of 31 May, a value of $109,000 on 5 June (which includes a cash contribution of $10,000 received that day), and an ending value of $110,550 on 30 June. Consider that the first sub-period ends and the second sub-period begins on the cash flow date, such that the ending value for Sub-period 1 is $99,000 ($109,000 less the contribution of $10,000) and the beginning value for Sub-period 2, including the $10,000 contribution, is $109,000. The portfolio's true time-weighted return using the intra-period valuation method is 0.41%, computed as follows:

$$r_{t,1} = \frac{V_1 - V_0}{V_0} = \frac{(109,000 - 10,000) - 100,000}{100,000} = \frac{99,000 - 100,000}{100,000} = -0.01$$

$$r_{t,2} = \frac{V_2 - V_1}{V_1} = \frac{110,550 - 109,000}{109,000} = 0.0142$$

$$r_{twr} = (1 + r_{t,1}) \times (1 + r_{t,2}) - 1 = [1 + (-0.01)] \times (1 + 0.0142) - 1$$
$$= 1.0041 - 1 = 0.0041 = 0.41\%$$

Geometric linking is used because returns are compounded and so are not additive but multiplicative.

If the portfolio experiences cash flows that are not large cash flows, and the firm does not calculate daily performance, portfolio returns must be calculated using a method that adjusts for daily weighted cash flows. Examples of acceptable approaches are the Modified Dietz method and the Modified Internal Rate of Return (Modified IRR) method, both of which weight each cash flow by the proportion of the measurement period it is held in the portfolio.

Equation 3 shows the formula for estimating the time-weighted rate of return using the Modified Dietz method:

$$r_{ModDietz} = \frac{V_1 - V_0 - CF}{V_0 + \sum_{i=1}^{n}(CF_i \times w_i)} \tag{3}$$

where $\sum_{i=1}^{n}(CF_i \times w_i)$ is the sum of each cash flow multiplied by its weight and $CF = \Sigma CF_i$. The weight ($w_i$) is simply the proportion of the measurement period, in days, that each cash flow has been in the portfolio, as shown in Equation 4:

$$w_i = \frac{CD - D_i}{CD} \tag{4}$$

where $CD$ is the total number of calendar days in the period and $D_i$ is the number of calendar days from the beginning of the period to the time cash flow $CF_i$ occurs. (Note that this formula assumes that cash flows occur at the end of the day.[1]) In our example, a \$10,000 contribution occurs on 5 June, so $D_i = 5$, and there are 30 days in June, so $CD = 30$. The proportion of the measurement period for which the \$10,000 is in the portfolio is thus

$$w_i = \frac{CD - D_i}{CD} = \frac{30 - 5}{30} = \frac{25}{30} = 0.83$$

Applying the Modified Dietz formula to the same example gives a return of 0.51%:

$$r_{ModDietz} = \frac{V_1 - V_0 - CF}{V_0 + \sum_{i=1}^{n}(CF_i \times w_i)} = \frac{110,550 - 100,000 - 10,000}{100,000 + [10,000 \times (25/30)]} = 0.0051 = 0.51\%$$

Note that this formula as given assumes that the portfolio is not valued at the time of the external cash flow.

The Modified IRR method is another estimation approach. This method determines the internal rate of return (IRR) for the period, adjusted to take into account the timing of cash flows. The Modified IRR is the value of $r$ that satisfies Equation 5:

$$\text{Ending Value} = V_1 = \sum_{i=1}^{n}\left[CF_i \times (1 + r)^{w_i}\right] + V_0(1 + r) \tag{5}$$

where the exponent, $w_i$, is as previously defined the ratio of the amount of time $CF_i$ is in the portfolio to the total time in the measurement period. The equation is solved iteratively by a trial-and-error procedure, settling on the value of $r$ that makes the series of cash flows equal to the ending fair value. The Modified IRR method is computationally intensive, but programs are available for solving the equation efficiently. (Some Modified IRR programs use the Modified Dietz return as an initial estimate or seed value.) Applying the Modified IRR method to the simple example used earlier in this section gives a result of 0.51%, the same as the rate of return found with the Modified Dietz method.

## TRUE VS. ESTIMATED TIME-WEIGHTED RETURNS

In the foregoing section, different methodologies for calculating a rate of return from a single set of input data gave different answers. To recapitulate:

## Inputs:

Fair value on 31 May: \$100,000

Cash flow on 5 June: + \$10,000

---

[1] Cash flows can also be assumed to occur at the beginning of the day. In that case, the weight factor is adjusted to add another day to the period that the cash flow is in the portfolio: $w_i = (CD - D_i + 1)/CD$. It is incumbent upon the firm to establish and consistently apply a policy, for each composite or pooled fund, related to the weighting of cash flows.

Fair value on 5 June: $109,000 (after the cash flow)

Fair value on 30 June: $110,550

## Solutions:

True time-weighted return: 0.41%

Modified Dietz method: 0.51%

Modified IRR method: 0.51%

In this particular example, the external cash flow causes the day-weighted estimates (0.51%) to vary by 10 basis points from the true time-weighted return (0.41%).

To appreciate the potentially distorting effect of external cash flows on estimated time-weighted rates of return, consider Exhibit 2 through Exhibit 4. The exhibits depict a "market index" with a value of 100 as of 31 May, and the data following each exhibit represent portfolios with a value of $100,000 on 31 May and contributions of $10,000 received on 5 June (on the left-hand side) and 15 June (on the right-hand side). In flat and steadily rising or falling markets (illustrated in Exhibit 2 and Exhibit 3), the timing of the cash flows has a relatively modest effect on the estimates' accuracy. We can observe this phenomenon by comparing the true time-weighted returns with those calculated using the Modified Dietz method. When markets are volatile, however, as illustrated in Exhibit 4, large external cash flows may have a material effect on the estimated return's accuracy. The reader should work through these examples using the formulas for the true time-weighted return and the Modified Dietz method. The calculations for the first example, on the left-hand side of Exhibit 2, were shown earlier.

### Exhibit 2: Effect of Cash Flows in a Flat Market

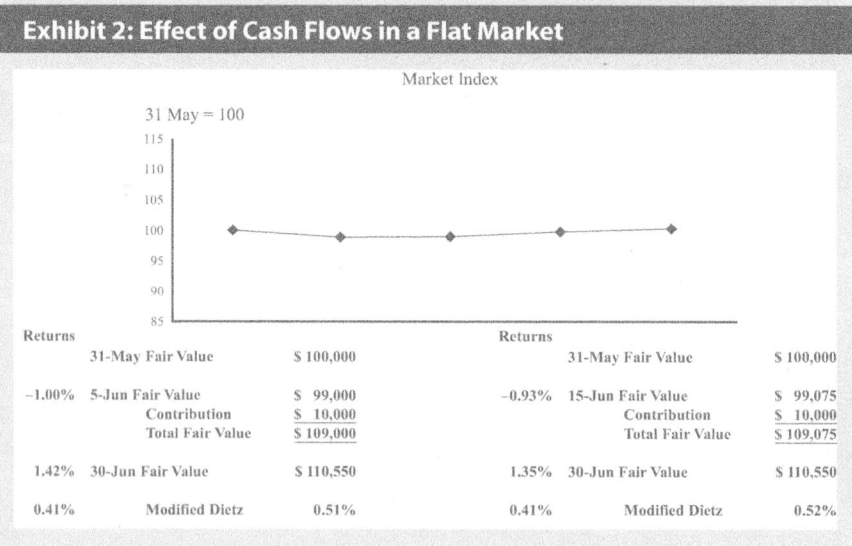

| Returns | | | | Returns | | |
|---|---|---|---|---|---|---|
| | 31-May Fair Value | $ 100,000 | | | 31-May Fair Value | $ 100,000 |
| –1.00% | 5-Jun Fair Value | $ 99,000 | | –0.93% | 15-Jun Fair Value | $ 99,075 |
| | Contribution | $ 10,000 | | | Contribution | $ 10,000 |
| | Total Fair Value | $ 109,000 | | | Total Fair Value | $ 109,075 |
| 1.42% | 30-Jun Fair Value | $ 110,550 | | 1.35% | 30-Jun Fair Value | $ 110,550 |
| 0.41% | Modified Dietz | 0.51% | | 0.41% | Modified Dietz | 0.52% |

Source: Paula Gehr

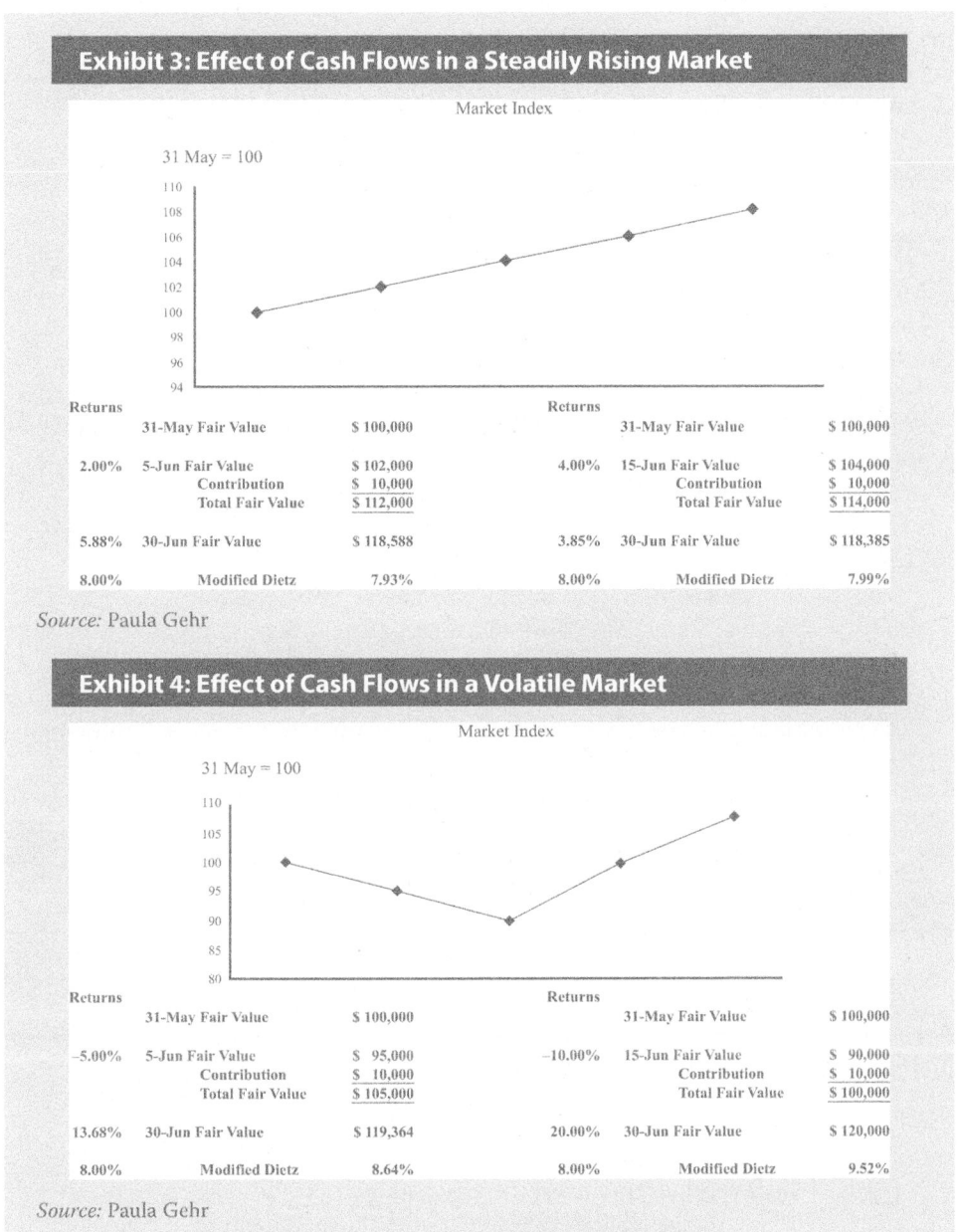

**Exhibit 3: Effect of Cash Flows in a Steadily Rising Market**

Market Index

31 May = 100

| Returns | | | Returns | | |
|---------|---|---|---------|---|---|
| | 31-May Fair Value | $ 100,000 | | 31-May Fair Value | $ 100,000 |
| 2.00% | 5-Jun Fair Value | $ 102,000 | 4.00% | 15-Jun Fair Value | $ 104,000 |
| | Contribution | $ 10,000 | | Contribution | $ 10,000 |
| | Total Fair Value | $ 112,000 | | Total Fair Value | $ 114,000 |
| 5.88% | 30-Jun Fair Value | $ 118,588 | 3.85% | 30-Jun Fair Value | $ 118,385 |
| 8.00% | Modified Dietz | 7.93% | 8.00% | Modified Dietz | 7.99% |

*Source:* Paula Gehr

**Exhibit 4: Effect of Cash Flows in a Volatile Market**

Market Index

31 May = 100

| Returns | | | Returns | | |
|---------|---|---|---------|---|---|
| | 31-May Fair Value | $ 100,000 | | 31-May Fair Value | $ 100,000 |
| −5.00% | 5-Jun Fair Value | $ 95,000 | −10.00% | 15-Jun Fair Value | $ 90,000 |
| | Contribution | $ 10,000 | | Contribution | $ 10,000 |
| | Total Fair Value | $ 105,000 | | Total Fair Value | $ 100,000 |
| 13.68% | 30-Jun Fair Value | $ 119,364 | 20.00% | 30-Jun Fair Value | $ 120,000 |
| 8.00% | Modified Dietz | 8.64% | 8.00% | Modified Dietz | 9.52% |

*Source:* Paula Gehr

The GIPS standards require firms to formulate and document composite-specific and pooled fund–specific policies for the treatment of external cash flows and to adhere to those policies consistently. Each policy should describe the firm's methodology for computing time-weighted returns and the firm's assumptions about the timing of capital inflows and outflows. If it is the firm's rule to value portfolios on the date of all external cash flows, as the GIPS standards recommend, then the firm should also state that policy.

As we have previously remarked, the GIPS standards do not specify a quantitative definition of large external cash flows. Taking into account the liquidity of the market segments or asset classes and the nature of the investment strategy, firms must make their own determinations for each composite. For example, a relatively high percentage of portfolio value might be easily deployed in a developed equity market, whereas a lower percentage of portfolio value might be deemed the appropriate criterion for a large external cash flow in a comparatively illiquid emerging debt market.

Whatever definition a firm adopts, it must document the policy and follow it without exception. If a portfolio receives a large external cash flow, as defined for the composite in which the portfolio is included, the firm is not at liberty to omit the valuation on the grounds that the market was not especially volatile during the measurement period. Inconsistent applications of firm policies constitute a breach of the GIPS standards.

---

**IMPLEMENTATION**

## Return Calculation Policies

Firms must calculate time-weighted rates of return that adjust for external cash flows. Both periodic and sub-period returns must be geometrically linked. External cash flows must be treated according to the firm's composite-specific policy. These portfolios must be valued on the date of all large cash flows, and firms must define what constitutes a large cash flow for each composite in order to determine when the portfolios in that composite must be valued. Here are examples of internal policy statements addressing these elements:

Portfolio return calculation methodology: "Eastern Institutional Asset Advisors calculates each portfolio's time-weighted rate of return on a monthly basis. For periods beginning on or after 1 January 2010, portfolios are valued monthly and when large cash flows occur. In the event of a large cash flow, a sub-period return will be calculated using the Modified Dietz method and sub-period returns will be geometrically linked to calculate the monthly return. Returns for longer measurement periods are computed by geometrically linking the monthly returns."

Large external cash flows: "Eastern Institutional Asset Advisors revalues portfolios that belong to the Large-Cap Domestic Equity composite when capital equal to 10% or more of fair value as of the end of the most recent measurement period is contributed or withdrawn."

---

# 4     MISCELLANEOUS RETURN CALCULATION TOPICS

☐     discuss requirements of the GIPS standards with respect to return calculation methodologies, including the treatment of external cash flows, cash and cash equivalents, and expenses and fees

☐     explain the recommended valuation hierarchy of the GIPS standards

A firm may choose to present MWRs instead of TWRs if the firm has control over the external cash flows *and*: (1) the portfolios are **closed-end**, **fixed life**, or **fixed commitment** or (2) **illiquid investments** are a significant part of the investment strategy. Annualized, since-inception MWRs must be calculated at least annually. For periods beginning with the effective date of the 2020 GIPS Standards, daily external cash flows must be used. (External cash flows for periods prior to this date must be reflected on at least a quarterly basis.) Portfolios for which a money-weighted return is calculated must be valued at least annually and as of the period end for which performance is calculated.

## Annualizing Returns

Returns for periods of less than one year must not be annualized. Extrapolating partial-year returns by annualizing them would amount to a prediction about investment results for the rest of the year.

## Treatment of Cash Equivalents

Returns from cash and cash equivalents held in portfolios must be included in all total return calculations. A primary purpose of performance measurement is to enable prospective clients and, by extension, their consultants to evaluate an investment management firm's results. Within the constraints established by a client's investment policy statement (IPS), active managers often have discretion to decide what portion of a portfolio's assets to hold in cash or cash equivalents. The portfolio return will be affected by how much cash the manager elects to hold, and thus return calculations must reflect the contribution of the cash and cash equivalents to investment results. Even if the management of cash balances is handled by another firm (as is often the case in manager-of-manager arrangements), cash and cash equivalents must be included in the total return calculation.

Consider the case of an institutional investor such as a defined benefit pension plan sponsor. The structure of the sponsor's investment program is generally based on an asset/liability study identifying the optimal mix of asset classes to meet the pension fund's financial objectives at an acceptable level of risk. The sponsor retains investment management firms to invest the fund's assets in specific markets in accordance with the study results. For example, within the domestic equity allocation, the sponsor might hire one firm to invest a certain portion of the fund's assets in small-cap growth stocks and another firm to invest a portion in large-cap value stocks. The sponsor expects the managers to remain fully invested in their mandated market sectors at all times. The sponsor's IPS may, however, allow the managers to hold some amount (e.g., up to 5% of portfolio assets) in cash and cash equivalents, if only to accommodate the frictional cash that arises in the process of buying and selling securities. (The client will usually define "cash equivalents," for example, as money market instruments and fixed-income securities with less than one year to maturity.) In this case, the manager has discretion over the size of the cash position, up to 5% of assets.

## Treatment of Expenses and Fees

The GIPS standards require that returns be calculated after the deduction of **transaction costs** incurred during the period. Transaction costs are the costs of buying or selling investments. These costs typically take the form of brokerage commissions, exchange fees and/or taxes, or spreads from either internal or external brokers. For private market investments, transaction costs include all legal, financial, advisory, and investment banking fees related to buying, selling, restructuring, and/or recapitalizing investments but do not include costs associated with investments that were considered but did not ultimately make it into the fund. **Custody fees** should not be considered transaction costs, even when they are charged on a per-transaction basis.

Commissions are explicit costs, generally a negotiated amount per share of common stock bought or sold, intended to compensate the broker, as the investor's agent, for arranging and settling trades. Bid–offer spreads are the difference between the price at which a dealer, acting for his firm's account, is willing to buy a security from a seller and the price at which he is willing to sell the security to a buyer. From the investor's perspective, the spread is the cost of immediacy or liquidity, and it compensates the dealer for both the cost of operations and the risk of adverse selection (the possibility that a well-informed trader has better information than the dealer has about the fundamental value of a security in the dealer's inventory). Transaction costs can be estimated for a specific portfolio only if actual transaction costs are not known.

Some portfolios may pay **bundled fees**, which can include any combination of **investment management fees**, transaction costs, custody fees, and/or **administrative fees**. **All-in fee** arrangements are common when a single company offers diverse services such as asset management, brokerage, and custody. If transaction costs cannot be identified (either actual transactions costs or estimated transactions costs based on a reasonable estimation method) and segregated from a bundle fee, composites for institutional investors must reduce the **gross-of-fees** return by the entire amount of the bundled fee or by that portion of the bundled fee that includes the transaction costs.

## Valuation Requirements

Meaningful performance measurement presupposes the validity of beginning and ending asset values. Section 2 of the GIPS Standards for Firms also addresses asset valuation. Firms are required to apply a fair value methodology when valuing assets. The GIPS standards define **fair value** as the amount at which an investment could be sold in an orderly, arm's-length transaction between willing parties. The valuation must be determined using the objective, observable, unadjusted quoted market price for an identical investment in an active market on the measurement date, if available. Fair value must include any accrued income on fixed-income securities and all other investments that earn interest income (the firm may choose to recognize income on cash and cash equivalents on a cash basis rather than an accrual basis).

If objective, observable, unadjusted quoted market prices for identical investments in active markets on the measurement date are not available, the GIPS standards recommend the following alternatives, in declining order of preference:

1. quoted prices for similar investments in active markets. If such inputs are not available or appropriate, then investments should be valued based on:

2. quoted prices for identical or similar investments in markets that are not active (markets in which there are few transactions for the investment, the prices are not current, or price quotations vary substantially over time and/ or between market makers). If such inputs are not available or appropriate, then investments should be valued based on:

3. market-based inputs, other than quoted prices, that are observable for the investment. If such inputs are not available or appropriate, then investments should be valued based on:

4. subjective, unobservable inputs.

### IMPLEMENTATION

## Valuation Policies and Procedures

Firms may enter transactions involving a wide range of financial instruments, including derivative securities, in many different markets. It is fitting, therefore, that the GIPS standards not only require firms to document their valuation policies, procedures, methodologies, and hierarchies but also recommend that the valuation hierarchies be composite-or pooled fund-specific. Normally, for investment strategies that employ plain-vanilla securities trading in robust markets, quoted prices are readily available. Other composites, however, may represent strategies that materially make use of securities that trade infrequently in relatively illiquid markets where values must be imputed or estimated. Real estate and private equity are obvious examples, but valuing investments in swaps, options, and other derivatives that are tied to underlying securities uniquely issued by specific companies may present difficulties, especially if the firm cannot refer to recent transactions in identical or similar assets. Implementing the GIPS standards offers firms an opportunity to re-examine their valuation policies, procedures, and methodologies and to define valuation hierarchies reflecting the characteristics of the securities held in each composite or pooled fund and the markets in which the strategy is executed. For assets valued using quantitative models, it is useful to list input factors such as discount rates and risk-adjusted cash flow projections and to review the basis for estimating them. Portfolio managers, security analysts, quantitative analysts, and traders should participate in these discussions. Once established, the valuation policies must be documented, followed consistently, and made available to prospective clients upon request.

# COMPOSITE TIME-WEIGHTED RETURN CALCULATIONS

**5**

☐ | explain requirements of the GIPS standards with respect to composite return calculations, including methods for asset-weighting portfolio returns

The notion of composites is central to the GIPS standards. The GIPS standards define a composite as an aggregation of one or more portfolios that are managed according to a similar investment mandate, objective, or strategy. Because composite returns convey the firm's investment results for a given investment mandate, objective, or strategy, proper composite construction is essential to achieving the ethical aims of the GIPS standards as well as the fair representation and full disclosure of the firm's performance. Provisions relating to the construction and maintenance of composites can be found in Section 3 of the GIPS standards.

*Candidates should read Section 3.A, Provisions 3.A.1 through 3.A.14 of the GIPS Standards for Firms for more complete understanding of the requirements for composite and pooled fund maintenance. Candidates are not responsible for the required provisions in Section 3 related to Wrap Fee and Carve-Outs (Provisions 3.A.14 through 3.A.19).*

To prevent firms from presenting only their best-performing portfolios to prospective clients, the GIPS standards require all actual, fee-paying, discretionary segregated accounts to be included in at least one composite. All actual, fee-paying, discretionary pooled funds must also be included in at least one composite if they meet a composite definition. Non-discretionary segregated accounts and pooled funds must not be included in composites. Non-fee-paying discretionary segregated accounts and pooled funds *may* be included in a composite, but additional disclosures may be required. (For example, in the interest of public service or community relations, a firm might waive the investment management fee on a charitable organization's portfolio, or a firm might use its own or its principals' capital to implement a new investment strategy.) If a strategy is offered as a pooled fund *and* a segregated account, the pooled fund must be included in a composite for that strategy. The firm does need not to create a composite for a strategy if it is offered only as a pooled fund.

## Composite Time-Weighted Return Calculations

Time-weighted composite returns must be calculated in one of three ways: asset-weighting the individual portfolio returns using beginning-of-period values; using a method that reflects both beginning-of-period values and external cash flows; or using the Aggregate Return method. Exhibit 5 displays the beginning asset values of four portfolios that, taken together, constitute a composite. The exhibit also shows the external cash flows experienced by each portfolio during the month of June. For completeness, the exhibit also shows each portfolio's ending fair value.

### Exhibit 5: A Composite Including Four Portfolios: Weighted External Cash Flows

|  | Cash Flow Weighting Factor | Portfolio ($ Thousands) | | | | |
|---|---|---|---|---|---|---|
|  |  | A | B | C | D | Total |
| Beginning assets (31 May) |  | 100.00 | 97.40 | 112.94 | 124.47 | 434.81 |
| *External cash flows* |  |  |  |  |  |  |
| 5 June | 0.83 | 10.00 | 15.00 |  |  | 25.00 |
| 8 June | 0.73 |  |  |  | −15.00 | −15.00 |
| 17 June | 0.43 |  | −5.00 |  |  | −5.00 |
| 24 June | 0.20 |  |  |  | −6.50 | −6.50 |
| 29 June | 0.03 |  | −2.50 |  | −4.00 | −6.50 |
| Ending assets (30 June) |  | 110.55 | 105.20 | 113.30 | 100.50 | 429.55 |
| Beginning assets + Weighted cash flows |  | 108.30 | 107.63 | 112.94 | 112.10 | 440.97 |
| Percentage of total beginning assets |  | 23.00% | 22.40% | 25.97% | 28.63% | 100.00% |
| Percentage of total beginning assets + Weighted cash flows |  | 24.56% | 24.41% | 25.61% | 25.42% | 100.00% |

*Note:* Weighted cash flows reflect two-decimal-place precision in the weighting factors.

Determining the relative weight of each portfolio in the composite at the beginning of the measurement period is straightforward. Portfolio A had a beginning fair value of $100,000, and all four portfolios combined had a beginning fair value of approximately $435,000, so the weight assigned to Portfolio A is 100/434.81 = 0.23 = 23%. As we will show in a moment, under a method reflecting only beginning-of-period values, we can calculate the composite return by multiplying the individual portfolio returns by the portfolio's beginning weight, then summing the products.

Determining a composite return when there are external cash flows is a little more complex. The cash flows must be weighted following the methodology introduced in our discussion of the Modified Dietz rate-of-return calculation. Each external cash flow is weighted in proportion to percentage of the time it is held in the portfolio during the measurement period as shown in Equation 4:

$$w_i = \frac{CD - D_i}{CD}$$

where $CD$ is the total number of calendar days in the period and $D_i$ is the number of calendar days since the beginning of the period until the time cash flow $CF_i$ occurs. Exhibit 5 showed the weighting factor computed to two decimal places with this formula for each of the days in the measurement period (the month of June) on which external cash flows occur that affect any of the portfolios in the composite. It also showed the weighted external cash flows under the two methods discussed. For the method incorporating weighted external cash flows, the sum of beginning assets and weighted external cash flows, $V_p$, is calculated as shown in Equation 6:

$$V_p = V_0 + \sum_{i=1}^{n}\left(CF_i \times w_i\right)$$

(6)

where $V_0$ is the portfolio's beginning value and $\sum_{i=1}^{n}(CF_i \times w_i)$ is the sum of each portfolio's weighted external cash inflows and outflows. Note that the right-hand side in Equation 6 is the denominator of the Modified Dietz formula (see Equation 4).

The composite return is the weighted-average return of the individual portfolios that belong to that composite. Under the "beginning assets" weighting method, the composite return calculation is shown in Equation 7:

$$r_C = \sum\left[r_{pi} \times \frac{V_{0,pi}}{\sum_{pi=1}^{n} V_{0,pi}}\right]$$

(7)

where $r_C$ is the composite return, $r_{pi}$ is the return of an individual portfolio $i$, $V_{0,pi}$ is the beginning value of portfolio $i$, and $\sum_{pi=1}^{n} V_{0,pi}$ is the total beginning fair value of all the individual portfolios in the composite. In other words, the composite return is the sum of the individual portfolio returns weighted in proportion to their respective percentages of aggregate beginning assets.

Under the alternate "beginning assets plus weighted cash flows" method, shown in Equation 8, the return calculation uses the individual portfolios' $V_p$, computed earlier, in place of $V_{0,p}$:

$$r_C = \sum\left(r_{pi} \times \frac{V_{pi}}{\sum V_{pi}}\right)$$

(8)

Exhibit 6 supplies each individual portfolio's return for the month of June and presents the composite returns resulting from these two weighting methods.

### Exhibit 6: Composite Returns

| | Percentage of Beginning Assets | Percentage of Beginning Assets + Weighted Cash Flows | Return for Month of June |
|---|---|---|---|
| Portfolio A | 23.00% | 24.56% | 0.51% |
| Portfolio B | 22.40% | 24.41% | 0.28% |
| Portfolio C | 25.97% | 25.61% | 0.32% |
| Portfolio D | 28.63% | 25.42% | 1.36% |
| | 100.00% | 100.00% | |
| Composite Return: | | | |
| Based on beginning assets | | | 0.65% |
| Based on beginning assets plus weighted cash flows | | | 0.62% |

Under the "beginning assets" weighting method, the composite return shown in Exhibit 6 is as follows:

$r_C = (0.0051 \times 0.23) + (0.0028 \times 0.224) + (0.0032 \times 0.2597) + (0.0136 \times 0.2863)$
$= 0.0065$

$$= 0.65\%$$

Similarly, the composite return under the "beginning assets plus weighted cash flows" method is as follows:

$$r_C = (0.0051 \times 0.2456) + (0.0028 \times 0.2441) + (0.0032 \times 0.2561)$$

$$+ (0.0136 \times 0.2542) = 0.0062 = 0.62\%$$

The Aggregate Return method combines all the composite assets and external cash flows to calculate returns as if the composite were one portfolio. Beginning assets and intra-period external cash flows can be summed and, treating the entire composite as though it were a single portfolio, the return can be computed directly with the Modified Dietz formula. This approach can be illustrated with data from Exhibit 5, using Equation 3:

$$r_{ModDietz} = \frac{V_1 - V_0 - CF}{V_0 + \sum_{i=1}^{n}(CF_i \times w_i)}$$

$$r_C = \frac{429.55 - 434.81 - 25 - (-15) - (-5) - (-6.5) - (-6.5)}{440.97}$$

$$= \frac{2.74}{440.97} = 0.0062 = 0.62\%$$

Composite time-weighted returns, except for private market investment composites, must be calculated at least monthly. The less frequently the asset-weighting exercise is conducted, the greater the likelihood that composite returns will inaccurately reflect the constituent portfolios' aggregate performance.

## 6     COMPOSITES: QUALIFYING PORTFOLIOS AND DEFINING INVESTMENT STRATEGIES

☐     explain the meaning of "discretionary" in the context of composite construction and, given a description of the relevant facts, determine whether a portfolio is likely to be considered discretionary

☐     explain the role of investment mandates, objectives, or strategies in the construction of composites

Investors commonly set forth investment restrictions in investment policy statements (IPSs). In addition to articulating the investor's overall financial objectives, an IPS normally expresses a number of constraints intended to limit the investment risks to which the assets are exposed. For example, the IPS may limit an individual equity portfolio's economic sector exposure to a certain percentage of portfolio assets or a certain relationship to the comparable benchmark weight: "No portfolio shall hold more than 15% of assets or 125% of the corresponding benchmark weight, whichever is greater, in any given sector, such as consumer discretionary stocks or information technology stocks." A fixed-income portfolio may be constrained to hold no securities rated below investment grade and to maintain the portfolio's weighted-average duration within a specified range, such as 75% to 125% of the benchmark duration. These restrictions are intended to preserve the portfolios from losses in value resulting from inadequate sector diversification, excessive credit quality risk, or unacceptable levels of interest rate risk.

Clearly, in addition to ensuring that the benchmark is appropriate, investors must be careful to formulate constraints that achieve their intended risk-control objectives without unduly impairing the portfolio managers' ability to act on their professional judgment regarding the relative attractiveness of sectors and securities. In other words, a well-written IPS meets the client's need for risk mitigation while respecting the portfolio manager's discretion. The manager is well advised to discuss with the client any restrictions that are incompatible with the intended investment strategy. Upon accepting the investment management assignment, however, the portfolio manager is ethically bound by the client's stated policies. Moreover, investment management agreements often incorporate the IPS, so the portfolio manager may also be legally required to comply with properly communicated client-specified constraints.

In some cases, the client's investment constraints may impinge on the portfolio manager's flexibility. Some clients may have environmental, social or governance (ESG) restrictions that prohibit investment in securities issued by companies operating in alcohol, tobacco, or gaming industries. Other clients might have restrictions that prohibit the sale of company stock. Additionally, legal restrictions may apply. For instance, a public fund might be statutorily precluded from investing in non-domestic securities. None of these constraints automatically renders a portfolio non-discretionary. Rather, in these and other cases, the portfolio manager must determine whether the client-imposed constraints are likely to materially affect her ability to execute the investment strategy. If the constraints are determined to not have a material effect, the manager could include the portfolio in a composite with portfolios that have no such restriction. If the constraint is material, the manager may include the portfolio in a composite with other, similarly constrained portfolios or classify it as non-discretionary and exclude the portfolio from all composites.

## IMPLEMENTATION

## Defining Discretion

The GIPS standards require that all actual fee-paying discretionary segregated accounts be included in at least one composite. (If a pooled fund meets the composite definition, it must be included in the composite.) Because discretion is a key variable that determines inclusion in or exclusion from a composite, a firm implementing the GIPS standards must have a clear, written definition of discretion. The firm must consistently apply its definition of discretion.

A client could insist that the manager retain specific holdings that might or might not otherwise be held in a portfolio. For example, the client could direct that legacy holdings with a low cost basis must not be sold because of the adverse tax consequences of realizing large gains. In such cases, retaining the asset in the portfolio may skew performance, and—whether the impact is favorable or unfavorable in any given measurement period—the outcome would not reflect the results of the manager's actual discretionary investment management. If holding the assets hinders the manager's ability to implement the intended strategy, either the entire portfolio should be considered non-discretionary and excluded from the firm's composites or the individual assets should be removed and the remaining assets for which the manager has full discretion should be included in the composite. Alternately, the firm might include a materiality threshold in its policy, enabling it to consider a portfolio discretionary if the non-discretionary assets consist of less than a certain percentage of portfolio assets.

Recognizing that degrees of discretion exist, the firm must consider the interactions among client-directed constraints, the portfolio's strategy or style, and the investment process, notably including the financial instruments used. For example, a client's investment policy might prohibit the use of derivative securities such as futures, swaps, and options. In this case, the firm must consider whether the restriction is pertinent. If a portfolio manager is managing a domestic mid-cap stock portfolio, the fact that the client prohibits the use of derivatives may be irrelevant if the manager's typical investment approach simply buys, holds, and sells common stocks. If the use of derivative securities is central to the firm's implementation of the investment mandate, however, then the client's policy may render the portfolio non-discretionary.

In some cases, the pattern of external cash flows might make a portfolio non-discretionary. For example, if a client frequently makes large withdrawals, perhaps on a regular schedule, a portfolio manager might have to maintain such a high level of liquidity that he cannot truly implement the investment strategy as he does for other portfolios with a similar stated investment mandate, objective, or strategy.

In the process of developing, testing, and refining new investment strategies, firms frequently construct model portfolios and use historical security prices to simulate hypothetical performance in past measurement periods. No model or hypothetical portfolios may be included in any composite. Firms may not link the **theoretical performance** of simulated or model portfolios with actual performance. (Model, hypothetical, backtested, or simulated returns are all considered theoretical performance. These returns can be shown as **supplemental information** but cannot be linked to actual composite or pooled fund returns.)

On the other hand, if the firm created a new strategy and managed portfolios in this strategy with its own assets—sometimes called seed money—it could include those portfolios from inception in appropriate composites (or, more likely, construct new composites reflecting the new strategies), subject to any presentation and reporting requirements related to the inclusion of non-fee-paying portfolios in composites.

To summarize the criteria for including portfolios in composites:

- All actual, fee-paying, discretionary segregated accounts must be included in at least one composite.

- Discretionary segregated accounts that are non–fee paying may be included in composites, but neither non-discretionary nor simulated or model portfolios may be included in any composite.

- Pooled funds must be included in any composite for which they meet the composite definition.

- A composite must include all portfolios that meet the composite definition.

## Composites—Defining Investment Strategies

Defining and constructing meaningful composites constitute a vital step toward achieving the ideal of fair representation and the goal of providing prospective clients with useful comparative information. Under the GIPS standards, composites must be defined according to investment mandate, objective, or strategy; composites must include all portfolios that meet the composite definition; and the composite definition, including detailed criteria that determine the assignment of portfolios to the composite, must be documented in the firm's policies and procedures. Well-defined composites will be objectively representative of the firm's products and consistent with the firm's marketing strategy.

One possible hierarchy that may be helpful for the firm considering how to define composites is outlined as follows.

Investment Mandate

    Asset Classes

        Style or Strategy

Benchmarks

Risk/Return Characteristics

A composite based on the investment mandate bears a summary product or strategy description, such as "Global Equities." This summary description may be an entirely acceptable composite definition as long as no significant strategic differences exist among the portfolios included in the composite. It is a guiding principle of composite definition that firms are not permitted to include portfolios with different investment mandates, objectives, or strategies in the same composite.

A composite based on the constituent portfolios' asset class, such as "equity" or "fixed income," may also be acceptable; however, asset classes are broadly inclusive, and because generic descriptions are not very informative, asset class composites should be offered only if they are legitimately and meaningfully representative of the firm's products.

To afford investors a better understanding of the nature of a composite, the firm may use an asset-class modifier indicating the composite's investment style or strategy. For example, equity portfolios may be restricted to a specific economic sector, such as telecommunication services. Stocks issued by corporations competing in the same economic sector are presumably affected more or less the same way by exogenous factors such as changes in raw material prices, consumer demand, or the general level of interest rates.

Portfolios might also be classified according to a defined style. An equity style matrix that classifies portfolios by capitalization (large cap, mid-cap, and small cap) and by style (value; core, also called neutral, market oriented, or blend; and growth) might be the starting point for defining a set of composites. Fixed-income portfolios may be classified by a combination of duration and/or market segment that generally aligns with the major fixed-income indexes.

A portfolio may be assigned to one of the style categories based on the money-weighted averages of pertinent characteristics of the portfolio's holdings. For example, a portfolio holding stocks with an average market capitalization of $5 billion along with a relatively high price-to-earnings multiple, a relatively high price-to-book ratio, and a relatively low dividend yield, would likely be identified as a mid-cap growth portfolio. Alternately, the portfolio's historical monthly or quarterly returns might be regressed against the returns of pertinent capital market indexes to determine which style-specific benchmarks best explain the portfolio's performance. Evaluating the comparative merits of these approaches falls outside the scope of this reading. Suffice it to say that, given the widespread acceptance of these categories, a firm may meaningfully and usefully define composites with reference to the capitalization range and the style in which the constituent portfolios are managed.

## IMPLEMENTATION

## Defining Composites

One of the greatest challenges in implementing the GIPS standards is devising the set of composites that will most meaningfully represent the firm's products. A firm must create composites for the firm's strategies that are managed for or offered as a segregated account. Composites must be defined according to investment mandate, objective, or strategy. What appears to be a straightforward exercise—defining composites and assigning portfolios to them—may prove rather difficult in practice.

A useful guideline is to build a set of composites that will accurately represent the firm's distinct investment strategies. With too few composites, a firm risks overlooking significant differences and grouping diverse portfolios together into a single, overly broad composite subject to a wide dispersion of portfolio returns. With too many composites, in addition to incurring unnecessary costs, the firm runs the risk of creating narrowly defined groupings that are too much alike in investment strategy, contain too few portfolios or assets to be useful, or compromise client confidentiality.

Assuming that the definitions of the "firm" and "discretion" have been agreed upon and that a master list of portfolios has been compiled, here is a common-sense strategy a firm might follow to reach agreement on composite definitions.

1. Review the firm's organizational structure and investment process to see if distinctive strategies can be readily identified. For instance, an equity advisor might have units specializing in one or more active management strategies as well as index fund construction and quantitatively driven enhanced indexing.

2. Review the firm's existing marketing materials to determine which strategies are offered as a segregated account. If possible, review marketing materials from competitors and recently received requests for proposals (RFPs) to determine how the industry defines products similar to those the firm offers.

3. Construct a provisional framework using descriptive captions to identify possible composites.

4. Taking into consideration the clients' investment policies, test how well the firm's fee-paying, discretionary portfolios would fit the provisional framework. The inevitable identification of exceptions—that is, the discovery that some segregated accounts do not really fit any composite defined in the provisional framework—will lead to the redefinition of proposed composites or the creation of new composites. Several iterations may be needed.

5. Review the proposed set of composites to ensure that, in the aggregate, the composites are likely to satisfy the requirements of the GIPS standards.

6. Document the composite definitions in detail and circulate the definitions for final review by all affected parties within the firm.

Of course, the most effective process for defining composites may differ from one firm to another in view of variables such as organizational structure, culture, and investment strategies, among other factors. Nonetheless, composite definitions have lasting consequences, and it is highly desirable to have a plan for reaching consensus.

Firms may also define composites based on the portfolios' benchmarks, as long as the benchmarks reflect the investment strategy and the firm has no other composites with the same characteristics. This approach is particularly appropriate if the portfolios are limited to holding stocks that are held in the index.

Finally, portfolios sharing distinctive risk/return profiles may reasonably be grouped together. For example, enhanced index funds with benchmark-specific targeted excess returns and tracking error tolerances might fall into natural groups.

Fixed-income composites can likewise be meaningfully and usefully defined in many dimensions. For example, composites might conform to asset classes or market segments such as government debt, mortgage-backed securities, convertible bonds, or high-yield bonds; investment strategies such as fundamental credit analysis, sector rotation, or interest rate anticipation; or investment styles such as indexing or core-plus. However a firm chooses to define the composites representing its investment products, those composites must consist of portfolios managed in accordance with similar investment strategies or objectives.

## COMPOSITES: INCLUDING AND EXCLUDING PORTFOLIOS

**7**

☐ | explain requirements of the GIPS standards with respect to composite construction, including switching portfolios among composites, the timing of the inclusion of new portfolios in composites, and the timing of the exclusion of terminated portfolios from composites

The GIPS standards governing composite construction require that composites include new portfolios on a timely and consistent basis after the portfolio comes under management. Firms are required to establish, document, and consistently apply a policy of including new portfolios in the appropriate composites on a timely basis. For many strategies, new portfolios should be included as of the beginning of the next full performance measurement period after the firm receives the funds. If composite returns are calculated monthly and a portfolio is funded on 20 May, the composite should include the new portfolio as of the beginning of June. It may take time to invest the assets of a new portfolio in accordance with the desired investment strategy, however, particularly when the portfolio is funded in kind (that is, with securities other than cash and cash equivalents) and the assets have to be redeployed, or when the securities to be purchased are relatively illiquid (e.g., in emerging markets). Accordingly, the GIPS standards give firms some discretion to determine when to add the new portfolio to a composite. In such cases, the firm must establish a policy on a composite-by-composite basis and apply it consistently to all new portfolios.

In addition to winning new business, firms routinely lose relationships. Under the GIPS standards, a firm must include a terminated portfolio in the historical performance of the appropriate composite through the last full measurement period in which the firm had the discretion to manage the portfolio to the strategy. In many cases, the firm loses its discretion over the portfolio upon being notified of a pending termination. For instance, the client may instruct the firm to stop buying securities immediately and to commence the liquidation of holdings in preparation for an outbound cash transfer on a specified date. Alternately, the client may halt trading and transfer control of the portfolio to a transition management organization to facilitate moving assets to a new firm. When the firm being terminated loses its discretion over the portfolio, it should include the portfolio in the composite through the last full measurement period prior to notification of termination. To use the same example, if a firm that calculates performance monthly is informed on 20 May that its management contract is being terminated effective 31 May and is instructed to stop trading forthwith, then the firm should include the portfolio in its composite only through 30 April. In any event, it is incumbent upon the GIPS-compliant firm to have defined and documented its policies governing the removal of terminated portfolios from composites and, of course, to apply those policies consistently.

**IMPLEMENTATION**

## Adding, Removing, and Switching Portfolios

GIPS-compliant firms must have written policies setting forth when portfolios may be added to or removed from composites. These policies should be composite-specific. For a firm that reports composite performance monthly, a policy statement could read as follows:

> "All new portfolios funded with cash or securities on or before the 15th day of the month shall be added to the appropriate composite at the beginning of the following month. All new portfolios funded with cash or securities after the 15th day of the month shall be added to the appropriate composite at the beginning of the second month after funding. All terminating portfolios will be removed from the composite at the end of the last full month for which the firm has full discretion. The historical performance of terminated portfolios shall remain in the appropriate composite."

Policies like the foregoing sample allow firms a reasonable amount of time to implement the strategy without delaying inclusion of the portfolio in the appropriate composite. Each firm must develop a policy that conforms to its own investment process while meeting the GIPS standards requirement to include portfolios in composites on a timely basis. Here is a sample statement for a policy:

> "Portfolios shall not be moved from one composite to another unless the composite is redefined or documented changes in the client's guidelines require restructuring the portfolio in such a way that another composite becomes more appropriate. The portfolio shall be removed from the original composite at the end of the last calendar month before the event causing the removal occurred and shall be added to the appropriate new composite at the beginning of the calendar month following the date on which the portfolio is substantially invested. The historical performance of the portfolio shall remain in the original composite."

The firm's policy for adding portfolios to or removing portfolios from a composite must also include language outlining conditions under which a portfolio may be switched from one composite to another. The GIPS standards stipulate that portfolios cannot be switched from one composite to another unless documented changes in the portfolio's investment mandate, objective, or strategy or the redefinition of the composite make it appropriate. The historical performance of the portfolio must remain with the original composite. This is an important requirement; if the GIPS standards permitted firms to transfer portfolios from one composite to another at will, an unethical firm might identify and exploit opportunities to improve the reported performance of selected composites by re-populating them with the portfolios whose investment results were most advantageous during the measurement period.

The GIPS standards describe two conditions under which portfolios can be reassigned. First, a portfolio can be switched from one composite to another if the client revises the mandate, objective, or strategy governing the investment of portfolio assets and the guideline changes are documented. For instance, a client might decide to modify the portfolio mandate from mid-cap value to large-cap value, or from domestic equity to global equity, with a corresponding change in the benchmark, while retaining the same investment advisor to restructure and manage the "same" portfolio in accordance with the new strategy. Or perhaps a client might decide to allow the use of derivative securities, previously prohibited, triggering a change in the investment strategy and making it suitable to assign the portfolio to a composite made up of portfolios that use derivatives.

Second, a portfolio can be reassigned to another composite if the original composite is redefined in such a way that the portfolio no longer fits it. Generally, if a strategy changes over time, it is most appropriate to create a new composite; accordingly, the redefinition of an existing composite should be a highly unusual event.

In the event of **significant cash flows**, a portfolio may be temporarily removed from the composite.

A significant cash flow is a client-directed cash flow sufficiently large that it may temporarily prevent the firm from implementing the strategy. Significant cash flows are more likely to be an issue for strategies such as fixed income and emerging markets, wherein the liquidity of the underlying securities inhibits the ability to quickly invest the incoming cash or to conduct an orderly sale of portfolio securities to meet a cash outflow. Firms must define "significant" on an *ex ante*, composite-specific basis and must consistently follow the composite-specific significant cash flow policy.

Alternatively, firms may use **temporary new accounts** to remove the effect of a significant cash flow. Firms adopting this approach place client-initiated incoming cash and securities into a temporary account that is not included in any composite until the external cash flows have been invested in accordance with the portfolio's investment mandate, objective, or strategy, at which time they would be transferred into the main portfolio and treated as an external cash flow. Relatedly, when the client initiates a large capital withdrawal, the firm transfers cash and securities in the desired amount to a temporary account until it liquidates the securities and the funds are distributed. The transfer is treated as an external cash outflow when calculating the portfolio's time-weighted total return.

The provisions governing composite construction additionally address the issue of minimum asset levels. A firm might decide that a particular composite will not include any portfolios whose value is below a specified level, on the grounds, for instance, that the investment strategy can be fully implemented only for portfolios above a certain size. Portfolios below the minimum asset level would be considered non-discretionary with respect to that composite. If a firm establishes a minimum asset level for a composite, it must document policies addressing how portfolios will be treated if they fall below the minimum. As an example, a firm may elect to remove portfolios the month after they fall below the minimum. As another example, the firm may determine that the minimum asset level required to *add* a portfolio to a composite is $1 million but that a portfolio will not be *removed* from a composite unless its assets fall below $900,000. The GIPS standards further state that any changes to a composite-specific minimum asset level must not be applied retroactively.

If a portfolio is removed from a composite because it fell below the minimum, its prior performance must remain in the composite. The firm must determine if the portfolio that has been removed meets any other composite definition and include it in the appropriate composite in a timely and consistent manner.

# PRESENTATION AND REPORTING REQUIREMENTS FOR COMPOSITES

**8**

☐ explain requirements of the GIPS standards with respect to presentation and reporting

☐ explain the conditions under which the performance of a past firm or affiliation may be linked to or used to represent the historical performance of a new or acquiring firm

Firms claiming compliance with the GIPS standards must make every reasonable effort to provide a GIPS Report to all prospective clients and limited distribution pooled fund investors. The GIPS Report must be one that represents the strategy being marketed to the prospect.

There are two types of GIPS Reports: a **GIPS Composite Report** and a **GIPS Pooled Fund Report**. A GIPS Composite Report includes all of the information required by the GIPS standards for a specific composite. A GIPS Pooled Fund Report includes all of the information required by the GIPS standards for a specific pooled fund. Sections 4 and 5 of the 2020 GIPS Standards for Firms address the requirements and recommendations for GIPS Composite Time-Weighted and Money-Weighted Return Reports, respectively. In this section, we will focus on certain required elements of the time-weighted return reports.

*Candidates should read Provisions 4.A.1 through 4.A.12 and 4.A.18 of the GIPS Standards for Firms for a more complete understanding of the requirements relating to Composite Time-Weighted Return Reports. Candidates are not responsible for Provisions 4.A.13 through 4.A.17 relating to carve-outs and overlay strategy and wrap fee composites.*

## Minimum Years of Performance

For each GIPS Composite Report that includes time-weighted returns, the GIPS standards require that firms show at least 5 years of annual performance (unless the composite has been in existence for less than 5 years) and that the GIPS-compliant performance record must then be extended each year until at least 10 years of performance have been presented. If the composite has been in existence for less than 5 years, the firm may present returns since inception and build over time to the 10 years of required returns.

## Required Elements of a GIPS Composite Report

The core elements of a GIPS Composite Report that presents a time-weighted return include the following:

- composite and benchmark annual returns for all years;
- the number of portfolios (if six or more) in the composite at each period end;
- the amount of assets in the composite;
- the amount of total firm assets at the end of each period;
- a measure of **internal dispersion** of individual portfolio returns for each annual period if the composite contains six or more portfolios for the full year; and
- if monthly composite returns are available, a three-year annualized *ex post* standard deviation of the composite and benchmark returns as of each annual period end.

### Dispersion Measures

The GIPS standards require that for each annual period a measure of internal dispersion of the returns earned by individual portfolios in the composite be presented. This important requirement is intended to allow users to see how consistently the firm implemented its strategy across individual portfolios. A wide range of results should prompt the recipient of the performance presentation to inquire about possible causes of the variability of returns to portfolios that are purportedly managed in accordance with the same strategy. It may suggest, among many other possibilities, that the composite is defined too broadly to provide meaningful information.

The dispersion of annual returns for individual portfolios within a composite can be measured in various ways. The GIPS Glossary entry for internal dispersion mentions several acceptable methods. Let us refer to the data in Exhibit 7, showing the beginning values (in euros) and the annual rates of return earned by the 14 portfolios that were in a German equity composite for the full year 20XX. (Note that only those portfolios in the composite for the entire year are included in the calculation of this dispersion measure.) The portfolios presented in Exhibit 7 are arrayed in descending order of returns.

### Exhibit 7: Data for Calculation of Dispersion

| Portfolio | Beginning Value | 20XX Return |
|:---:|:---:|:---:|
| A | €118,493 | 2.66% |
| B | €79,854 | 2.64% |
| C | €121,562 | 2.53% |
| D | €86,973 | 2.49% |
| E | €105,491 | 2.47% |
| F | €112,075 | 2.42% |
| G | €98,667 | 2.38% |
| H | €92,518 | 2.33% |
| I | €107,768 | 2.28% |
| J | €96,572 | 2.21% |
| K | €75,400 | 2.17% |
| L | €77,384 | 2.07% |
| M | €31,264 | 1.96% |
| N | €84,535 | 1.93% |

The Glossary in the GIPS Standards for Firms defines **internal dispersion** as "a measure of the spread of the annual returns of individual portfolios within a composite" and indicates that acceptable measures include, but are not limited to, high/low, range, and the equal-weighted or asset-weighted standard deviation of portfolio returns. Using the data in Exhibit 7, we will consider each of these measures.

The simplest method of expressing internal dispersion for an annual period is to disclose the highest and lowest returns earned by portfolios that were in the composite for the full year. In the case of the German equity composite, the highest return was 2.66% and the lowest was 1.93%. As an alternative, the high/low range—the arithmetic difference between the highest and the lowest return—might also be presented. In this case it was 0.73%, or 73 bps. In either form, the high/low disclosure is easy to understand. It has a potential disadvantage, however. In any annual period, an outlier—that is, one portfolio with an abnormally high or low return—may be present, resulting in a measure of dispersion that is not entirely representative of the distribution of returns. Although they are more difficult to calculate and to interpret, other dispersion measures may convey better information.

The standard deviation of returns for portfolios included in the composite is another acceptable measure of internal dispersion. As applied to composites, standard deviation measures the cross-sectional dispersion of returns for portfolios included in the composite for the full year. The standard deviation for a composite in which the constituent portfolios are equally weighted is calculated using Equation 9:

$$S_c = \sqrt{\frac{\sum_{i=1}^{n} (r_i - \bar{r}_c)^2}{n}} \tag{9}$$

where $r_i$ is the return of each individual portfolio, $\bar{r}_c$ is the equal-weighted mean or arithmetic mean return to the portfolios in the composite, and $n$ is the number of portfolios in the composite. Applying Equation 9 to the portfolio data given in Exhibit 7, assuming equal weighting, the mean return is 2.32% and the standard deviation is 22 bps (0.22%). If the individual portfolio returns are normally distributed around the mean return, then approximately two-thirds of the portfolios will have returns falling between the mean plus the standard deviation (2.32% + 0.22% = 2.54%) and the mean minus the standard deviation (2.32% − 0.22% = 2.10%).

Some firms prefer to present the asset-weighted standard deviation rather than the equal-weighted standard deviation. The asset-weighted standard deviation of individual portfolio returns within a composite can be calculated using Equation 10:

$$S_{C_{aw}} = \sqrt{\sum_{i=1}^{n} \left[ \left( r_i - \bar{r}_{proxy} \right)^2 \times w_i \right]} \tag{10}$$

where $\bar{r}_{proxy}$ is the asset-weighted mean return of portfolios 1 through $n$ (see Equation 9); $w_i$ is the weight of portfolio $i$, calculated as the ratio of the beginning value of portfolio $i$ to the total beginning value of the assets of portfolios 1 through $n$, that is, $w_i = \frac{V_{0,i}}{V_{0,\,Total}}$; and the sum of the weights $w_1$ through $w_n$ is 1.

$$\bar{r}_{proxy} = \sum_{i=1}^{n} \left( w_i \times r_i \right) \tag{11}$$

Applying Equation 11 and 12 to the data given in Exhibit 7, we find that the asset-weighted standard deviation is 21 bps (0.21%).

Note that the GIPS standards do not limit firms to using one of the measures of internal dispersion described here. A firm may prefer another way of expressing composite dispersion. The method chosen should, however, fairly represent the range of returns for each annual period.

The 2020 GIPS Standards for Firms also require that firms present information about the historical variability of composite and benchmark returns. Specifically, the GIPS standards state that, where monthly composite returns are available, firms must present, as of each annual period end, the three-year annualized *ex post* standard deviation of the monthly returns of both the composite and the benchmark. The rationale is to give prospective clients an indication of the risk of an investment strategy as executed by the firms under consideration. Because all GIPS Composite Reports include the same risk measure, and that measure is based on historical experience rather than subjective inputs, the GIPS standards allow for some degree of comparability among firms that claim compliance.

## Portability

The "portability" of past performance is a complex and sometimes contentious subject. Performance from a past firm or affiliation may be linked to the performance of the new or acquiring firm if the new or acquiring firm meets certain requirements. The requirements, which apply on a composite-specific basis, are that (1) substantially all the investment decision makers are employed by the new or acquiring firm, (2) the decision-making process remains substantially intact and independent within the new or acquiring firm, (3) the new or acquiring firm has records that document and support the reported performance, and (4) there must be no break in the track record between the past firm or affiliation and the new or acquiring firm. If there is a break in the track record between the past firm and the new or acquiring firm, and if the first three portability tests are met, then the performance from the past firm or affiliation may be used to represent the historical performance of the new or acquiring firm—but the two performance records may not be linked. If a GIPS-compliant firm acquires another firm or affiliation, the firm is given a one-year "grace period" to bring any non-compliant assets into compliance for future reporting periods.

## Sample Reports

Appendices A and B of the 2020 GIPS Standards for Firms contain several sample GIPS Composite and Pooled Fund Reports. We have included Sample 1 in Exhibit 8.

### Exhibit 8: Composite with Time-Weighted Returns

#### Spinning Top Investments Large-Cap Growth Composite, 1 February 2011–31 December 2020

| Year | Composite Gross Return TWR (%) | Composite Net Return TWR (%) | Benchmark Return (%) | 3-Year Std Deviation Composite Gross (%) | 3-Year Std Deviation Benchmark (%) | Number of Portfolios | Internal Dispersion (%) | Composite Assets ($ M) | Firm Assets[b] ($ M) |
|---|---|---|---|---|---|---|---|---|---|
| 2011[a] | 2.18 | 1.25 | 1.17 | | | 31 | n/a | 165 | n/a |
| 2012 | 18.66 | 17.49 | 15.48 | | | 34 | 2 | 235 | n/a |
| 2013 | 41.16 | 39.90 | 33.36 | | | 39 | 5.7 | 344 | n/a |
| 2014 | 14.50 | 13.37 | 13.03 | 11.30 | 9.59 | 45 | 2.8 | 445 | 1,032 |
| 2015 | 6.52 | 5.47 | 5.67 | 12.51 | 10.68 | 48 | 3.1 | 520 | 1,056 |
| 2016 | 8.22 | 7.15 | 7.09 | 12.95 | 11.15 | 49 | 2.8 | 505 | 1,185 |
| 2017 | 33.78 | 32.48 | 30.18 | 12.29 | 10.53 | 44 | 2.9 | 475 | 1,269 |
| 2018 | -0.84 | -1.83 | -0.65 | 13.26 | 11.91 | 47 | 3.1 | 493 | 1,091 |
| 2019 | 33.08 | 31.78 | 29.76 | 12.81 | 11.71 | 51 | 3.5 | 549 | 1,252 |
| 2020 | 7.51 | 6.44 | 6.30 | 13.74 | 12.37 | 54 | 2.5 | 575 | 1,414 |

[a]*Returns are for the period 1 February 2011 to 31 December 2011.*
[b]*Spinning Top investments acquired the composite through an acquisition of ABC Capital in May 2014. Firm assets prior to 2014 are not presented because the composite was not part of the firm.*

*Disclosures*

1. Spinning Top Investments claims compliance with the Global Investment Performance Standards (GIPS®) and has prepared and presented this report in compliance with the GIPS standards. Spinning Top Investments has been independently verified for the periods 1 January 2011 to 31 December 2020. The verification report is available upon request. A firm that claims compliance with the GIPS standards must establish policies and procedures for complying with all the applicable requirements of the GIPS standards. Verification provides assurance on whether the firm's policies and procedures related to composite and pooled fund maintenance, as well as the calculation,

presentation, and distribution of performance, have been designed in compliance with the GIPS standards and have been implemented on a firm-wide basis. Verification does not provide assurance on the accuracy of any specific performance report.

2. Spinning Top Investments is an equity investment manager that invests solely in US-based securities. Spinning Top Investments is defined as an independent investment management firm that is not affiliated with any parent organization. Spinning Top Investments acquired ABC Capital in May 2014.

3. The Large Cap Growth Composite includes all institutional portfolios that invest in large-cap US stocks that are considered to have growth in earnings prospects that are superior to that of the average company within the XYZ Large Cap Growth Index. Key material risks include the risks that stock prices will decline and that the composite will underperform its benchmark. The account minimum for the composite is $5 million. Prior to July 2016, the account minimum was $2 million. Prior to March 2020, the name of the composite was the Growth Composite.

4. Performance prior to May 2014 occurred while the investment management team was affiliated with another firm. The investment management team has managed the composite since its inception, and the investment process has not changed. The historical performance has been linked to performance earned at Spinning Top Investments.

5. The benchmark is the XYZ Large Cap Growth Index, a market-capitalization-weighted equity index of all US stocks with a market cap greater than $10 billion and a growth tilt.

6. Returns presented are time-weighted returns. Valuations are computed and performance is reported in US dollars.

7. Gross-of-fees returns are presented before management and custodial fees but after all trading expenses. Composite and benchmark returns are presented gross of non-reclaimable withholding taxes. Net-of-fees returns are calculated by deducting a model management fee of 0.083%, 1/12th of the highest management fee of 1.00%, from the monthly gross composite return. The management fee schedule for separate accounts is as follows: 1.00% on the first $25 million; 0.60% thereafter. The management fee schedule and total expense ratio for the Large Cap Collective Fund, which is included in the composite, are 0.65% on all assets and 0.93%, respectively.

8. Policies for valuing investments, calculating performance, and preparing GIPS reports are available upon request.

9. A list of composite descriptions and a list of broad distribution pooled funds are available upon request.

10. The composite was created in November 2011, and the inception date is 1 February 2011.

11. As of 1 January 2014, internal dispersion is calculated using the equal-weighted standard deviation of annual gross returns of those portfolios that were included in the composite for the entire year. Prior to 2014, internal dispersion was calculated using asset-weighted standard deviation.

12. The three-year annualized standard deviation measures the variability of the composite gross returns and the benchmark returns over the preceding 36-month period.

13. Effective 1 November 2011, portfolios are removed from the composite if they have a significant cash flow. A significant cash flow is defined as a contribution or withdrawal greater than 25% of the beginning market value of a portfolio. The portfolio is removed from the composite for the month in which the significant cash flow occurred.

14. GIPS® is a registered trademark of CFA Institute. CFA Institute does not endorse or promote this organization, nor does it warrant the accuracy or quality of the content contained herein.

# VERIFICATION

9

☐ | discuss the purpose, scope, and process of verification

Verification may be informally and unofficially characterized as a process in which an independent expert assesses a firm's policies and procedures for constructing composites and calculating and presenting performance in light of the requirements of the GIPS standards. Verification is intended to provide the firm and the users of its GIPS Reports greater confidence in its claim of compliance with the GIPS standards. Verification does not provide assurance as to the accuracy of any particular composite or pooled fund presentation. In addition to making the claim of compliance on a firm-wide basis more credible, however, the verification process may benefit the firm in other ways: increased knowledge in the performance measurement team, consistently higher quality of performance presentations, improved internal processes and procedures, and potential marketing advantages. Above all, verification supports the guiding principles of fair representation and full disclosure of investment performance.

The GIPS standards recommend that firms undergo verification.

## IMPLEMENTATION

### Selecting a Verification Firm

Verification is a major undertaking, and it is crucial for the investment management firm to choose an independent verifier whose resources match the firm's needs. At the outset of the selection process, the investment management firm approaching verification should consider the scope of its operations and the nature of its products. The requirements of a large investment management organization with a presence in markets around the world will differ from those of a firm operating in only a single country. Similarly, a hedge fund manager, a manager who engages in real estate or private equity investing, a quantitatively oriented manager whose investment strategies rely heavily on the use of derivative securities, or a manager who manages tax-aware portfolios for individuals may have more specialized requirements than a manager who manages funds for tax-exempt institutions such as pension plans and charitable foundations. These factors should be communicated to potential verifiers and reflected in the selection criteria.

Some organizations have standard RFP templates that can be adapted for specific purposes. The RFP should include a description of the issuing organization and a statement on the scope of the project. Firms investigating verifiers' qualifications might consider conducting an internet search and initially asking RFP respondents for the following information:

- a description of the verification firm, including its history, ownership, and organizational structure; a description of the performance-related services it offers; and a representative list of verification assignments completed indicating the nature of the investment management firm verified (e.g., "institutional client division of a regional bank");

- an explanation of the firm's approach to project management, sampling, and testing;

- the roles and biographies, including professional designations, of the verifiers who will be assigned to this project;

- client references, including contact details, and information about the number of clients added and lost over a specific period (for instance, the last three years);

- the verification firm's fees; and

- a preliminary project plan setting forth the major tasks and estimated timeframes for completion of the verification.

## Scope of Verification

Verification, which must be performed by a qualified and independent third party, provides assurance on whether the firm's policies and procedures related to composite and pooled fund maintenance, as well as the calculation, presentation, and distribution of performance have been designed in compliance with the GIPS standards and have been implemented on a firm-wide basis. A verifier must conduct the verification in accordance with the GIPS Standards for Verifiers.

A single verification report is issued only with respect to the whole firm; verification cannot be carried out on a single composite or pooled fund. If a firm does not meet *all* the requirements of the GIPS standards, it may not state or in any other way represent that it is in compliance with the GIPS standards—a firm cannot claim that a single composite is "in compliance," or that all the equity strategies are "in compliance."

A firm that is verified may choose to have a detailed **performance examination** conducted on one or more specific composites or pooled funds, and it may state that a composite has been examined *if* a performance examination report has been issued for the specific composite.

## Verification Process

The GIPS Standards for Verifiers outlines various procedures that verifiers must follow in the course of conducting a verification. We will focus here on the requirements for planning, sample selection and testing, as these elements will help the reader understand the scope and process of verification.

Verifiers must learn about the firm, including its corporate structure and how it operates, and they must understand the firm's policies and procedures for complying with all applicable requirements and adopted recommendations of the GIPS standards. Verifiers must not only obtain a copy of the firm's GIPS-related policies and procedures but also ensure that all applicable policies and procedures are properly included and adequately documented. Finally, verifiers must understand the policies, procedures, and methodologies the firm uses to value portfolios and compute investment performance.

Although verification is conducted on a firm-wide basis, verifiers may use a sampling methodology to conduct the required testing. When selecting sample portfolios, verifiers must take into consideration the number of composites and pooled funds at the firm and the number of portfolios in each composite. In addition, verifiers must also take into account the total assets under management, the internal control structure at the firm, the number of years being verified, the systems used in the construction and maintenance of composites, the method of calculating performance, and whether the firm uses external performance measurement services. The selection of sample accounts for testing is a critical step in the verification process. If the verifier encounters errors or discovers that the firm's record-keeping is deficient, a larger sample or additional verification procedures may be warranted.

---

**IMPLEMENTATION**

## Preparing for Verification

The investment management firm undertaking verification should gather the following information. The verifiers may use this information to prepare a fee estimate and a project plan, and they will need it in the course of the review.

- information about the firm, including its corporate structure and the types of investment product it manages;
- sample GIPS Reports and marketing materials;
- *all* of the firm's policies and procedures used to establish and maintain compliance with the GIPS standards, such as the firm's definition of discretion, the sources, methods, and review procedures for asset valuations, the time-weighted rate-of-return calculation methodology, the treatment of external cash flows, the computation of composite returns, the correction of errors, etc.;
- the complete list of composite and limited distribution pooled fund descriptions and a list of all broad distribution pooled funds (descriptions are not required for broad distribution pooled funds);
- composite definitions, including benchmarks and the criteria for including portfolios;
- a list of all portfolios under management, with each portfolio's value;
- a list of all the portfolios that have been in each composite during the verification period, the dates they were in the composites, and documentation supporting any changes to the portfolios in the composites; and
- a list of all portfolios excluded from all composites.

The verifiers will require the investment management agreements and investment policy statements for selected portfolios and historical portfolio- and composite-level performance data for sampling and testing. Although the items listed here represent a good starting point for initiating a verification, other information requirements will likely surface during the course of the verification.

---

Verifiers must perform sufficient testing procedures to determine that the firm satisfies certain fundamental requirements with respect to recordkeeping, policies and procedures (including error correction policies), the definition of the firm, the completeness of the list of composite and limited distribution pooled fund descriptions, and the calculation of total firm assets. Verifiers must conduct a series of tests to determine that portfolios are properly assigned to composites and that portfolios not included in composites have been properly excluded. They must evaluate outlier returns within a sample of the firm's composites for possible indications of errors in return calculation and/or mis-assignment of a portfolio to the composite.

Verifiers must review selected portfolios to determine that the treatment of certain input data is consistent with the firm's policies and the requirements of the GIPS standards. The GIPS standards specifically identify the classification of portfolio flows (for example, receipts, disbursements, dividends, interest, fees, and taxes) as one such item. Other items to evaluate include the treatment of: dividend and interest income; taxes, tax reclaims, and tax accruals; fees and expenses; and the accounting treatment and valuation methodologies for investments.

The verifier must determine that portfolio holdings, income, and cash flows used in calculating returns are supported by documentation from independent third parties, such as custodial or brokerage statements, as applicable.

We have already stressed that verification does not provide assurance that specific composite or pooled fund returns are correctly calculated and presented. Nonetheless, testing the firm's performance-related calculations is an important element of the verification process. Verifiers must determine that the firm has calculated and presented performance in accordance with the requirements of the GIPS standards as well as with the firm's policies and procedures. In so doing, they must recalculate rates of return for selected portfolios and composites to confirm that a return formula that meets the requirements of the GIPS standards is used and that fees and expenses have been treated in conformity with both the GIPS standards and the firm's policies and procedures.

Testing the construction and maintenance of composites is central to the verification process. Verifiers must obtain a list of all portfolios in the composite, including closed portfolios; select a sampling of new, existing, and closed portfolios for review; and perform sufficient procedures to determine that the selected portfolios are appropriately classified as discretionary or non-discretionary. In making this determination, verifiers will refer to the firm's policies and procedures related to investment discretion and the selected portfolios' investment management agreements and/or investment guidelines.

Verifiers must determine that portfolios sharing the same investment mandate, objective, or strategy are included in the same composite and that the timing of portfolios' inclusion in and exclusion from composites is in accordance with the firm's policies and procedures. Finally, verifiers must determine that portfolios' movements from one composite to another are appropriate and consistent with the redefinition of the composite or documented changes to the investment mandate, objective, or strategy.

Finally, verifiers must test a sample of GIPS Reports to ensure that the calculations are accurate and that the report includes all the required information and disclosures. Moreover, the information and disclosures must be consistent with the firm's documented policies and procedures and the firm's records. The verifier must also evaluate a sample of the firm's marketing materials to ensure that when an advertisement references the GIPS standards, the reference to the GIPS standards is proper, calculations in the advertisement are correct, and the advertisement includes all the required information and disclosures.

We have remarked that verification alone, without a specifically focused performance examination, does not ensure that any particular presentation of composite or pooled fund performance meets the requirements of the GIPS standards or represents investment results fairly, completely, and accurately. A verification report issued by a verifier who meets or exceeds the required verification procedures, as summarized here, lends additional credibility to the firm's claim of compliance with the GIPS standards.

# SUMMARY

The Global Investment Performance Standards for Firms meet the need for globally accepted standards for investment management firms in calculating and presenting their results to clients and prospective clients. The GIPS standards will continue to evolve to address additional aspects of performance presentation. Firms that claim compliance must meet all applicable requirements, including not only the provisions of the GIPS standards but also any Guidance Statements, interpretations, and Questions & Answers published by CFA Institute and the GIPS standards governing bodies. Practitioners should register for the GIPS Newsletter to stay informed about existing and new requirements and recommended best practices. CFA Institute and other organizations offer publications and conduct conferences and workshops designed to help practitioners implement and maintain compliance with the GIPS standards.

This reading has made the following points:

- Only investment management firms and asset owners that manage assets on a discretionary basis—and compete for business—may claim compliance with the GIPS Standards for Firms.

- The objectives of the GIPS standards are as follows: (1) Promote investor interests and instill investor confidence; (2) ensure accurate and consistent data; (3) obtain worldwide acceptance of a single standard for calculating and presenting performance; (4) promote fair, global competition among investment firms; and (5) promote industry self-regulation on a global basis.

- When the GIPS standards conflict with law and/or regulations regarding the calculation and presentation of performance, firms must comply with the law or regulations and disclose the conflict in the GIPS Report.

- Required fundamentals of compliance with the GIPS standards include properly defining the firm, providing GIPS Reports to all prospective clients/investors, adhering to applicable laws and regulations, and ensuring that information presented is not false or misleading.

- A "firm" is an investment firm, subsidiary, or division held out to the public as a distinct business entity.

- A composite is an aggregation of one or more portfolios managed according to a similar investment mandate, objective, or strategy. The composite return is the weighted average of the return of all portfolios in the composite.

- All discretionary, fee-paying, segregated accounts must be included in at least one composite. All discretionary, fee-paying pooled funds must be included in any composite for which they meet the composite definition. A portfolio is discretionary if the firm is able to implement the intended investment strategy.

- Firms must formulate, document, and adhere to composite- and pooled fund–specific policies for the treatment of external cash flows and to adhere to those policies consistently.

- The GIPS standards mandate the use of certain calculation methodologies to facilitate comparability of results among firms. Time-weighted returns are required for all portfolios except portfolios meeting certain criteria.

- Money-weighted returns may be presented instead of time-weighted returns if the firm has control over the external cash flows into the portfolios in the composite or the pooled fund and at least one of the following conditions is met: the portfolios in the composite are (or the pooled fund is): 1) closed-end; 2) fixed life; 3) fixed commitment; or 4) have illiquid investments as a significant part of the investment strategy.

- Returns for periods of less than one year must not be annualized.

- Returns from cash and cash equivalents must be included in all total return calculations.

- Returns must be calculated after the deduction of transaction costs.

- Assets must be valued using a fair value methodology. If objective, observable, unadjusted quoted market prices for identical investments in active markets on the measurement date are available, they must be used. If they are not available, firms may use, in this order: (1) quoted prices for similar investments in markets that are active; (2) quoted prices for identical or similar investments in markets that are not active; (3) market-based inputs, other than quoted prices, that are observable for the investment; or (4) subjective, unobservable inputs.

- A firm must have a clear, written definition of discretion that is consistently applied.

- Firms may not link the theoretical performance of simulated or model portfolios with actual performance.

- GIPS Composite Reports that present TWRs must include the following key items:

    - at least five years of annual performance (unless the composite has been in existence for a shorter period), building to a minimum of 10 years of returns;

    - composite and benchmark annual returns for all years;

    - the number of portfolios (if six or more) in the composite at each period end;

    - the amount of assets in the composite;

    - the amount of total firm assets at the end of each period;

    - a measure of internal dispersion of individual portfolio returns for each annual period and, where monthly returns are available; and

    - the three-year annualized *ex post* standard deviation of the composite and of the benchmark as of each annual period end.

- Performance from a past firm or affiliation may be linked to the performance of the new or acquiring firm if (1) substantially all the investment decision makers are employed by the new or acquiring firm, (2) the decision-making process remains substantially intact and independent within the new or acquiring firm, (3) the new or acquiring firm has records that document and support the reported performance, and (4) there is no break in the track record between the past firm or affiliation and the new or acquiring firm.

- Verification provides assurance on whether the firm's policies and procedures related to composite and pooled fund maintenance, as well as the calculation, presentation, and distribution of performance have been designed in compliance with the GIPS standards and have been implemented on a firm-wide basis.

- Verifiers must determine if the firm satisfies the GIPS standards requirements with respect to recordkeeping, policies and procedures, the definition of the firm, the completeness of the list of composites and limited distribution pooled fund descriptions, and the calculation of total firm assets.

- A verification report may be issued only with respect to the whole firm.

## PRACTICE PROBLEMS

1. Company C manages money for both retail and institutional clients. There are two autonomous groups within the company: "Company C Institutional Investment Management," which manages institutional assets, and "Company C Retail Investors," which manages retail assets. How should Company C define itself as a firm to comply with the GIPS standards?

2. Firm A is a multinational investment firm with offices around the world, including Japan, Australia, the United Kingdom, and the United States. Although all of its offices are part of the global parent firm, each office is registered with the appropriate national regulatory authority and each is held out to clients and prospective clients as a distinct business entity. Firm A (United States) claims compliance with the GIPS standards. Can the US entity claim compliance with the GIPS standards?

3. Which statement *most accurately* expresses a requirement of the GIPS standards?

   A. Non-fee-paying portfolios must not be included in composites.

   B. All actual fee-paying discretionary segregated accounts must be included in at least one composite.

   C. All actual fee-paying discretionary segregated accounts must be included in only one composite.

4. Use the information in the following table to answer this question (amounts in €):

| Date | Fair Value | External Cash Flow | Fair Value Post Cash Flow |
|---|---|---|---|
| 31 December 2018 | 200,000 | | |
| 31 January 2019 | 208,000 | | |
| 16 February 2019 | 217,000 | +40,000 | 257,000 |
| 28 February 2019 | 263,000 | | |
| 22 March 2019 | 270,000 | −30,000 | 240,000 |
| 31 March 2019 | 245,000 | | |

   Calculate the rate of return for this portfolio for January, February, March, and the first quarter of 2019 using revaluing for large cash flows methodology (assume "large" is defined as greater than 5%).

5. The GIPS standards do **not** require firms to value portfolios in accordance with:

   A. the definition of fair value.

   B. composite-specific valuation policies.

   C. generally accepted principles of financial accounting.

6. Convenable Capital Management manages an equity portfolio for the Flender Company. Cash held in the portfolio is invested by Flender's existing custodial bank. Must Convenable include cash and cash equivalents in the portfolio return calculations?

   A. Yes

**B.** No, the cash is not invested by Convenable

**C.** No, Convenable does not have discretion over the selection of the custodian

7. Under the GIPS standards, the *most* accurate statement is that transaction costs do **not** include:

   **A.** spreads from internal brokers.

   **B.** brokerage commissions.

   **C.** custody fees charged per transaction.

# The following information relates to questions 8-10

A European equity composite contains three portfolios whose cash flow weighting factors are as follows.

|  | Cash Flow Weighting Factor | Portfolio (€ millions) | | |
|---|---|---|---|---|
|  |  | A | B | C |
| Fair value as of 31 July |  | 74.9 | 127.6 | 110.4 |
| External cash flows: |  |  |  |  |
| 8 August | 0.742 |  | −15 |  |
| 12 August | 0.613 | 7.5 |  |  |
| 19 August | 0.387 |  | −5 | 15 |
| Fair value as of 31 August |  | 85.3 | 109.8 | 128.4 |

8. Calculate the returns of Portfolio A, Portfolio B, and Portfolio C for the month of August using the Modified Dietz formula.

9. Calculate the August composite return by asset-weighting the individual portfolio returns using beginning-of-period values.

10. Calculate the August composite return by asset-weighting the individual portfolio returns using a method that reflects both beginning-of-period values and external cash flows.

11. Can a firm include a single portfolio in more than one of the firm's composites?

12. In March 2016, Tan/Lim Asset Management, a GIPS-compliant firm, introduced a new technical analysis model that management believed would be a powerful tool in tactical asset allocation. After extensive backtesting, Tan/Lim began to use the model to manage actual "live" portfolios in June 2016, and managers constructed a composite composed of actual, fee-paying, discretionary portfolios managed in accordance with the model. In 2019, after three very successful years of managing client funds in this way, management decided that because the actual performance of live portfolios validated the model's performance, the firm should present the simulated performance of the model through the backtesting period to prospective clients. Tan/Lim proceeded to link the backtested returns to the actual performance of the composite and to present 3-, 5- and 10-year

performance as a continuous record in GIPS Reports. Does this practice comply with the GIPS standards?

13. Midwest National Bank manages a domestic equity portfolio for the Springfield Municipal Employees' Retirement Fund (SMERF), a mature defined benefit pension plan. The SMERF portfolio is included in Midwest's Institutional Equity composite. The composite description states, "Portfolios included in the Institutional Equity composite are actively managed for long-term capital appreciation." SMERF's investment policy statement includes the following provisions:

All security transactions must be approved in advance by the SMERF Investment Committee. SMERF anticipates making regular net withdrawals in substantial amounts from the portfolio to meet pension liabilities. SMERF staff will prepare a schedule of withdrawals at the beginning of each fiscal year. The portfolio manager must manage liquidity so as to disburse funds in accordance with the withdrawal schedule.

In view of these restrictions, discuss whether Midwest National Bank can justify including the SMERF portfolio in the composite.

14. A fixed-income portfolio is *most likely* to be considered non-discretionary if the client's investment policy states that:

   A. securities held at a gain must not be sold.

   B. the average credit quality must be investment grade.

   C. securities held in the portfolio must be issued in developed markets.

15. A charitable foundation transfers securities in kind to Taurus Asset Management Ltd. to fund a new bank loan portfolio. Taurus estimates that after liquidating the transferred securities, it will take five months to invest the foundation's assets in bank loans. Which statement *best* describes a requirement of the GIPS standards? Taurus must include the foundation's portfolio in the appropriate composite:

   A. on a timely and consistent basis.

   B. when the assets are substantially invested.

   C. as of the beginning of the next full measurement period.

16. Ord Capital Management, an investment management firm that claims compliance with the GIPS standards, manages a global equity portfolio for a pension plan sponsored by Chimie Bio-Industrielle. On 15 April, the plan sponsor notifies Ord that the firm will be terminated as of the end of the month and instructs the manager to stop trading immediately. Assuming Ord calculates composites using monthly portfolio returns, Ord must include the Chimie portfolio in the historical returns of the composite to which it belongs up to:

   A. 31 March.

   B. 15 April.

   C. 30 April.

17. Southwest Capital Advisors LLC manages a fixed-income composite in accordance with an enhanced indexing strategy that makes strategic use of high-yield and emerging market bonds in addition to investment grade bonds issued in developed markets. The Merrimack Company, a family office, has a portfolio that is

included in the firm's fixed-income enhanced indexing composite. Merrimack informs Southwest in writing that, because of changes in its investment policy, the portfolio can no longer hold high-yield or emerging market bonds. In accordance with the GIPS standards, Southwest decides to switch the Merrimack portfolio to another composite. The historical performance of the portfolio must be:

A. reflected in both composites.

B. switched to the new composite.

C. retained in the enhanced indexing composite.

## The following information relates to questions 18-20

Bamako Investment Management defines its core-plus fixed-income composite as containing all discretionary portfolios of more than $10 million that are invested in accordance with a strategy that includes domestic high-yield debt in addition to US government and agency securities and investment-grade bonds issued by US corporations. The composite benchmark is 75% Bloomberg Barclays Capital US Government/Credit Index and 25% Bloomberg Barclays Capital US High Yield Index, rebalanced monthly.

18. The core-plus fixed-income composite includes a portfolio managed on behalf of the Bida Academy endowment fund. The trustees of Bida inform Bamako in writing that because of a change in investment policy, the endowment fund is no longer permitted to hold below-investment-grade securities. Bamako determines that henceforth, the Bida portfolio should be included in the core fixed-income composite rather than the core-plus fixed-income composite. The historical record of the portfolio must be:

A. included in both composites.

B. kept in the core-plus fixed-income composite.

C. excluded from the core-plus fixed-income composite.

19. After an extended period of rising interest rates, the value of Bouwa Special Equipment Company's core-plus fixed-income portfolio falls below the composite minimum of $10 million. The Bouwa portfolio remains below the composite-specific minimum asset level for nine months, at which point the client makes an additional contribution that brings it back above $10 million in assets. During the nine months the portfolio is below the composite minimum asset level, Bamako must:

A. temporarily switch the Bouwa portfolio to the firm's miscellaneous composite.

B. include the Bouwa portfolio in the core-plus fixed-income composite in all measurement periods.

C. exclude the Bouwa portfolio from the core-plus fixed-income composite for the period it was below the minimum asset level.

20. Mahe Manufacturing Company, a core-plus fixed-income client, informs Bamako in writing that, in the future, all security transactions must be approved in

advance by Mahe's controller. The *most likely* consequence is that Bamako must prospectively exclude the Mahe portfolio from:

**A.** all composites.

**B.** total firm assets.

**C.** the core-plus fixed-income composite only.

---

21. What is the minimum number of portfolios that a composite must contain to comply with the GIPS standards? Must a firm disclose the number of portfolios in a composite?

22. Macondo Institutional Asset Management has been managing equity, fixed-income, and balanced accounts since 2007. The firm became GIPS-compliant on 1 January 2012 and has prepared GIPS Composite Reports using time-weighted returns for the 2007–2019 period. Fixed-income performance was poor prior to 2015, when a new team of managers was brought on board. When Jorge Garcia joins Macondo as marketing director in June 2020, he suggests showing performance starting with calendar 2015, the first year that performance started to improve. He proposes to show composites with returns for the five calendar years 2015 through 2019. Does this course of action comply with the GIPS standards?

23. Dylan O'Connor is a portfolio manager at JEMStone Asset Management. He makes all the investment decisions for the portfolios in the firm's Emerging Market composite, supported by JEMStone's research department and trading desk. Acella Investment Advisors is seeking to establish an emerging market investment strategy and hires O'Connor to join Acella. Can Acella link O'Connor's historical performance while at JEMStone to the performance of its new strategy and comply with the GIPS standards?

24. It is *most* accurate to say that verification:

**A.** makes the claim of compliance more credible.

**B.** certifies that the firm has adequate internal controls.

**C.** ensures the accuracy of specific composite presentations.

25. Renner, Williams & Woods decides to have its equity and balanced composites verified. Because the firm has only a handful of fixed-income accounts and does not present fixed-income management results in marketing materials shown to prospects, management decides that it would be a waste of time and money to hire a verification firm to verify such a small composite. Is it possible for Renner, Williams & Woods to obtain a firm-wide verification that covers only the equity and balanced composites?

## SOLUTIONS

1.  The GIPS standards encourage firms to adopt the broadest, most meaningful definition of a firm. Company C should consider defining itself to include the assets managed by both the institutional entity and the retail entity for the purposes of claiming compliance with the GIPS standards. Company C could define the two autonomous entities as separate firms, however, if each subsidiary is held out to clients and prospective clients as a distinct business unit.

2.  Yes, the US entity is a distinct business entity and thus meets the definition of a firm under the GIPS standards.

3.  B is correct. The GIPS standards require that all actual, fee-paying, discretionary segregated accounts must be included in at least one composite. Although non-fee-paying discretionary accounts may be included in a composite (with appropriate disclosure), non-discretionary segregated accounts must not be included in a firm's composites.

4.  January:

    $R_{Jan} = (208{,}000 - 200{,}000)/200{,}000 = \textbf{4.00\%}$

    February:

    $R_{Feb1-15} = (217{,}000 - 208{,}000)/208{,}000 = 4.33\%$

    $R_{Feb16-28} = (263{,}000 - 257{,}000)/257{,}000 = 2.33\%$

    $R_{Feb1-28} = [(1 + 0.0433) \times (1 + 0.0233)] - 1 = \textbf{6.76\%}$

    March:

    $R_{Mar1-21} = (270{,}000 - 263{,}000)/263{,}000 = 2.66\%$

    $R_{Mar22-31} = (245{,}000 - 240{,}000)/240{,}000 = 2.08\%$

    $R_{Mar1-31} = [(1 + 0.0266) \times (1 + 0.0208)] - 1 = \textbf{4.80\%}$

    Quarter 1:

    $R_{QT1} = [(1 + 0.0400) \times (1 + 0.0676) \times (1 + 0.0480)] - 1 = \textbf{16.36\%}$

5.  C is correct. The GIPS standards state that portfolios must be valued in accordance with the definition of fair value, and that firms must value portfolios in accordance with the composite-specific valuation policy. The GIPS standards do not require firms to adhere to the principles of financial accounting.

6.  A is correct. The GIPS standards state, "Returns from cash and cash equivalents must be included in all return calculations, even if the firm does not control the specific cash investment(s)."

7.  C is correct. The GIPS Glossary defines transaction costs as "the costs of buying or selling investments" and states, "These costs typically take the form of brokerage commissions, exchange fees and/or taxes, and/or bid–offer spreads from either internal or external brokers. Custodial fees charged per transaction should be considered custody fees and not transaction costs."

8.  Portfolio returns:

$$r_A = \frac{85.3 - 74.9 - 7.5}{74.9 + (7.5 \times 0.613)} = \frac{2.9}{79.5} = 0.0365 = 3.65\%$$

$$r_B = \frac{109.8 - 127.6 - (-15) - (-5)}{127.6 + (-15 \times 0.742) + (-5 \times 0.387)} = \frac{2.2}{114.535} = 0.0192 = 1.92\%$$

$$r_C = \frac{128.4 - 110.4 - 15}{110.4 + (15 \times 0.387)} = \frac{3}{116.205} = 0.0258 = 2.58\%$$

9. To calculate the composite return based on beginning assets, first determine the percentage of beginning composite assets represented by each portfolio; then determine the weighted-average return for the month:

Beginning composite assets = 74.9 + 127.6 + 110.4 = 312.9

Portfolio A = 74.9/312.9 = 0.239 = 23.9%

Portfolio B = 127.6/312.9 = 0.408 = 40.8%

Portfolio C = 110.4/312.9 = 0.353 = 35.3%

$r_{Comp}$ = (0.0365 × 0.239) + (0.0192 × 0.408) + (0.0258 × 0.353)

= 0.0257 = 2.57%

10. To calculate the composite return based on beginning assets plus cash flows, first use the denominator of the Modified Dietz formula to determine the percentage of total beginning assets plus weighted cash flows represented by each portfolio, and then calculate the weighted-average return:

Beginning composite assets + Weighted cash flows = [74.9 + (7.5 × 0.613)] + [127.6 + (−15 × 0.742) + (−5 × 0.387)] + [110.4 + (15 × 0.387)] = 79.5 + 114.535 + 116.205

= 310.24

Portfolio A = 79.5/310.24 = 0.256 = 25.6%

Portfolio B = 114.535/310.24 = 0.369 = 36.9%

Portfolio C = 116.205/310.24 = 0.375 = 37.5%

$r_{Comp}$ = (0.0365 × 0.256) + (0.0192 × 0.369) + (0.0258 × 0.375)

= 0.0261 = 2.61%

The Aggregate Return method is calculated by summing beginning assets and intra-period external cash flows, treating the entire composite as though it were a single portfolio and then computing the return directly with the Modified Dietz formula.

$$r_{Comp} = \frac{323.5 - 312.9 - (-15 + 7.5 + 10)}{312.9 + [(-15) \times 0.742 + 7.5 \times 0.613 + 10 \times 0.387]}$$
= 0.0261 = 2.61%

11. Yes. The GIPS standards state that firms must include all actual, discretionary, fee-paying segregated accounts in at least one of the firm's composites. If the segregated account meets the defined criteria for inclusion in more than one composite, the firm must include the account in all the firm's appropriate composites. For example, a firm may have a large-cap composite and a large-cap growth composite. If the firm manages a segregated account that meets the criteria for inclusion in the large-cap composite as well as the large-cap growth composite,

the firm must include the account in both composites.

12. No, Tan/Lim may not claim compliance with the GIPS standards if model performance is linked to actual performance. The GIPS standards state that composites must include only actual assets under management within the defined firm, and they expressly prohibit linking the performance of simulated or model portfolios with actual performance.

13. The GIPS standards prohibit including non-discretionary portfolios in composites. IPS restrictions do not necessarily render a portfolio non-discretionary. It is up to the investment management firm to define discretion and to determine whether it has the discretion to implement the investment strategy, given the restrictions of the IPS. In this case, however, it appears likely that SMERF's policy requiring transactions to be approved in advance by the Investment Committee and the pension plan's liquidity needs prevent Midwest National Bank from fully implementing the investment objective of achieving long-term capital appreciation through active management. If so, Midwest National Bank must classify the SMERF portfolio as non-discretionary and exclude it from all composites.

14. A is correct. Such a restriction would most likely lead to the composition of this portfolio differing materially from other fixed-income portfolios run by the firm and, as such, the manager could reasonably classify this portfolio as non-discretionary. The restrictions stated in answers B and C are constraints that are likely to be specified as part of a fixed-income strategy.

15. A is correct. The GIPS standards state, "Composites must include new portfolios on a timely and consistent basis after each portfolio comes under management." In this case, it is expected to take an extended period to invest the new client's assets in accordance with the composite strategy. Assuming Taurus complies with the GIPS standards, its documented policy would provide for the inclusion of new bank loan portfolios in the composite on a timely basis. For example, Taurus's policy may require new portfolios to be included in the composite as of the first full measurement period that the assets are fully invested. Taurus must apply its policy consistently.

16. A is correct. Terminated portfolios must be included in the historical performance of the composite through the last full measurement during which the firm had discretion. The last full measurement period during which the Chimie Bio-Industrielle portfolio was under the management of Ord Capital Management was the month of March.

17. C is correct. The portfolio's historical performance must remain with the original composite. Portfolios must not be switched from one composite to another unless either documented changes to a portfolio's investment mandate, objective, or strategy or the redefinition of the composite make it appropriate.

18. B is correct. The portfolio's historical performance must remain with the original composite. Portfolios must not be switched from one composite to another unless either documented changes to a portfolio's investment mandate, objective, or strategy or the redefinition of the composite make it appropriate.

19. C is correct. The GIPS standards state, "If the firm sets a minimum asset level for portfolios to be included in a composite, the firm must not include portfolios below the minimum asset level in that composite." However, a firm may set one minimum asset level at which to *add* a portfolio to a composite and another level at which a portfolio must be *removed* from a composite. Unless Bamako's policies specify different minimum asset levels for adding and removing portfolios

from composites, Bamako must remove the Bouwa portfolio from the core-plus fixed-income composite when the portfolio's assets fall below the minimum and return it to the composite when it once again qualifies for inclusion. A is incorrect because composites must be defined according to similar investment mandates, objectives, and/or strategies; there should be no "miscellaneous" composite.

20. A is correct. The client's prior approval authority for security transactions most likely renders the portfolio non-discretionary. The GIPS standards state "non-discretionary portfolios must not be included in composites." B is incorrect because total firm assets must include all discretionary and non-discretionary assets managed by the firm.

21. Under the GIPS standards, there is no minimum or maximum number of portfolios that a composite may include. The GIPS standards require that firms disclose the number of portfolios in each composite as of the end of each annual period presented, unless there are five or fewer portfolios.

22. The GIPS standards require that when a firm initially claims compliance with the GIPS standards, it must present at least five years of GIPS-compliant performance (or for the period since the composite inception date if the composite has been in existence less than five years). After presenting a minimum of five years of GIPS-compliant performance (or for the period since the composite inception date if the composite has been in existence less than five years), the firm must present an additional year of performance each year, building up to a minimum of 10 years of GIPS-compliant performance. In 2020, Macondo must present performance from 2010 through 2019. Macondo Institutional Asset Management thus cannot drop the years prior to 2015 at the time Garcia suggests it do so. In addition to violating a specific requirement, Garcia's suggestion was not in the spirit of fair representation and full disclosure of performance. The firm may eliminate returns from more than 10 years ago from its GIPS Report, as long as it continues to show at least the most recent 10 years. It is recommended, however, that Macondo show its entire GIPS-compliant performance record.

23. Acella must determine if O'Connor's performance track record meets all of the portability requirements. Acella must have records supporting the performance of portfolios currently in the composite and those that were previously managed to the strategy but have since terminated. The firm must also be comfortable that Mr. O'Connor was the primary decision maker for the strategy while at JEM-Stone and that the strategy will remain substantially intact and independent once at Acella. If these requirements are met, Acella may port the track record, but the ported composite must pass one more test if the firm wishes to link performance: There must not be a break in the track record between the past firm and Acella. For example, if O'Connor left his prior firm at the end of February 2019 and did not start with Acella until 1 May 2019, there will be a break in the track record and Acella must not link to the prior performance.

24. A is correct. Verification brings additional credibility to the claim of compliance, but it "does not provide assurance on the accuracy of any specific performance report." Verification also does not provide assurance on the adequacy of a firm's internal controls.

25. No, a firm may not choose to have only a portion of the firm verified. A firm that has been verified may choose to have a detailed performance *examination* conducted on one or more specific composites, but verification cannot be carried out on only select composites, pooled funds, or portfolios. Firms must not state that a particular composite has been "verified."

# Level III Core Glossary

**Absolute return benchmark**  A minimum target return that an investment manager is expected to beat.

**Accrual taxes**  Taxes levied and paid on a periodic basis.

**Accumulation phase**  Phase where the government predominantly contributes to a sovereign wealth pension reserve fund.

**Active management**  A portfolio management approach that allows risk factor mismatches relative to a benchmark index causing potentially significant return differences between the active portfolio and the underlying benchmark.

**Active return**  The return on a portfolio minus the return on the portfolio's benchmark.

**Active risk**  The standard deviation of active returns.

**Active risk budgeting**  Risk budgeting that concerns active risk (risk relative to a portfolio's benchmark).

**Active share**  A measure of how similar a portfolio is to its benchmark. A manager who precisely replicates the benchmark will have an active share of zero; a manager with no holdings in common with the benchmark will have an active share of one.

**Aggregate wealth**  The total value of all assets owned, encompassing personal property, financial assets, real assets, and rights.

**Arithmetic attribution**  An attribution approach which explains the arithmetic difference between the portfolio return and its benchmark return. The single-period attribution effects sum to the excess return, however, when combining multiple periods, the sub-period attribution effects will not sum to the excess return.

**Ask price**  The price at which a trader will sell a specified quantity of a security. Also called *ask*, *offer price*, or *offer*.

**Asset-only**  With respect to asset allocation, an approach that focuses directly on the characteristics of the assets without explicitly modeling the liabilities.

**Authority bias**  A behavioral bias which involves groups deferring to a group member that is a subject matter expert or in a position of authority.

**Aversion to complexity**  A behavioral phenomenon of groups in many professional contexts, in which disproportionate attention is given to trivial issues at the expense of important but harder-to-grasp or contested topics.

**Back-fill bias**  The distortion in index or peer group data which results when returns are reported to a database only after they are known to be good returns.

**Base**  With respect to a foreign exchange quotation of the price of one unit of a currency, the currency referred to in "one unit of a currency."

**Basis risk**  The possibility that the expected value of a derivative differs unexpectedly from that of the underlying.

**Bear spread**  An option strategy that becomes more valuable when the price of the underlying asset declines, so requires buying one option and writing another with a *lower* exercise price. A put bear spread involves buying a put with a higher exercise price and selling a put with a lower exercise price. A bear spread can also be executed with calls.

**Best ask**  The offer to sell with the lowest ask price. Also called *best offer* or *inside ask*.

**Best bid**  The highest bid in the market.

**Best offer**  The lowest offer (ask price) in the market.

**Best-in-class**  An ESG implementation approach that seeks to identify the most favorable companies in an industry based on ESG considerations.

**Bid price**  In a price quotation, the price at which the party making the quotation is willing to buy a specified quantity of an asset or security.

**Bid–ask spread**  The ask price minus the bid price.

**Buffering**  Establishing ranges around breakpoints that define whether a stock belongs in one index or another.

**Bull spread**  An option strategy that becomes more valuable when the price of the underlying asset rises, so requires buying one option and writing another with a *higher* exercise price. A call bull spread involves buying a call with a lower exercise price and selling a call with a higher exercise price. A bull spread can also be executed with puts.

**Business cycle**  Fluctuations in GDP in relation to long-term trend growth, usually lasting 9-11 years.

**Calendar rebalancing**  Rebalancing a portfolio to target weights on a periodic basis; for example, monthly, quarterly, semi-annually, or annually.

**Calendar spread**  A strategy in which one sells an option and buys the same type of option but with different expiration dates, on the same underlying asset and with the same strike. When the investor buys the more distant (near-term) call and sells the near-term (more distant) call, it is a long (short) calendar spread.

**Canada model**  Characterized by a high allocation to alternatives. Unlike the endowment model, however, the Canada model relies more on internally managed assets. The innovative features of the Canada model are the: a) reference portfolio, b) total portfolio approach, and c) active management.

**Capital market expectations (CME)**  Expectations concerning the risk and return prospects of asset classes.

**Capital sufficiency analysis**  The process of evaluating whether a client has sufficient capital resources to achieve their financial goals and objectives; it considers the client's assets, liabilities, income, expenses, risk tolerance, time horizon, and other relevant factors.

**Capture ratio**  A measure of the manager's gain or loss relative to the gain or loss of the benchmark.

**Carhart model**  A four factor model used in performance attribution. The four factors are: market (RMRF), size (SMB), value (HML), and momentum (WML).

**Carry trade**  A trading strategy that involves buying a security and financing it at a rate that is lower than the yield on that security.

**Cash flow matching**  Immunization approach that attempts to ensure that all future liability payouts are matched precisely by cash flows from bonds or fixed-income derivatives.

**Cash-secured put**   An option strategy involving the writing of a put option and simultaneously depositing an amount of money equal to the exercise price into a designated account (this strategy is also called a fiduciary put).

**Collar**   An option position in which the investor is long shares of stock and then buys a put with an exercise price below the current stock price and writes a call with an exercise price above the current stock price. Collars allow a shareholder to acquire downside protection through a protective put but reduce the cash outlay by writing a covered call.

**Contingent immunization**   Hybrid approach that combines immunization with an active management approach when the asset portfolio's value exceeds the present value of the liability portfolio.

**Cost basis**   The initial cost of acquiring an investment including expenses incurred to acquire the investment. Also referred to as simply basis.

**Covered call**   An option strategy in which a long position in an asset is combined with a short position in a call on that asset.

**Cross hedge**   A hedge involving a hedging instrument that is imperfectly correlated with the asset being hedged; an example is hedging a bond investment with futures on a non-identical bond.

**Cross-currency basis swap**   A swap in which notional principals are exchanged because the goal of the transaction is to issue at a more favorable funding rate and swap the amount back to the currency of choice.

**Cross-sectional consistency**   A feature of expectations setting which means that estimates for all classes reflect the same underlying assumptions and are generated with methodologies that reflect or preserve important relationships among the asset classes, such as strong correlations. It is the internal consistency across asset classes.

**Currency overlay programs**   A currency overlay program is a program to manage a portfolio's currency exposures for the case in which those exposures are managed separately from the management of the portfolio itself.

**Custom security-based benchmark**   Benchmark that is custom built to accurately reflect the investment discipline of a particular investment manager. Also called a *strategy benchmark* because it reflects a manager's particular strategy.

**Decision-reversal risk**   The risk of reversing a chosen course of action at the point of maximum loss.

**Decumulation phase**   Phase where the government predominantly withdraws from a sovereign wealth pension reserve fund.

**Deferred taxes**   Taxes postponed until some future date.

**Defined benefit**   A retirement plan in which a plan sponsor commits to paying a specified retirement benefit.

**Defined benefit plan**   Retirement plan that is funded by the employer that guarantees a retirement benefit based on factors such as years of service, salary, and age.

**Defined contribution**   A retirement plan in which contributions are defined but the ultimate retirement benefit is not specified or guaranteed by the plan sponsor.

**Defined contribution plan**   Retirement plan in which the employer, employee, or both contribute to an account in which the employee bears the investment risk.

**Delay costs**   Implicit trading costs that arise from the inability to complete desired trades immediately. Also called *slippage*.

**Delta**   The relationship between the option price and the underlying price, which reflects the sensitivity of the price of the option to changes in the price of the underlying. Delta is a good approximation of how an option price will change for a small change in the stock.

**Delta hedging**   Hedging that involves matching the price response of the position being hedged over a narrow range of prices.

**Demand deposits**   Accounts that can be drawn upon regularly and without notice. This category includes checking accounts and certain savings accounts that are often accessible through online banks or automated teller machines (ATMs).

**Diffusion index**   Reflects the proportion of the index's components that are moving in a pattern consistent with the overall index.

**Dividend capture**   A trading strategy whereby an equity portfolio manager purchases stocks just before their ex-dividend dates, holds these stocks through the ex-dividend date to earn the right to receive the dividend, and subsequently sells the shares.

**Domestic asset**   An asset that trades in the investor's domestic currency (or home currency).

**Domestic currency**   The currency of the investor, i.e., the currency in which he or she typically makes consumption purchases, e.g., the Swiss franc for an investor domiciled in Switzerland.

**Domestic-currency return**   A rate of return stated in domestic currency terms from the perspective of the investor; reflects both the foreign-currency return on an asset as well as percentage movement in the spot exchange rate between the domestic and foreign currencies.

**Drawdown**   A percentage peak-to-trough reduction in net asset value.

**Drawdown duration**   The total time from the start of the drawdown until the cumulative drawdown recovers to zero.

**Due diligence**   Investigation and analysis in support of a recommendation; the failure to exercise due diligence may sometimes result in liability according to various securities laws.

**Duration matching**   Immunization approach based on the duration of assets and liabilities. Ideally, the liabilities being matched (the liability portfolio) and the portfolio of assets (the bond portfolio) should be affected similarly by a change in interest rates.

**Duration times spread**   Weighting of spread duration by credit spread in order to incorporate the empirical observation that spread changes for lower-rated bonds tend to be consistent on a percentage, rather than absolute, basis.

**Dynamic asset allocation**   Dynamic asset allocation is an investment strategy premised on long-term asset allocation but employing short-term, tactical trading to maintain investment allocation targets.

**Dynamic hedge**   A hedge requiring adjustment as the price of the hedged asset changes.

**Econometrics**   The application of quantitative modeling and analysis grounded in economic theory to the analysis of economic data.

**Economic balance sheet**   An extended balance sheet that includes the present values of both lifetime earnings and future consumption.

**Economic indicators**   Economic statistics provided by government and established private organizations that contain information on an economy's recent past activity or its current or future position in the business cycle.

**Effective federal funds (FFE) rate** The fed funds rate actually transacted between depository institutions, not the Fed's target federal funds rate.

**Effective spread** Two times the difference between the execution price and the midpoint of the market quote at the time an order is entered.

**Endowment model** Characterized by a high allocation to alternative investments (private investments and hedge funds), significant active management, and externally managed assets.

**Enhanced indexing approach** Maintains a close link to the benchmark but attempts to generate a modest amount of outperformance relative to the benchmark.

**Excess return** Used in various senses appropriate to context: 1) The difference between the portfolio return and the benchmark return, which may be either positive or negative; 2) The return in excess of the risk-free rate, thus representing the return for bearing risk.

**Exhaustive** Covering or containing all possible outcomes.

**Extended portfolio assets and liabilities** Assets and liabilities beyond those shown on a conventional balance sheet that are relevant in making asset allocation decisions; an example of an extended asset is human capital.

**Factor-model-based benchmarks** Benchmarks constructed by examining a portfolio's sensitivity to a set of factors, such as the return for a broad market index, company earnings growth, industry, or financial leverage.

**Family offices** Private firms that offer a range of wealth management services tailored specifically for ultra-high-net-worth individuals.

**Foreign assets** Assets denominated in currencies other than the investor's home currency.

**Foreign currency** Currency that is not the currency in which an investor makes consumption purchases, e.g., the US dollar from the perspective of a Swiss investor.

**Foreign-currency return** The return of the foreign asset measured in foreign-currency terms.

**Forward rate bias** An empirically observed divergence from interest rate parity conditions that active investors seek to benefit from by borrowing in a lower-yield currency and investing in a higher-yield currency.

**Funding currencies** The low-yield currencies in which borrowing occurs in a carry trade.

**Gamma** A numerical measure of how sensitive an option's delta (the sensitivity of the derivative's price) is to a change in the value of the underlying.

**General account** Account holding assets to fund future liabilities from traditional life insurance and fixed annuities, the products in which the insurer bears all the risks—particularly mortality risk and longevity risk.

**Gini coefficient** A measure of inequality of wealth, or $i$, that ranges from 0 (perfect equality) to 1 (perfect inequality).

**Goals-based** With respect to asset allocation or investing, an approach that focuses on achieving an investor's goals (for example, related to supporting lifestyle needs or aspirations) based typically on constructing sub-portfolios aligned with those goals.

**Goals-based investing** An investment industry term for approaches to investing for individuals and families focused on aligning investments with goals (parallel to liability-driven investing for institutional investors).

**Grinold–Kroner model** An expression for the expected return on a share as the sum of an expected income return, an expected nominal earnings growth return, and an expected repricing return.

**Groupthink** A behavioral bias that occurs when a team minimizes conflict and dissent in reaching and maintaining a consensus.

**Hedge ratio** The proportion of an underlying that will offset the risk associated with a derivative position.

**High-net-worth individuals (HNWIs)** Individuals with investable assets exceeding a certain minimum level, often as low as USD1 million, but typically more.

**High-water mark** A measure that reflects the fund's maximum value as of a performance fee payment date net of fees.

**Holdings-based attribution** A "buy and hold" attribution approach which calculates the return of portfolio and benchmark components based upon the price and foreign exchange rate changes applied to daily snapshots of portfolio holdings.

**Holdings-based style analysis** A bottom-up style analysis that estimates the risk exposures from the actual securities held in the portfolio at a point in time.

**Home bias** A preference for securities listed on the exchanges of one's home country.

**Home currency** See *domestic currency*.

**Home-country bias** The favoring of domestic over non-domestic investments relative to global market value weights.

**Human capital** The present value of an individual's future expected labor income.

**Impact investing** Refers to investments made with the specific intent of generating positive, measurable social and environmental impact alongside a financial return (which differentiates it from philanthropy).

**Implementation shortfall** (IS) The difference between the return for a notional or paper portfolio, where all transactions are assumed to take place at the manager's decision price, and the portfolio's actual return, which reflects realized transactions, including all fees and costs.

**Implied volatility** The standard deviation that causes an option pricing model to give the current option price.

**Implied volatility surface** A three-dimensional plot, for put and call options on the same underlying asset, of days to expiration ($x$-axis), option strike prices ($y$-axis), and implied volatilities ($z$-axis). It simultaneously shows the volatility skew (or smile) and the term structure of implied volatility.

**Inflation-linked bonds** Debt instruments that link the principal and interest to inflation.

**Input uncertainty** Uncertainty concerning whether the inputs are correct.

**Inside ask** See *best ask*.

**Inside bid** See *best bid*.

**Inside spread** The spread between the best bid price and the best ask price. Also called the *market bid-ask spread*, *inside bid-ask spread*, or *market spread*.

**Interaction effect** The impact of overweighting and underweighting individual securities within sectors that are themselves overweighted or underweighted.

**Intertemporal consistency** A feature of expectations setting which means that estimates for an asset class over different horizons reflect the same assumptions with respect to the potential paths of returns over time. It is the internal consistency over various time horizons.

**Intrinsic value**   The amount gained (per unit) by an option buyer if an option is exercised at any given point in time. May be referred to as the exercise value of the option.

**Investable net worth**   The sum of liquid assets, such as savings and investment accounts, and less short-term liabilities such as credit card debt.

**Investable wealth**   The sum of liquid assets such as savings and investment accounts.

**Investment currencies**   The high-yielding currencies in a carry trade.

**Investment policy statement (IPS)**   A description of a client's unique investment objectives, risk tolerance, investment time horizon, and other applicable constraints.

**Investment style**   A natural grouping of investment disciplines that has some predictive power in explaining the future dispersion of returns across portfolios.

**Key person risk**   The risk that results from over-reliance on an individual or individuals whose departure would negatively affect an investment manager.

**Knock-in/knock-out**   Features of a vanilla option that is created (or ceases to exist) when the spot exchange rate touches a pre-specified level.

**Latency**   The elapsed time between the occurrence of an event and a subsequent action that depends on that event.

**Leading economic indicators**   Turning points that usually precede those of the overall economy; they are believed to have value for predicting the economy's future state, usually near-term.

**Liability driven investing (LDI) model**   In the LDI model, the primary investment objective is to generate returns sufficient to cover liabilities, with a focus on maximizing expected surplus return (excess return of assets over liabilities) and managing surplus volatility.

**Liability glide path**   A specification of desired proportions of liability-hedging assets and return-seeking assets and the duration of the liability hedge as funded status changes and contributions are made.

**Liability-based mandates**   Mandates managed to match or cover expected liability payments (future cash outflows) with future projected cash inflows.

**Liability-driven investing**   An investment industry term that generally encompasses asset allocation that is focused on funding an investor's liabilities in institutional contexts.

**Liability-relative**   With respect to asset allocation, an approach that focuses directly only on funding liabilities as an investment objective.

**Limit order book**   The book or list of limit orders to buy and sell that pertains to a security.

**Limited-life foundations**   A type of foundation where founders seek to maintain control of spending while they (or their immediate heirs) are still alive.

**Longevity risk**   The risk of exhausting an individual's financial resources before passing away, thereby leaving insufficient capital for living expenses and unmet needs.

**Lorenz curve**   A measure of the cumulative percentage of wealth owned by each percentage of the population.

**Macro attribution**   Attribution at the sponsor level.

**Manager peer group**   See *manager universe.*

**Manager universe**   A broad group of managers with similar investment disciplines. Also called *manager peer group.*

**Marginal tax rate**   The highest rate of tax applied to taxable income.

**Market fragmentation**   Trading the same instrument in multiple venues.

**Market impact**   The effect of the trade on transaction prices. Also called *price impact.*

**Micro attribution**   Attribution at the portfolio manager level.

**Midquote price**   The average, or midpoint, of the prevailing bid and ask prices.

**Minimum-variance hedge ratio**   A mathematical approach to determining the optimal cross hedging ratio.

**Mission-related investing**   Investing aimed at causes promoting positive societal or environmental change.

**Model uncertainty**   Uncertainty as to whether a selected model is correct.

**Negative screening**   An ESG investment approach that consists of excluding investments in certain sectors, companies, or practices in a fund or portfolio based on specific ESG criteria.

**Net worth**   The difference between assets and liabilities.

**Non-deliverable forwards**   Forward contracts that are cash settled (in the non-controlled currency of the currency pair) rather than physically settled (the controlled currency is neither delivered nor received).

**Nonstationarity**   A characteristic of series of data whose properties, such as mean and variance, are not constant through time. When analyzing historical data it means that different parts of a data series reflect different underlying statistical properties.

**Norway model**   Characterized by an almost exclusive reliance on public equities and fixed income (the traditional 60/40 equity/bond model falls under the Norway model), with largely passively managed assets and with very little to no allocation to alternative investments.

**Offer price**   The price at which a counterparty is willing to sell one unit of the base currency.

**Opportunity cost**   The value that investors forgo by choosing a particular course of action; the value of something in its best alternative use.

**Optional stock dividends**   A type of dividend in which shareholders may elect to receive either cash or new shares.

**Overbought**   When a market has trended too far in one direction and is vulnerable to a trend reversal, or correction.

**Oversold**   The opposite of overbought; see *overbought.*

**Packeting**   Splitting stock positions into multiple parts.

**Parameter uncertainty**   Uncertainty arising because a quantitative model's parameters are estimated with error.

**Participant-switching life-cycle options**   Automatically switch DC plan members into a more conservative asset mix as their age increases. There may be several automatic de-risking switches at different age targets.

**Participant/cohort option**   Pools the DC plan member with a cohort that has a similar target retirement date.

**Passive management**   A buy-and-hold approach to investing in which an investor does not make portfolio changes based upon short-term expectations of changing market or security performance.

**Percent-range rebalancing**   An approach to rebalancing that involves setting rebalancing thresholds or trigger points, stated as a percentage of the portfolio's value, around target values.

**Performance attribution**   The process of disaggregating a portfolio's return to determine the drivers of its performance.

**Personal assets**   Nonbusiness, on-investment assets including personal property and real property.

**Personal property**   Property owned by individuals that are not real property and not considered investments.

**Planned goals**   Financial objectives that can be reasonably estimated or quantified at the onset and can be achieved within an expected time horizon.

**Position delta**   The overall or portfolio delta. For example, the position delta of a covered call, consisting of long 100 shares and short one at-the-money call, is +50 (= +100 for the shares and -50 for the short ATM call).

**Positive screening**   An ESG investment approach that consists of including investments in sectors or companies in a fund or portfolio typically based on ESG performance relative to industry peers.

**Price improvement**   When trade execution prices are better than quoted prices.

**Private wealth management**   Financial planning and investment management to help individual investors, particularly high-net-worth individuals (HNWIs) and ultra-high-net-worth individuals (UHNWIs), manage their wealth.

**Protective put**   A strategy of purchasing an underlying asset and purchasing a put on the same asset.

**Pure indexing**   Attempts to replicate a bond index as closely as possible, targeting zero active return and zero active risk.

**Put spread**   A strategy used to reduce the upfront cost of buying a protective put, it involves buying a put option and writing another put option.

**Re-base**   With reference to index construction, to change the time period used as the base of the index.

**Realized volatility**   Historical volatility, the square root of the realized variance of returns, which is a measure of the range of past price outcomes for the underlying asset.

**Rebalancing**   In the context of asset allocation, a discipline for adjusting the portfolio to align with the strategic asset allocation.

**Rebalancing range**   A range of values for asset class weights defined by trigger points above and below target weights, such that if the portfolio value passes through a trigger point, rebalancing occurs. Also known as a corridor.

**Rebate rate**   The portion of the collateral earnings rate that is repaid to the security borrower by the security lender.

**Reduced form models**   Statistical credit models that solve for the probability of default over a specific time period, using observable company-specific and market-based variables.

**Regime**   The governing set of relationships (between variables) that stem from technological, political, legal, and regulatory environments. Changes in such environments or policy stances can be described as changes in regime.

**Relative value**   A concept that describes the selection of the most attractive individual securities to populate the portfolio with, using ranking and comparing.

**Repo rate**   The interest rate on a repurchase agreement.

**Repurchase agreements**   In repurchase agreements, or repos, a security owner agrees to sell a security for a specific cash amount while simultaneously agreeing to repurchase the security at a specified future date (typically one day later) and price.

**Reserve portfolio**   The component of an insurer's general account that is subject to specific regulatory requirements and is intended to ensure the company's ability to meet its policy liabilities. The assets in the reserve portfolio are managed conservatively and must be highly liquid and low risk.

**Resistance levels**   Price points on dealers' order boards where one would expect to see a clustering of offers.

**Return attribution**   A set of techniques used to identify the sources of the excess return of a portfolio against its benchmark.

**Returns-based attribution**   An attribution approach that uses only the total portfolio returns over a period to identify the components of the investment process that have generated the returns. The Brinson–Hood–Beebower approach is a returns-based attribution approach.

**Returns-based benchmarks**   Benchmarks constructed by examining a portfolio's sensitivity to a set of factors, such as the returns for various style indexes (e.g., small-cap value, small-cap growth, large-cap value, and large-cap growth).

**Returns-based style analysis**   A top-down style analysis that involves estimating the sensitivities of a portfolio to security market indexes.

**Reverse repos**   Repurchase agreements from the standpoint of the lender.

**Risk attribution**   The analysis of the sources of risk.

**Risk aversion**   The dislike for risk such that compensation is required in terms of higher expected returns for assuming higher risk.

**Risk budgeting**   The establishment of objectives for individuals, groups, or divisions of an organization that takes into account the allocation of an acceptable level of risk.

**Risk capacity**   The ability to bear financial risk.

**Risk premiums**   Extra returns expected by investors for bearing some specified risk.

**Risk reversal**   A strategy used to profit from the existence of an implied volatility skew and from changes in its shape over time. A combination of long (short) calls and short (long) puts on the same underlying with the same expiration is a long (short) risk reversal.

**Risk tolerance**   The level of risk an investor is willing and able to bear.

**Seagull spread**   An extension of the risk reversal foreign exchange option strategy that limits downside risk.

**Securities lending**   A form of collateralized lending that may be used to generate income for portfolios.

**Selective**   An index construction methodology that targets only those securities with certain characteristics.

**Separate accounts**   Accounts holding assets to fund future liabilities from variable life insurance and variable annuities, the products in which customers make investment decisions from a menu of options and themselves bear investment risk.

**Sharpe ratio**   The ratio of mean excess return to standard deviation (excess return).

**Shortfall probability**   The probability of failing to meet a specific liability or goal.

**Shrinkage estimation**   Estimation that involves taking a weighted average of a historical estimate of a parameter and some other parameter estimate, where the weights reflect the analyst's relative belief in the estimates.

**Special dividends**   Dividends paid by a company that does not pay dividends on a regular schedule, or dividends that supplement regular cash dividends with an extra payment.

**Spread duration**   The change in bond price for a given change in yield spread. Also referred to as OAS duration when the option-adjusted spread (OAS) is the yield measure used.

**Static hedge**   A hedge that is not sensitive to changes in the price of the asset hedged.

**Stock lending**   Securities lending involving the transfer of equities.

**Stops**   Stop-loss orders involve leaving bids or offers away from the current market price to be filled if the market reaches those levels.

**Straddle**   An option combination in which one buys *both* puts and calls, with the same exercise price and same expiration date, on the same underlying asset. In contrast to this long straddle, if someone *writes* both options, it is a short straddle.

**Strangle**   A variation on a straddle in which the put and call have different exercise prices; if the put and call are held long, it is a long strangle; if they are held short, it is a short strangle.

**Strategic asset allocation**   A long-term strategy that establishes target allocations for various asset classes and aims to optimize the balance between risk and reward by diversifying investments.

**Structural models**   Models that specify functional relationships among variables based on economic theory. The functional form and parameters of these models are derived from the underlying theory. They may include unobservable parameters.

**Support levels**   Price points on dealers' order boards where one would expect to see a clustering of bids.

**Surplus**   The difference between assets and liabilities, analogous to shareholders' equity on a corporate balance sheet.

**Surplus portfolio**   The component of an insurer's general account that is intended to realize higher expected returns than the reserve portfolio and so can assume some liquidity risk. Surplus portfolio assets are often managed aggressively with exposure to alternative assets.

**Survivorship bias**   Relates to the inclusion of only current investment funds in a database. As such, the returns of funds that are no longer available in the marketplace (have been liquidated) are excluded from the database. Also see *backfill bias*.

**Synthetic long forward position**   The combination of a long call and a short put with identical strike price and expiration, traded at the same time on the same underlying.

**Synthetic short forward position**   The combination of a short call and a long put at the same strike price and maturity (traded at the same time on the same underlying).

**Tactical asset allocation**   A proactive strategy that adjusts asset class allocations within a portfolio based on short-term market trends, economic conditions, or valuation changes to capitalize on temporary market inefficiencies or opportunities to improve returns or manage risk more effectively.

**Tax drag**   The negative effect of taxes on an investment's net returns.

**Taylor rule**   A rule linking a central bank's target short-term interest rate to the rate of growth of the economy and inflation.

**Term deposits**   Interest-bearing accounts that have a specified maturity date. This category includes savings accounts and certificates of deposit (CDs). Also see *time deposits*.

**Term structure of volatility**   The plot of implied volatility (*y*-axis) against option maturity (*x*-axis) for options with the same strike price on the same underlying. Typically, implied volatility is not constant across different maturities – rather, it is often in contango, meaning that the implied volatilities for longer-term options are higher than for near-term ones.

**Thematic investing**   An ESG investment approach with a focus on assets relating to ESG factors or themes, such as clean energy, green technology, sustainable agriculture, gender diversity, and affordable housing.

**Theta**   The change in a derivative instrument for a given small change in calendar time, holding everything else constant. Specifically, the theta calculation assumes nothing changes except calendar time. Theta also reflects the rate at which an option's time value decays.

**Threshold-based rebalancing policy**   The manager rebalances the portfolio when asset class weights deviate from their target weights by a prespecified percentage regardless of timing and frequency.

**Time deposits**   Interest-bearing accounts that have a specified maturity date. This category includes savings accounts and certificates of deposit (CDs). Also see *term deposits*.

**Time value**   The difference between an option's premium and its intrinsic value.

**Time-based rebalancing policy**   The manager rebalances the portfolio regularly, at a certain given time interval such as quarterly, semi-annually, or annually, regardless of any difference between prevailing asset class weights and target asset class weights.

**Time-series estimation**   Estimators that are based on lagged values of the variable being forecast; often consist of lagged values of other selected variables.

**Total factor productivity**   A scale factor that reflects the portion of growth unaccounted for by explicit factor inputs (e.g., capital and labor).

**Total return payer**   Party responsible for paying the reference obligation cash flows and return to the receiver but that is also compensated by the receiver for any depreciation in the index or default losses incurred by the portfolio.

**Total return receiver**   Receives both the cash flows from the underlying index and any appreciation in the index over the period in exchange for paying the MRR plus a predetermined spread.

**Tracking risk**   The standard deviation of the differences between a portfolio's returns and its benchmarks returns. Also called tracking error.

**Transactions-based attribution**   An attribution approach that captures the impact of intra-day trades and exogenous events such as a significant class action settlement.

**Trigger points**   In the context of portfolio rebalancing, the endpoints of a rebalancing range (corridor).

**Ultra-high-net-worth individuals (UHNWIs)**   Individuals with net worth usually exceeding USD30 million or more.

**Unplanned goals**   Unforeseen financial needs that are difficult to quantify because either the funding need, the timing of the financial need, or both may not be estimated.

**Unsmoothing**   An adjustment to the reported return series if serial correlation is detected. Various approaches are available to unsmooth a return series.

**Variance notional**   The notional amount of a variance swap; it equals vega notional divided by two times the volatility strike price [i.e., (vega notional)/(2 × volatility strike)].

**Vega**   The change in a given derivative instrument for a given small change in volatility, holding everything else constant. A sensitivity measure for options that reflects the effect of volatility.

**Vega notional**   The trade size for a variance swap, which represents the average profit and loss of the variance swap for a 1% change in volatility from the strike.

**Vesting**   The process of an employee becoming unconditionally entitled to, and an employer becoming obligated to pay, compensation.

**Volatility clustering**   The tendency for large (small) swings in prices to be followed by large (small) swings of random direction.

**Volatility skew**   The skewed plot (of implied volatility ($y$-axis) against strike price ($x$-axis) for options on the same underlying with the same expiration) that occurs when the implied volatility increases for OTM puts and decreases for OTM calls, as the strike price moves away from the current price.

**Volatility smile**   The U-shaped plot (of implied volatility ($y$-axis) against strike price ($x$-axis) for options on the same underlying with the same expiration) that occurs when the implied volatilities priced into both OTM puts and calls trade at a premium to implied volatilities of ATM options.

**Wealth**   The value of all the assets owned by an individual.

**Wealth life cycle**   Stages of an individual investor's wealth in terms of human capital, financial capital, and economic net worth.

# Portfolio Management Pathway Glossary

**Accounting defeasement**　A way of extinguishing a debt obligation by setting aside sufficient high-quality securities to repay the liability. Also called *in-substance defeasance*.

**Active management**　A portfolio management approach that allows risk factor mismatches relative to a benchmark index causing potentially significant return differences between the active portfolio and the underlying benchmark.

**Active return**　The return on a portfolio minus the return on the portfolio's benchmark.

**Active risk**　The standard deviation of active returns.

**Active share**　A measure of how similar a portfolio is to its benchmark. A manager who precisely replicates the benchmark will have an active share of zero; a manager with no holdings in common with the benchmark will have an active share of one.

**Agency trade**　A trade in which the broker is engaged to find the other side of the trade, acting as an agent. In doing so, the broker does not assume any risk for the trade.

**Alpha decay**　In a trading context, alpha decay is the erosion or deterioration in short term alpha after the investment decision has been made.

**Alternative trading systems**　Trading venues that function like exchanges but that do not exercise regulatory authority over their subscribers except with respect to the conduct of the subscribers' trading in their trading systems. Also called *electronic communications networks* or *multilateral trading facilities*.

**Arrival price**　In a trading context, the arrival price is the security price at the time the order was released to the market for execution.

**Asset swap spread (ASW)**　The spread over MRR on an interest rate swap for the remaining life of the bond that is equivalent to the bond's fixed coupon.

**Asset swaps**　Convert a bond's fixed coupon to MRR plus (or minus) a spread.

**Authorized participants**　(APs) A special group of institutional investors who are authorized by the ETF issuer to participate in the creation/redemption process. APs are large broker/dealers, often market makers.

**Barbell**　A fixed-income investment strategy combining short- and long-term bond positions.

**Bear flattening**　A decrease in the yield spread between long- and short-term maturities across the yield curve, which is largely driven by a rise in short-term bond yields-to-maturity.

**Bear steepening**　An increase in the yield spread between long- and short-term maturities across the yield curve, which is largely driven by a rise in long-term bond yields-to-maturity.

**Breadth**　The number of truly independent decisions made each year.

**Bull flattening**　A decrease in the yield spread between long- and short-term maturities across the yield curve, which is largely driven by a decline in long-term bond yields-to-maturity.

**Bull steepening**　An increase in the yield spread between long- and short-term maturities across the yield curve, which is largely driven by a decline in short-term bond yields-to-maturity.

**Bullet**　A fixed-income investment strategy that focuses on the intermediate term (or "belly") of the yield curve.

**Butterfly spread**　A measure of yield curve shape or curvature equal to double the intermediate yield-to-maturity less the sum of short- and long-term yields-to-maturity.

**Butterfly strategy**　A common yield curve shape strategy that combines a long or short bullet position with a barbell portfolio in the opposite direction to capitalize on expected yield curve shape changes.

**Carry trade across currencies**　A strategy seeking to benefit from a positive interest rate differential across currencies by combining a short position (or borrowing) in a low-yielding currency and a long position (or lending) in a high-yielding currency.

**Cash drag**　Tracking error caused by temporarily uninvested cash.

**CDS curve**　Plot of CDS spreads across maturities for a single reference entity or group of reference entities in an index.

**Cell approach**　See *stratified sampling*.

**Closet indexer**　A fund that advertises itself as being actively managed but is substantially similar to an index fund in its exposures.

**Completion overlay**　A type of overlay that addresses an indexed portfolio that has diverged from its proper exposure.

**Conditional value at risk**　(CVaR) Also known as expected loss The average portfolio loss over a specific time period conditional on that loss exceeding the value at risk (VaR) threshold.

**Contingent immunization**　Hybrid approach that combines immunization with an active management approach when the asset portfolio's value exceeds the present value of the liability portfolio.

**Covered interest rate parity**　The relationship among the spot exchange rate, the forward exchange rate, and the interest rates in two currencies that ensures that the return on a hedged (i.e., covered) foreign risk-free investment is the same as the return on a domestic risk-free investment. Also called *interest rate parity*.

**Credit cycle**　The expansion and contraction of credit over the business cycle, which translates into asset price changes based on default and recovery expectations across maturities and rating categories.

**Credit default swap (CDS) basis**　Yield spread on a bond, as compared to CDS spread of same tenor.

**Credit loss rate**　The realized percentage of par value lost to default for a group of bonds equal to the bonds' default rate multiplied by the loss severity.

**Credit migration**　The change in a bond's credit rating over a certain period.

**Credit valuation adjustment (CVA)**　The present value of credit risk for a loan, bond, or derivative obligation.

**Cross-currency basis swap**　A swap in which notional principals are exchanged because the goal of the transaction is to issue at a more favorable funding rate and swap the amount back to the currency of choice.

**Currency overlay**   A type of overlay that helps hedge the returns of securities held in foreign currency back to the home country's currency.

**Decision price**   In a trading context, the decision price is the security price at the time the investment decision was made.

**Default intensity**   POD over a specified time period in a reduced form credit model.

**Default risk**   See *credit risk*.

**Delay cost**   The (trading related) cost associated with not submitting the order to the market in a timely manner.

**Direct market access**   (DMA) Access in which market participants can transact orders directly with the order book of an exchange using a broker's exchange connectivity.

**Discount margin**   The discount (or required) margin is the yield spread versus the MRR such that the FRN is priced at par on a rate reset date.

**Duration Times Spread (DTS)**   Weighting of spread duration by credit spread to incorporate the empirical observation that spread changes for lower-rated bonds tend to be consistent on a percentage rather than absolute basis.

**Empirical duration**   Estimation of the price–yield relationship using historical bond market data in statistical models.

**Enhanced indexing strategy**   A method investors use to match an underlying market index in which the investor purchases fewer securities than the full set of index constituents but matches primary risk factors reflected in the index.

**Evaluated pricing**   See *matrix pricing*.

**Excess spread**   Surplus difference of yield remaining after payments to bondholders are made after expenses are made and losses are covered.

**Execution cost**   The difference between the (trading related) cost of the real portfolio and the paper portfolio, based on shares and prices transacted.

**Expected shortfall**   The average loss conditional on exceeding the VaR cutoff; sometimes referred to as *conditional VaR* or *expected tail loss*.

**Expected tail loss**   See *expected shortfall*.

**Forward rate bias**   An empirically observed divergence from interest rate parity conditions that active investors seek to benefit from by borrowing in a lower-yield currency and investing in a higher-yield currency.

**Full replication approach**   When every issue in an index is represented in the portfolio and each portfolio position has approximately the same weight in the fund as in the index.

**G-spread**   Yield spread in basis points between a bond's yield-to-maturity and that of an actual or interpolated government bond. It represents the return for bearing risks relative to the government bond.

**Green bonds**   Bonds used in green finance whereby the proceeds are earmarked toward environmental-related products.

**Hazard rate**   The probability that an event will occur, given that it has not already occurred.

**I-spread (interpolated spread)**   Yield spread measure using swaps or constant maturity Treasury YTMs as a benchmark.

**Immunization**   An asset/liability management approach that structures investments in bonds to match (offset) liabilities' weighted-average duration; a type of dedication strategy.

**Implementation shortfall**   (IS) The difference between the return for a notional or paper portfolio, where all transactions are assumed to take place at the manager's decision price, and the portfolio's actual return, which reflects realized transactions, including all fees and costs.

**Incremental VaR (or partial VaR)**   The change in the minimum portfolio loss expected to occur over a given time period at a specific confidence level resulting from increasing or decreasing a portfolio position.

**Information coefficient**   Formally defined as the correlation between forecast return and actual return. In essence, it measures the effectiveness of investment insight.

**Key rate duration**   Also known as partial duration, is a measure of a bond's sensitivity to a change in the benchmark yield at a specific maturity.

**Liquidity budget**   The portfolio allocations (or weightings) considered acceptable for the liquidity categories in the liquidity classification schedule (or time-to-cash table).

**Liquidity classification schedule**   A liquidity management classification (or table) that defines portfolio liquidity "buckets" or categories based on the estimated time necessary to convert assets in that particular category into cash.

**Loss severity**   Portion of a bond's value (including unpaid interest) an investor loses in the event of default.

**Matrix pricing**   An estimation process for financial instruments based on the prices of comparable instruments.

**Multilateral trading facilities**   See *alternative trading systems*.

**Negative butterfly**   An increase in the butterfly spread due to lower short- and long-term yields-to-maturity and a higher intermediate yield-to-maturity.

**OAS duration**   The change in bond price for a given change in OAS.

**Opportunity cost**   The value that investors forgo by choosing a particular course of action; the value of something in its best alternative use.

**Option-adjusted spread (OAS)**   A generalized constant yield spread over the zero curve that incorporates bond option pricing based on assumed interest rate volatility and may be used for callable, putable, and non-callable bonds.

**Options on bond futures contracts**   Instruments that involve the right, but not the obligation, to enter into a bond futures contract at a pre-determined strike (bond price) on a future date in exchange for an up-front premium.

**Overlay**   A derivative position (or derivative positions) used to adjust a pre-existing portfolio closer to its objectives.

**Passive investment**   In the fixed-income context, it is investment that seeks to mimic the prevailing characteristics of the overall investments available in terms of credit quality, type of borrower, maturity, and duration rather than express a specific market view.

**Portfolio overlay**   An array of derivative positions managed separately from the securities portfolio to achieve overall intended portfolio characteristics.

**Positive butterfly**   A decrease in the butterfly spread due to higher short- and long-term yields-to-maturity and a lower intermediate yield-to-maturity.

**Present value of distribution of cash flows methodology**   Method used to address a portfolio's sensitivity to rate changes along the yield curve. This approach seeks to approximate and match the yield curve risk of an index over discrete time periods.

**Principal trade**   A trade in which the market maker or dealer becomes a disclosed counterparty and assumes risk for the trade by transacting the security for their own account. Also called *broker risk trades*.

**Probability of default**   The likelihood that a borrower defaults or fails to meet its obligation to make full and timely payments of principal and interest.

**Program trading**    A strategy of buying or selling many stocks simultaneously.

**Pure indexing**    Attempts to replicate a bond index as closely as possible, targeting zero active return and zero active risk.

**Quoted margin**    Specified spread of a floating rate instrument over a market reference rate or benchmark.

**Rebalancing overlay**    A type of overlay that addresses a portfolio's need to sell certain constituent securities and buy others.

**Reduced form credit models**    Credit models that solve for default probability over a specific time period using observable company-specific variables such as financial ratios and macroeconomic variables.

**Relative VaR**    See *ex ante tracking error*.

**Request for quote**    (RFQ) A non-binding quote provided by a market maker or dealer to a potential buyer or seller upon request. Commonly used in fixed income markets these quotes are only valid at the time they are provided.

**Scenario analysis**    A variation of the valuation process combining a base case with alternative outcomes, allowing the incorporation of more favorable or adverse scenarios in the valuation process.

**Smart beta**    Involves the use of transparent, rules-based strategies as a basis for investment decisions.

**Smart order routers**    (SOR) Smart systems used to electronically route small orders to the best markets for execution based on order type and prevailing market conditions.

**Spread duration**    The change in bond price for a given change in yield spread. Also referred to as OAS duration when the option-adjusted spread (OAS) is the yield measure used.

**Stratified sampling**    A sampling method that guarantees that subpopulations of interest are represented in the sample. Also called *representative sampling* or *cell approach*.

**Structural credit models**    Credit models that apply market-based variables to estimate the value of an issuer's assets and the volatility of asset value.

**Structural risk**    Risk that arises from portfolio design, particularly the choice of the portfolio allocations.

**Surplus**    The difference between assets and liabilities, analogous to shareholders' equity on a corporate balance sheet.

**Swaption**    This instrument grants a party the right, but not the obligation, to enter into an interest rate swap at a pre-determined strike (fixed swap rate) on a future date in exchange for an up-front premium.

**Time-to-cash table**    See *liquidity classification schedule*.

**Total return swap**    A swap in which one party agrees to pay the total return on a security. Often used as a credit derivative, in which the underlying is a bond.

**Tracking error**    The standard deviation of the differences between a portfolio's returns and its benchmark's returns; a synonym of active risk. Also called *tracking risk*.

**Tracking risk**    The standard deviation of the differences between a portfolio's returns and its benchmarks returns. Also called tracking error.

**Trade urgency**    A reference to how quickly or slowly an order is executed over the trading time horizon.

**Transfer coefficient**    The ability to translate portfolio insights into investment decisions without constraint.

**Uncovered interest rate parity**    The proposition that the expected return on an uncovered (i.e., unhedged) foreign currency (risk-free) investment should equal the return on a comparable domestic currency investment.

**Value at risk (VaR)**    The minimum loss that would be expected a certain percentage of the time over a certain period of time given the assumed market conditions.

**Yield spread**    The difference in yield-to-maturity between a bond and that of a another bond.

**Z-score**    A reduced-form statistical credit measure that uses company-specific and market-based ratios to create a composite score used to determine whether a firm is likely to default or remain solvent.

**Zero-discount margin (Z-DM)**    A yield spread calculation for FRNs that incorporates forward MRR.

**Zero-volatility spread (Z-spread)**    A constant spread which is estimated using the market prices of comparable bonds for issuers of similar credit quality of a bond over the benchmark rate.

# Private Markets Pathway Glossary

**100/10/1 rule of thumb** A VC investor's rule of thumb that demonstrates the high selectivity required, as one may review 100 startup pitches, conduct due diligence on 10 of those reviewed, and select just one for investment.

**Acquisition and development loan** A loan used to purchase and prepare land for a specific construction use.

**Agency cost of equity** A principal–agent problem which arises when company managers have more information about a company than public shareholders, limiting the ability to assess performance and take corrective action.

**Agreement among lenders** A contractual arrangement among lenders in a unitranche debt facility which may reallocate interest and principal payments, priority of claims, or voting rights on covenant or other credit agreement changes.

**Angel investors** High-net-worth investors who are also often entrepreneurs that provide seed financing to startup companies.

**Arbitrage spread** The difference between an announced acquisition price and the post-announcement market price, which represents the potential return to a merger arbitrage strategy prior to considering transaction costs.

**Asset impairment** An adverse change in the market value of an asset that falls below its balance sheet carrying value.

**Asset swap** Converts a bond's fixed coupon to MRR plus (or minus) a spread using an interest rate swap for the remaining life of the bond.

**Asset-based lending** Revolving credit facility extended on a secured basis using accounts receivable, inventory, or equipment as collateral.

**Bankruptcy** Legal proceedings, which vary by jurisdiction, allowing a firm whose liabilities exceed its assets to restructure existing debt obligations or liquidate assets in an orderly manner.

**Bond tender offer** An offer from a fixed-income issuer to repurchase outstanding loans or bonds.

**Brownfield investment** Infrastructure investments that involve existing rather than to-be-built facilities, which may involve the privatization or repurposing of existing public assets or an expansion of existing facilities.

**Build-operate-transfer (BOT) project** Infrastructure project whose construction and development is conducted by private entities sponsored by a public entity and transferred to public control after a finite operating period.

**Business development companies** A type of closed-end investment vehicle in the United States which are publicly traded and specialize in private debt.

**Buyout equity** Private equity investment in a mature company with the intent to transform, divest, or acquire businesses and sell the reorganized firm at a higher price to public or private investors.

**Capital structure arbitrage** An investment approach that combines long or short debt, equity, and/or credit default swap positions to exploit mispricing in a single issuer's obligations.

**Capitalization rate** A measure of the required rate of return on a property, also known as *cap rate*.

**Capitalization table** A detailed summary of changes in firm value, fractional ownership dilution, and prices paid by investors or stakeholders over the course of multiple equity rounds typically shown on a fully diluted basis.

**Carbon offset** Investments that reduce or remove carbon dioxide and other greenhouse gases to compensate for emissions produced elsewhere to achieve reduction or net-zero emission goals.

**Carried interest** A performance or incentive fee applied to private market fund investments based on returns above a hurdle rate.

**Catch-up clause** A clause in a limited partner agreement that specifies that a general partner will receive 100% of the distributions above a prespecified hurdle *until* the GP receives the carried interest percentage (such as 20%) of the returns generated and then every excess dollar will be split between the LPs and GP based on the carried interest percentage.

**CDS basis** Differences in bond and CDS spreads that arise because of bond price differences from par, accrued interest, and varying contract terms.

**Change of control** A debt clause that requires an issuer to repurchase outstanding bonds at a fixed price at or above par if a new owner acquires a predetermined percentage of voting shares.

**Change of control clause** Debt provision that requires an issuer to offer to repay outstanding debt if a new owner acquires a predetermined percentage of voting shares.

**Change of control provision** A restrictive covenant typically included in a high-yield bond indenture that requires the issuer to offer to repurchase outstanding bonds at a fixed price (above par) if a new owner acquires a predetermined percentage of voting shares.

**Circulation** Zoning requirement mandating provisions for security and emergency access to buildings or facilities.

**Clawback provisions** Limited partnership agreement provisions that involve returning GP performance fees to LPs in cases where transactions that are initially successful later face losses.

**Closed-end funds** Funds with a finite life requiring an initial capital commitment with a lockup period and eventual sale of the property or properties for distribution to investors.

**Collateralized loan obligations (CLOs)** Investment vehicle with exposure to a portfolio of leveraged loans separated into tranches with different cash flow claims and exposure to losses based on a waterfall.

**Concession agreement** A contractual arrangement under which an entity (also known as a grantor) establishes terms and conditions with a developer or operator (referred to as a concessionaire) to plan, build, operate, finance, and maintain an infrastructure asset for a specific period.

**Concessionaire** A developer or operator that is provided the right under a concession agreement to charge user fees over an operating period to recover construction, maintenance, and operational costs and compensate investors.

**Construction and development (C&D) loan**   Debt financing for real estate development which is committed prior to project initiation and drawn through a construction phase, accruing interest over time, and typically repaid with a mortgage loan.

**Construction and development loan**   A loan used to provide funds during the building phase of a real estate project.

**Continuation funds**   New private investment funds established by GPs through the sale of existing assets in another limited partnership in GP-led secondary transactions.

**Contracts for difference (CfDs)**   Contracts used as an income stabilization measure under which the difference between a pre-agreed, fixed contractual price (or strike price) for a service or good is exchanged for the current prevailing market price (or so-called reference price).

**Contractual subordination**   Use of contract or intercreditor agreement between senior and subordinated lenders to establish seniority ranking of debt obligations.

**Conversion period**   The period over which a convertible bond may be exchanged for equity at a predetermined price.

**Conversion price**   Predetermined share price at which convertible debt may be fully exchanged for common shares during the conversion period.

**Conversion ratio**   The number of common shares a convertible bond or noteholder may receive in exchange for a specific bond par value.

**Conversion value**   The current contingency feature value derived by comparing a convertible bond's price with its value if a bondholder were to exchange bonds for shares.

**Convertible arbitrage**   A special situations investment approach that involves capitalizing on the perceived mispricing of the underlying risk components of a convertible bond.

**Convertible debt**   A fixed-income instrument which combines the features of debt with equity via a contingent feature, allowing debtholders to exchange their claim for common shares at a predetermined fixed price in the future.

**Convertible preferred shares (CPS)**   A form of preferred stock that may pay a dividend and be converted into common shares at a fixed conversion ratio, or number of common shares received for each preferred share.

**Convexity**   The second order, usually a positive change in the price of a bond for a given change in yield, which can be negative for a callable bond such as a high-yield bond.

**Covenant-lite**   Debt transactions involving a relatively weak set of restrictive covenants imposed on an issuer due to competitive market pressures.

**Credit event**   An occurrence that triggers the settlement of a CDS contract, including failure to make a debt payment, debt restructuring, or a bankruptcy filing.

**Credit loss rate**   The realized percentage of par value lost to default for a group of bonds equal to the bonds' default rate multiplied by the loss severity.

**Credit valuation adjustment (CVA)**   The present value of credit risk for a loan, bond, or derivative obligation.

**Data room**   A repository used to store confidential company documents that may be accessed by potential bidders who sign a non-disclosure agreement.

**Debt profile**   A detailed breakdown of short-term and long-term liabilities by tenor, seniority, and other features, used in a private debt market strategy.

**Debt service coverage ratio**   A ratio in which the net operating income of a real estate investment for a specific period is divided by the amount of debt service to be paid during the same time period.

**Debt service reserve account (DSRA)**   A separate fund established to accumulate the cash flow necessary to meet debt service requirements from which cash is released when debt interest and principal payments are due.

**Debt-for-equity exchange**   An exchange executed by distressed firms in which new shares are issued to debtholders in exchange for the extinguishment of existing debt claims.

**Debtor in possession (DIP)**   A debtor that has filed for Chapter 11 US bankruptcy protection but remains in possession of company assets for the purpose of maintaining operations as a going concern.

**Delay option**   Developers may increase a project's present value by postponing property construction until market conditions improve.

**DIP financing**   Super senior debt financing obtained on a short-term basis to cover ongoing bankruptcy costs and provide funding to maintain operations as a company completes the bankruptcy process.

**Direct capitalization approach**   A property valuation approach that divides a single year's net operating income by the cap rate to estimate a property's value.

**Direct co-investment**   The direct purchase of an ownership stake or private debt investment with the use of one or more partners, one or more of whom may be a private fund manager.

**Direct investment**   The purchase of an ownership stake or debt investment without the use of a partner or an investment intermediary.

**Direct lending**   A type of senior secured leveraged loan privately issued on a floating-rate basis by non-bank lenders, usually to small and medium-sized companies.

**Distressed debt**   Loans or bonds which face a high likelihood of non-payment or bankruptcy.

**Distressed debt exchange**   An exchange of existing bonds for new securities from the same issuer that involve lower par values, longer maturities, and/or fewer protective financial covenants than current outstanding bonds.

**Distributed to paid-in (DPI)**   Also referred to as the cash-on-cash return, this ratio gauges an investor's realized rate of return via the ratio of cumulative distributions to limited partners to the capital invested.

**Dividend recapitalization**   A change in the mix of debt and equity outstanding for an existing corporate issuer which increases leverage via debt-financed dividends or share repurchases to benefit existing shareholders.

**Down round**   Venture capital financing of an early-stage company which takes place at a share price below that of the previous financing round.

**Duration**   The first-order, linear change in a bond's price for a given yield change in yield, which is a negative or inverse relationship.

**Effective spread duration**   Change in a loan or bond price for a given change in yield spread, with the spread typically defined as OAS.

**Empirical duration**   Estimation of the price–yield relationship using historical bond market data in statistical models.

**Equity dividend rate** A ratio in which a real estate investment's before-tax cash flow (equal to net operating income minus debt service) is divided by the difference between the investment's purchase price and the amount of debt outstanding.

**Exit value of equity** The expected terminal value of an early-stage firm at the end of a holding period is determined by using the required return on investment or a market multiple if the firm is expected to be profitable.

**Export credit agencies (ECAs)** Quasi-government entities sponsored by developed market governments to promote the export of domestic goods and services via credit insurance, political risk insurance, or subsidized or guaranteed debt financing.

**Fallen angels** Formerly investment-grade-rated issuers whose bonds are downgraded to high yield due to credit deterioration.

**Feed crops** Crops such as grain used as either raw material in food production or as an intermediate good.

**Financial buyer** An owner seeking to earn investment returns from an existing company without identifying or capitalizing on synergies from a controlling interest.

**Financial dislocation** A situation in which market prices are misaligned on an absolute or relative basis due to financial market stress, changes in liquidity, market constraints, or other industry- or company-specific factors.

**Financial sponsor** A private equity buyout fund which purchases a controlling stake in a firm distributed to investors in the form of limited partnerships.

**First lien** Also known as a priority lien, this investor protection grants a lender the right to take possession of property from a borrower which fails to repay debt.

**First-out tranche** Senior debt tranche in a unitranche facility which is typically at an interest rate below the blended facility rate and repaid earlier than subordinated debt claims.

**Fraudulent conveyance** An unlawful transfer of assets by an issuer to a third party to prevent creditors from reaching a borrower's assets, which in some cases may be voided by a court under bankruptcy law.

**Free cash flow to the firm (FCFF)** Free cash flow to both debt and equity holders composed of after-tax EBITDA plus tax benefits of depreciation less changes in long-term assets and working capital.

**Free fall bankruptcy** A situation in which an issuer enters the bankruptcy process without a reorganization plan in place.

**General partners (GPs)** Private fund managers responsible for sourcing and deploying capital from limited partner investors over an investment life cycle and distributing returns to those investors over a finite investment holding period.

**Go-shop process** Provision in a sale or merger agreement in which the seller solicits bids from potential third-party buyers for a limited period after extending the offer to an initial buyer.

**Governance rights** Powers extended to preferred or minority shareholders which may include board seats, special voting rights, or the ability to observe board meetings, among others.

**GP-led secondary** A form of private market sale in which a general partner sells a private asset from an existing portfolio into a new fund.

**Grantor** Another word for "settlor," who is a person who creates a trust.

**Greenfield investment** New "to be built" infrastructure projects and assets created to provide a specific essential service or to supply a public good.

**Growth equity** Private equity investment in a young company with a business model and growing revenue used to reach its total addressable market and reduce concentrated ownership of founders and initial investors.

**Growth equity method** Valuation approach used for private companies engaging in profitable expansion which incorporates cash flow projections over an investment horizon required to achieve a desired exit valuation and initial capital necessary to reach a targeted investor ROI.

**Hard hurdle rate** The minimum rate of return in a performance-based fee arrangement in which the GP earns only fees on annual returns that exceed the hurdle rate.

**Heavily indebted poor countries (HIPCs)** A specific group of developing countries eligible for support from the International Monetary Fund (IMF) and the World Bank.

**High-water mark** A measure that reflects the fund's maximum value as of a performance fee payment date net of fees.

**High-yield bonds** Fixed-income securities issued on a fixed-rate basis by sub-investment grade companies, which are typically subordinate to leveraged loans and include call features.

**Hurdle rate** A predetermined minimum rate of return an investment fund must reach before a GP receives incentive-based compensation.

**Incurrence covenants** Restrictive debt covenants involving financial metrics which only must be met at the time the issuer seeks to take on additional debt.

**Infrastructure Company Classification Standard (TICCS)** A standard developed to categorize infrastructure investments based on key characteristics affecting relative risk and return with the input of asset owners and asset managers.

**Insolvency** A situation in which an issuer's total liabilities exceed the market value of its assets.

**Intercreditor agreement** Legal contract specifying details of the priority of claims and other key terms governing separate debt claims to the same assets and legal entity.

**Intermittent market reference price (IMRP)** The UK market reference price for intermittently produced power determined daily based on the prior day's hourly electricity rates.

**Internal rate of return (IRR)** The uniform discount rate for a series of cash flows over $n$ periods that returns a net present value of zero.

**Interval funds** Open-end funds with certain constraints that have no predetermined maturity date but include liquidity restrictions, such as limits on the fraction of total assets available for redemption on a periodic basis.

**J-curve effect** Net income over a multiyear private investment holding period characterized by negative returns in an initial phase, followed by cash flow and income growth toward the end of the holding period.

**Land expectation value** Value of an acre of bare land in perpetual timberland production.

**Last-out tranche** Junior debt tranche in a unitranche facility which is at an interest rate above the blended facility rate and repaid after senior debt claims.

**LBO model** Valuation approach used for buyout equity which uses expected cash flows of a target acquisition, as well as expected capital structure composition and cost, to establish the maximum price that can be paid to a seller while satisfying targeted financing returns.

**Leveraged buyout (LBO)**   Buyout equity transaction that uses a high proportion of debt financing to make a company acquisition.

**Leveraged loan**   Term debt extended to sub-investment-grade borrowers with a floating-rate periodic coupon based on market reference rates plus a spread that usually is secured and involves restrictive covenants.

**Leveraged loans**   Term debt extended to sub-investment grade borrowers with a floating-rate periodic coupon based upon market reference rates plus a spread, which usually are secured and involve restrictive covenants.

**Limited partner co-investment**   Involves the purchase of an ownership stake or private debt investment in a single investment that is managed by a private fund manager or general partner.

**Limited partners (LPs)**   Outside investors in a private market fund who own a fractional interest in a limited, closed-end partnership managed by a general partner based on the investment commitment and other terms set out in a limited partner agreement.

**Limited partnership**   Closed-end form of ownership frequently used in private market funds in which private market fund investors, or limited partners, commit capital that is invested, managed, and distributed by a private market fund manager, or general partner, over an investment holding period.

**Liquidation preference payout**   Predefined distribution of cash proceeds to preferred shareholders made in full before any distributions are made to common shareholders.

**Liquidity financing**   Private debt funds which seek to generate income by investing in a portfolio of short-term obligations in order to maintain a stable net asset value.

**Loan to value (LTV)**   A measure of leverage used by debt investors that equals the loan amount outstanding divided by the project value.

**Loan-to-value ratio**   A ratio in which the amount of debt outstanding on a real estate investment is divided by the current value of the investment.

**Lockup agreement**   A provision requiring a private equity investor to retain a material interest in the shares of a new public company for a predetermined period to protect the interests of institutional investors.

**Loss given default (LGD)**   The amount a debtholder fails to recover if a default occurs, usually expressed as a percentage of par value.

**Low Carbon Contracts Company (LCCC)**   UK government-owned counterparty for qualified low-carbon energy contracts for difference.

**Maintenance covenants**   Restrictive debt covenants requiring an issuer to meet certain financial metrics for each financial reporting period.

**Management buyout**   A private sale to a strategic buyer that includes a company's existing management. The management team commits their own equity capital along with other investors as an incentive to grow the firm's cash flows and value.

**Merchant payment scheme**   Also referred to as a commercial payment scheme, under this structure frequently used for power generation and toll road assets, an operator has the right to collect service or user fees over an operating period but remains exposed to the asset's business risk based on demand and other economic factors.

**Merger arbitrage**   Special situations investments related to business combinations in which investors seek to capitalize on price discrepancies of securities issued by the target company.

**Mezzanine debt**   Debt claims that are serviced after all senior debt claims, but before common shares and other forms of equity in the capital structure.

**Mezzanine loan**   A debt claim that is serviced after all senior debt claims but before common shares and other forms of equity in the capital structure.

**Multiple of invested capital**   A ratio in which the total value of all realized investments and residual asset values (assets that may still be awaiting sale) are divided by capital invested.

**Multiple of invested capital (MOIC)**   Also referred to as the multiple of money or total value to paid-in, this private market performance measure incorporates both the cumulative distributions received and the net asset value of a fund as a proportion of invested capital.

**Multiple of money (MOM)**   Also referred to as the multiple of invested capital or total value to paid-in, this private market return measure incorporates both the cumulative distributions received and the fund's net asset value as a proportion of invested capital.

**Net operating income**   A key property income measure that ignores financing costs and taxes and is measured as NOI = Effective gross income – Operating expenses – Property maintenance allowance.

**Non-disclosure agreement**   A legal contract specifying that any confidential information received by a prospective company buyer is used only to evaluate a possible transaction.

**Non-sponsored loans**   Direct loans to small- or medium-sized firms which lack a controlling financial sponsor and involve greater search, due diligence, and monitoring costs.

**Open-end diversified core equity (ODCE) funds**   Private investment funds that hold portfolios of core income-producing properties.

**Open-end funds**   Funds which allow investors to contribute or withdraw capital freely and have no predetermined end date.

**Optimal conversion point**   The implied equity price at which convertible preferred shareholders are better off exercising their right to convert preferred shares into common shares.

**Option-adjusted spread (OAS)**   A generalized constant yield spread over the zero curve that incorporates bond option pricing based on assumed interest rate volatility and may be used for callable, putable, and non-callable bonds.

**Own–lease**   A farmland investing model more common among financial investors in which an owner or lessor receives fixed rental payments for undeveloped tillable acreage under a multiyear lease agreement from a farm operator lessee who assumes all other business risks.

**Own–operate**   A farmland investing model which involves owning land, buildings, equipment, and other assets as well as operating an agricultural business.

**P90 level**   Probability-weighted measure of the minimum amount of electricity an average wind turbine is 90% likely to produce over an average period given changing weather conditions.

**Paid-in capital (PIC)**   Reflects the proportion of the limited partners' total committed capital that the general partner has so far deployed, following any capital calls, to total committed capital.

**Participation rights**   Preferred share feature which offers upside gains to investors via similar distributions to those received by common shareholders instead of a conversion to common equity.

**Payment in kind (PIK)**   Interest paid not in cash, but via accrual, increasing the debt principal outstanding, which is then paid at maturity.

**Permanent crops**   Agricultural crops planted for many seasons, such as orchards or vineyards, which typically generate a higher return per acre or hectare.

**Post-money valuation**   A combination of the pre-money valuation and new equity invested.

**Pre-money valuation**   Estimated current value of a startup company prior to new financing derived using the VC method.

**Pre-seed capital**   Initial equity capital for a new business, most often sourced from founders and angel investors, which is used to establish the feasibility of a product or market need.

**Prepackaged bankruptcy**   A detailed business plan and exit strategy with a new capital structure proposal that is formulated and agreed on with major creditors prior to entering the bankruptcy process.

**Price step-up**   Change in a company's price per share over a series of financings.

**Private asset investment life cycle**   Refers to the multiyear investment holding period common among private investments that consists of capital commitment, deployment, distribution and exit phases.

**Probability of default (POD)**   The likelihood that a borrower fails to make full and timely payments of principal and interest according to debt terms, usually expressed in annual percentage terms.

**Public market equivalent**   A theoretical public market investment in which private fund cash outflows are invested in a public market index while cash inflows are sold from a public market index.

**Public–private partnerships (PPPs)**   A long-term contractual relationship between the public and private sectors involving a concession agreement or other form of compensation in exchange for delivering an essential service or public good.

**Pulpwood**   A timber product consisting of lower-quality, small, and often thinned trees that is the primary input for paper products.

**Quoted margin (QM)**   Spread over the market reference rate for a floating-rate loan established at the time of issuance to compensate investors for issuer credit and liquidity risk.

**Ratchet provision**   Antidilution provision negotiated by investors in early-stage companies that partially or fully reduces the conversion price of existing options or preferred shares to the price at which new shares are issued in a subsequent financing round.

**Real options**   Refers to the right but not the obligation to take future action. The existence of such options may affect the value of a real estate investment.

**Recurring revenue financing**   A form of venture debt in which a private loan is offered to a startup firm with an established subscriber base in the form of a discounted upfront monthly payment of expected subscription revenue in exchange for all monthly subscriber cash flows.

**Redemption rights**   Grant an investor the right to redeem preferred shares for cash as a form of downside protection against adverse events.

**Reduced form models**   Statistical credit models that solve for the probability of default over a specific time period, using observable company-specific and market-based variables.

**Reference price**   The current prevailing market price for a service or good whose difference from a pre-agreed, fixed contractual price (or strike price) determines the settlement amount in a contract for difference.

**Request for proposal (RFP)**   Standardized document used by public entities to choose parties involved in the development, construction, operation, and financing of infrastructure projects that outlines project details, requirements, and timing, as well as assessment criteria used to award contracts to successful bidders.

**Required margin**   Also known as discount margin. The market-determined yield spread over or under the market reference rate such that a floating-rate loan is priced at par on a rate reset date following issuance.

**Reserve currencies**   Freely floating currencies issued by central banks in major developed markets that are widely held by external parties, including central banks.

**Residual value to paid-in (RVPI)**   A measure of an investor's unrealized return on investment equal to the fund's net asset value as a proportion of the total invested capital.

**Retained cash flow (RCF)**   Net cash from operating activities less dividends, and often compared to net debt as a measure of financial leverage.

**Return on investment (ROI)**   A simple performance measure equal to the ratio or multiplier of cash flows received versus those invested that ignores the time value of money and length of an investment holding period.

**Revolving credit agreement**   The most reliable form of a short-term bank borrowing facility, which can be drawn and repaid based upon working capital needs and in effect for multiple years on either a secured or unsecured basis. Also known as revolvers.

**Row crops**   Agricultural crops harvested annually and rotated.

**Sawtimber**   Top-quality timber used for construction lumber, as well as other building products, such as plywood or particleboard.

**Scenario analysis**   A variation of the valuation process combining a base case with alternative outcomes, allowing the incorporation of more favorable or adverse scenarios in the valuation process.

**Second lien**   An investor protection which increases the recovery rate in the event of default versus unsecured debt. A second lien loan is secured by an asset with an existing lien and will only be repaid once the first lien creditor receives payment.

**Secondaries**   Limited partnership stakes in existing mid-cycle private market funds that are purchased and sold among LPs, which in many cases involves the fund GP as an intermediary.

**Seed capital**   Equity investment(s) used to launch a startup company once it has a proven business idea.

**Sensitivity analysis**   A form of analysis used to determine the impact of a change in one or more key variables affecting investment returns or valuation.

**Sequencing option**   Dividing and executing a project in staggered phases rather than all at once, which may increase a project's risk-adjusted return by reducing exposure to market oversupply during the lease-up period.

**Series financing**   One or more stages of equity investment in young companies which occurs after the firm is established and before it is sold or goes public.

**Setback**   Zoning requirement mandating provisions for distance to property lines.

**Social infrastructure**   Infrastructure investments directed toward essential government services, such as education and health care.

**Soft hurdle rate**   The minimum rate of return in a performance-based fee arrangement in which the entire return is subject to the fee once the hurdle is exceeded.

**Sovereign immunity**   A principle that limits legal recourse of lenders from forcing a sovereign borrower to declare bankruptcy or liquidate its assets to settle debt claims.

**Special purpose entity (SPE)**   Also referred to as a special purpose vehicle (SPV), this legal entity is created for a specific economic purpose. In the case of a project SPV, the entity's sole purpose is to facilitate the construction, operation, and financing of an infrastructure asset over its contractual life.

**Special situations**   An area of private capital investment that targets return by investing in stressed, distressed, or event-driven opportunities.

**Specialty financing**   Involves forms of non-bank lending to commercial and consumer borrowers such as credit card receivables, leasing, and installment loans.

**Sponsored loans**   Debt funding in which a private equity firm with a large equity investment in a prospective borrower directly solicits debt investors for the company.

**Stabilized NOI**   A more permanent level of the property's earnings potential over time, as opposed to the amount of NOI observed during a specific time period that may result from temporary market cycles.

**Strategic buyer**   An investor seeking to capitalize on synergies by extending the value creation process initiated by a GP, combining a business with another portfolio company, or taking other actions to increase firm value.

**Strike price**   A pre-agreed, fixed contractual price per period whose difference from the current prevailing market price (or so-called reference price) determines the settlement amount in a contract for difference.

**Structural credit risk models**   Option-based models of a firm's market value of assets over time versus its fixed obligations used to link an issuer's likelihood of default to its equity price.

**Structural subordination**   Refers to the positioning of debt, which is issued by a legal entity, typically a holding company, which is separate and therefore one step removed from an operating company, which holds assets pledged under a security agreement to senior secured debtholders.

**Stumpage fee**   A fee paid to timberland owners by private firms for the right to harvest timber.

**Subscription lines**   Short-term lines of credit extended to private market funds that are secured by LP investor fund commitments prior to drawdown.

**Sum-of-the-parts valuation**   A valuation approach that considers the value of a firm's business segments if they are sold separately.

**Switching option**   The option to choose among alternative projects for a given plot of land or switch economic uses for an existing project, such as a mixed-use facility, which may increase value.

**Take-private transaction**   Also referred to as a *go-private transaction*, this involves the purchase of a public company by private investors in which the target company's shares are no longer publicly traded.

**Technical default**   A violation of the terms and conditions of a credit, loan, or bond agreement, such as the breach of a financial covenant.

**Tender process**   Early bond repayment mechanism in which a voluntary offer is extended to bondholders by an issuer to repurchase outstanding bonds prior to maturity.

**Total addressable market**   A measure of the industry-wide revenue potential for the company's product or service.

**Total value to paid-in (TVPI)**   Also referred to as multiple of invested capital or multiple of money, this measure reflects the overall value to the limited partner by incorporating both the cumulative distributions received and the net asset value as a proportion of invested capital. TVPI is the sum of distributed to paid-in and residual value to paid-in.

**Turnkey**   A type of construction project in which a general contractor agrees to deliver a project on a fully completed basis.

**Unitranche debt**   A hybrid loan combining senior and subordinated debt in one facility, typically issued to small- or medium-sized corporate borrowers by private debt funds.

**VC method**   Valuation method for startup companies in which the current value is determined using the expected terminal value of the firm (or exit value of equity) and the required return on investment.

**Venture capital**   Private equity investment in a startup or early-stage company involving high risk and a high rate of failure.

**Venture debt**   Unsecured debt from non-bank lenders offered to startup companies, often in anticipation of follow-on equity offerings, which typically involves a loan plus a warrant.

**Vintage year**   Year in which capital is initially deployed to a specific investment or project or a private market fund, used for benchmarking purposes and to seek diversification over time in a private market allocation.

**Voidable preference**   A situation in which an issuer grants a preference to one creditor over another in violation of a loan agreement or bond indenture, which may be reversed in bankruptcy court.

**Warrant**   Debt feature or security granting the right to purchase additional common equity shares issued by the company at a predetermined price for a given period.

**Weighted average cost of capital (WACC)**   The expected cost of debt and equity weighted by the proportion of each used in a company's capital structure.

**Z-score**   A reduced-form statistical credit measure that uses company-specific and market-based ratios to create a composite score used to determine whether a firm is likely to default or remain solvent.

**Zero-volatility spread (Z-spread)**   A constant spread which is estimated using the market prices of comparable bonds for issuers of similar credit quality of a bond over the benchmark rate.

# Private Wealth Pathway Glossary

**Accumulation** The process of saving for retirement.

**Accumulation period** In a lifetime or period-certain annuity, the accumulation period is the phase during which the annuitant makes regular premium payments to build up the annuity's investment value.

**Acquirer's dilemma** The process of incorporating a new identity as a wealthy person into the identity that an individual already has from their formative years.

**Advanced-life deferred annuity** An annuity purchased in later life, providing deferred income initiated by a lump-sum payment.

**Agreeableness** A personality trait that describes the degree to which a person has a kind and empathic orientation to others.

**Allocation effect** The impact of overweighting and under-weighting sectors relative to the benchmark on the return of the portfolio.

**Alternative minimum tax (AMT)** A special regime of taxation under which an individual calculates their taxes under two sets of rules—one being the conventional and an alternative one, usually more conservative with respect to deductions and tax credits, which is referred to as AMT. The taxable entity will pay the tax calculated under the method that results in the higher tax amount.

**Anchoring** A type of cognitive bias that makes individuals focus on the first idea or value they are presented with as a baseline for subsequent evaluations of a decision.

**Annuity** A decumulation vehicle that requires an upfront payment for a stream of periodic payments.

**Anstalt** A structure combining the attributes of a company and a foundation that is used in civil law jurisdictions for wealth transfer purposes.

**Arithmetic active return** The arithmetic difference between the return of the portfolio and the return of its benchmark.

**Arm's-length transaction** Both buyer and seller act independently without any preexisting relationship that may sway their decision making.

**Asset structuring** The process of structuring a collection of investments, business interests, or other financial holdings to maximize wealth.

**Availability heuristic** A type of cognitive bias that makes individuals overweight information that is readily available when making decisions.

**Beneficiary** A person who has beneficial ownership of trust assets and to whom the trustee is accountable.

**Bequest** The act of giving or leaving property to a specified person(s) through the provisions of a will.

**Centralized portfolio management (CPM)** A paradigm of total portfolio construction and investment operation whereby the assets of a single beneficiary are managed by multiple managers, internal or external, who act in a coordinated fashion with the goal of improving the optimality of the investment outcome. The coordination involves trading, information sharing, and aggregation that reduces turnover, taxes, and improves the risk-return profile of the overall portfolio.

**Charitable incorporated organizations** Legally incorporated entities established for non-profit purposes, like social welfare, education, and environmental protection, under the law of Japan.

**Charitable lead trust (CLT)** A US philanthropic vehicle that inverts the sequence of benefits provided by a CRT. A CLT focuses on offering an immediate income stream to charitable causes while preserving the remainder of the trust's assets for the donor's heirs.

**Charitable remainder trust (CRT)** A US philanthropic vehicle that provides an income stream to the donor while committing the remaining assets to a future gift to charity.

**Choice overload bias** This cognitive bias occurs when an individual feels paralyzed into inaction because of the variety and abundance of options.

**Citizenship-based tax systems** Tax their citizens regardless of their residential status.

**Civil law system** The elected legislatures, derived from Roman jurisprudence, that enact laws; the courts interpret and apply these laws to each particular case through their judges.

**Cohabitation agreement** A legal and financial framework for a relationship between two unmarried adults that defines how assets and debts will be treated during cohabitation and in the event of separation or death.

**Common law system** A case law system derived from the British legal tradition in which previously adjudicated cases influence pending and future cases.

**Community foundation** A charitable organization that makes social or educational grants for the benefit of a local community as is typically funded by public donations.

**Community property** Property acquired by a spouse during a marriage that is owned jointly by both spouses and is divided upon divorce, annulment, or the death of a spouse.

**Community property regimes** Regimes that treat marital assets as jointly owned and thus divided equally in the event of divorce.

**Comprehensive wealth planning** Focuses on integrated management of all of a client's financial and business affairs.

**Concentrated position** A holding that, due to its low tax basis and implicit large potential capital gains or personal association with the client, inhibits the development of an efficient, diversified portfolio.

**Confirmation bias** A type of cognitive bias that makes individuals view information that confirms beliefs they already hold as more salient.

**Conscientiousness** A personality trait characterizing the ability to exercise discipline and self-control to achieve goals.

**Cost-push inflation** Inflation triggered by an increase in the costs of production inputs, such as labor and materials, which leads businesses to raise their prices.

**Credit method** A method that offsets domestic tax liability with the taxes already paid to a foreign country.

**Cross-Border Financial Center** A financial hub that specializes in providing financial services, like banking, asset management, or investment opportunities, to clients located in different jurisdictions. Unlike OFCs, the emphasis is not necessarily on tax advantages but on serving diverse geographic markets.

**Custodian** A specialized financial institution responsible for safeguarding an investor's financial assets and is not typically involved in asset management activities. The custodian may offer additional services like performance analytics to assist in portfolio evaluation.

**Decumulation** The process of spending down savings in retirement.

**Deduction method** A method that reduces taxable income by the amount already paid to a foreign government.

**Deemed disposition** A tax event upon death, among others, in certain countries, including Canada, which treats property as if it were sold upon death and imposes a capital gains tax on the assets as if they were sold.

**Deferred fixed annuity** Provides an annuity payout at a future date, not immediately.

**Deferred variable annuities** Annuities that initiates payments at a future date, allowing contributions to an investment account whose performance affects payouts.

**Demand-pull inflation** Inflation triggered by increased consumer demand for goods and services, resulting in upward pressure on prices.

**Digital Security** Technologies and best practices employed to protect sensitive financial information and digital assets from unauthorized access, data breaches, or cyberattacks. For high-net-worth individuals, robust digital security measures are essential to safeguard not only investment portfolios but also personal data, as these clients are often prime targets for cybercriminals.

**Disability** A temporary or permanent impairment that substantially limits an individual's employment, employability, and human capital.

**Discretionary financial goals** Non-essential objectives that are desirable but not critical for maintaining one's lifestyle.

**Discretionary trust** A trust that provides the trustee discretion in determining what distributions may be made to a beneficiary.

**Discretionary wealth** The difference between the sum of explicit and implied assets less the sum of current and implied liabilities.

**Disposition effect** A type of cognitive bias that makes individuals unwilling to sell their possessions at a loss.

**Donative intent** The making of a transfer without any expectation of anything in exchange.

**Donee** The person receiving the gift.

**Donor** A person making a lifetime gift.

**Donor-advised fund (DAF)** A philanthropic fund that allows donors to make charitable contributions, immediately benefit from tax deductions, and subsequently recommend grants to other qualified charities over time.

**Double taxation** Income is taxed twice.

**Dynasty trusts** Trusts that can last for multiple generations, perhaps perpetually, usually created in a jurisdiction that has abolished its rule against perpetuities.

**Embedded family office (EFO)** A dedicated space within the family business with a small number of staff who handle the financial, legal, and tax matters of the owners.

**Endowment effect** A type of cognitive bias that makes individuals value an object more highly if they own it than if they did not.

**Endowment life insurance** A hybrid insurance product that combines features of term and whole life insurance, offering a set coverage period after which the policy matures and pays out the cash value to the policy owner if the insured has not died by that time.

**Entrepreneurial personality profile** A set of personality traits described in Bill Wagner's book, The Entrepreneur Next Door: Discover the Secrets to Financial Independence, that differentiate entrepreneurs from an average person.

**Equivalency determination** The determination by the tax authorities that a donee non-US charity is the equivalent of a US public charity.

**Estate** A person's assets at death.

**Estate tax** A tax imposed on the value of the estate of a decedent payable by the estate, not the recipient.

**Excess return** Used in various senses appropriate to context: 1) The difference between the portfolio return and the benchmark return, which may be either positive or negative; 2) The return in excess of the risk-free rate, thus representing the return for bearing risk.

**Exemption method** A method that allows for offsetting taxes; the home country relinquishes its taxation rights on foreign-source income.

**Expenditure responsibility** The determination by the tax authorities that a donee non-US charity will use a grant for appropriate purposes as stated in the grant agreement.

**External Asset Managers (EAMs)** Independent firms or individuals that manage assets on behalf of a client but use the infrastructure and services of a larger financial institution for trade execution, custody, and other operational needs. EAMs offer a personalized touch and can provide a more boutique experience than traditional asset management services.

**Externally managed assets** Financial and investment assets managed by a hired external manager who the client has determined can add more value to than the client themselves.

**Extroversion** A personality trait characterizing the degree to which an individual is comfortable in social environments.

**Family advisory board** A group of family members and non-family members that assist in setting a strategic direction and establishing priorities for overseeing the family's wealth.

**Family constitution** A formal written agreement among family members that sets out the principles, values, and guidelines by which the family will interact with its wealth, including its family business(es), investments, and philanthropic endeavors.

**Family council** A select group of family members who act as a representative body that makes decisions on issues concerning family wealth and family business.

**Family extended balance sheet** Comprehensively accounts for a client's explicit and implicit financial assets, current and future expected liabilities, and net worth.

**Family foundation** A platform for focused philanthropy. It unites family members toward achieving common charitable goals.

**Family limited partnership (FLP)** A family limited partnership is a limited partnership created by a family to pool assets. While FLPs have non-tax reasons for their creation, often interests in the FLP can be transferred to family members for estate planning purposes at a valuation discount.

**Family mission statement** An aspirational statement that reflects a family's shared values and commitments.

**Family office**   A private wealth management advisory firm serving very wealthy clients.

**Fideicomiso**   A trust-like entity that holds and manages assets for specific purposes, including charitable ones, within certain civil law jurisdictions in Latin America.

**Fiduciary standard of care**   States that an advisor must put their clients' interests above their own over the entire course of a relationship.

**Fixed annuity**   An annuity offering a predetermined, fixed annual income derived from an initial lump-sum investment.

**Fixed trust**   A trust that, by its terms, provides for fixed distributions to a beneficiary.

**Fondation**   An independent legal entity used in European civil law countries for philanthropic activities and charitable grantmaking in which founders benefit from income tax deductions for contributions, and the Fondation typically enjoys tax exempt status.

**Forced heirship**   The regime in civil law jurisdictions that requires disposing of a portion of one's estate to one's spouse and descendants.

**Forced inheritance rules**   Rules that establish a legal obligation to leave a portion of one's estate to certain family members, typically children or descendants.

**Framing effects**   A type of cognitive bias that makes the way in which a choice is presented affect decisions.

**Funding ratio**   The ratio of assets to liabilities.

**Funding ratio return**   The ratio of funding ratio at time $t$ to funding ratio at time $t-1$.

**Generation skipping**   The process of transferring capital directly to the third generation to avoid a double layer of taxation.

**Generation-skipping transfer tax**   A tax imposed in the United States on transfers that skip a generation, which is intended to impose a tax at each generational level.

**Gift tax**   A tax imposed on the donor of a gift based on the value of the gift.

**Goals-based planning**   Aligns an individual's financial resources with their unique goals and circumstances, with the aim of achieving specific financial objectives.

**Golden visas**   Visas that provide initial residency, work rights, and a path to permanent residency, and potentially citizenship, through significant investments in areas like real estate, government debt, or business ventures.

**Grantor**   Another word for "settlor," who is a person who creates a trust.

**Grantor retained annuity trust (GRAT)**   A trust that provides the grantor with an annuity for a period of years.

**Health risk**   Risk that encompasses both direct and indirect costs stemming from unexpected illness or injury, affecting human capital.

**Healthspan**   The number of years of life from birth to the onset of chronic disease or disability.

**Hindsight bias**   A type of cognitive bias that makes individuals misremember the past in ways that make them appear to have made better and more well-informed choices.

**Immediate variable annuities**   Annuities beginning payments immediately after a lump-sum investment, where payment amounts vary based on underlying investment performance.

**Income yield**   The fixed annual income, expressed as a percentage of the initial annuity investment, that the annuitant receives.

**Individualism versus collectivism**   A Hofstede cultural dimension that considers the degree to which individuals are supposed to look out for themselves versus relying on the community for support and sustenance.

**Indulgence versus restraint**   A Hofstede cultural dimension that refers to society's willingness to accept and encourage the gratification of desires versus discouraging the gratification of desires within a relatively rigid set of norms. Another way of looking at this is the degree of permissiveness within a society.

**Inflation-adjusted payments**   Payments that allow annuitants to counter inflation erosion by choosing payments that adjust for inflation or grow by a fixed percentage, although the latter provides a weaker protection against inflation.

**Information ratio**   The ratio of mean active return to standard deviation (active return).

**Inheritance**   Assets that a person receives as a beneficiary after someone's death.

**Inheritance tax**   A tax imposed on the recipient of an inheritance.

**Inheritor's dilemma**   The combination of financial and emotional challenges faced by individuals inheriting significant wealth. It is marked by the pressure to manage and uphold the legacy responsibly.

**Institutional family office (IFO)**   See Professional family office (PFO).

**Intentionally defective grantor trust**   A trust that is created in the United States whereby the gift is not part of the estate of the grantor, but the grantor continues to pay income tax on the assets in the trust.

**Inter vivos trust**   A trust created during the settlor's lifetime.

**Interaction effect**   The impact of overweighting and underweighting individual securities within sectors that are themselves overweighted or underweighted.

**Internally managed assets**   Businesses in which the individual or family holds controlling or direct ownership, privately owned residential real estate, or other properties that generate value through the client's activities; human capital is an important component of internally managed assets.

**Intestacy**   Dying without a will.

**Investor visa**   A visa that offers temporary residency in exchange for specified investments in local businesses or industries, without guaranteeing a route to full citizenship.

**Irrevocable trust**   A trust that cannot be changed or revoked by the settlor.

**Joint life annuity**   An annuity that covers two annuitants, typically spouses with lifetime payments. Also called *survivor option*.

**Joint tenants with right of survivorship (JTWROS)**   A form of ownership of property in which two or more individuals own the property together, and upon the death of one of the owners, the deceased owner's share automatically passes to the surviving owner(s).

**Kinecon group**   A network of individuals that share both a kinship bond and economic interests.

**Liability risk**   The risk of financial losses due to legal responsibility for property damage or personal injury.

**Life annuity with period certain**   An annuity in which the annuitants are guaranteed a minimum number of payments even if they die prematurely, with any remaining payments going to a designated beneficiary.

**Life annuity with return-of-premium**   An annuity that ensures that if the annuitant passes away before recouping the initial investment, the unpaid principal balance, after subtracting any fees and adjustments, is disbursed to a designated beneficiary.

**Life insurance wrappers**   A type of financial product that allows investors to house a variety of assets, such as equities or hedge funds, within a life insurance policy coverage structure and to benefit from tax advantages on investment income generated by these assets.

**Lifespan**   The number of years of life from birth to death.

**Lifetime annuity**   An annuity in which annuitants can opt to receive payments for their entire lives. Also called *period-certain payments*.

**Lifetime gifts**   Gifts made during lifetime, usually for tax purposes.

**Liquidity event**   Converts heretofore illiquid assets into more liquid assets either in the form of cash or securities.

**Liquidity premium**   The compensation for liquidity risk that increases in proportion to the investment's illiquidity.

**Liquidity risk**   The risk that an investment may not be readily sold at its true value.

**Logarithmic active return**   The natural log of 1+Arithmetic active return.

**Long-term versus short-term orientation**   A Hofstede cultural dimension that refers to the degree to which cultures encourage delayed gratification of material, social, and emotional needs.

**Longevity risk**   The risk of exhausting an individual's financial resources before passing away, thereby leaving insufficient capital for living expenses and unmet needs.

**Loss control**   Strategies implemented to mitigate or prevent a loss.

**Loss prevention**   Strategies implemented to mitigate the likelihood of incurring a loss.

**Loss reduction**   Strategies implemented to mitigate the impact after a loss occurs.

**Masculine versus feminine**   A Hofstede cultural dimension that defines "masculine values" as success, wealth, and personal accomplishment and "feminine values" as those that emphasize caring for others and a holistic quality of life.

**Mission-related investing**   Investing aimed at causes promoting positive societal or environmental change.

**Money scripts**   Function as unconscious "tapes" consisting of beliefs and attitudes about money that are informed and shaped by one's experiences as a child or a young adult.

**Multi-family office**   Unlike a single-family office that serves one affluent family, a multi-family office (MFO) provides comprehensive wealth management services to multiple high-net-worth families. The scale allows for a diversified service offering and potential cost efficiencies.

**Multi-partiality**   A facilitation technique in which the advisor takes the sides of all participants simultaneously, thus giving equal attention to the many identities and experiences of the dialogue participants.

**Net New Business Volume**   The volume of new business across new and existing clients.

**Net New Money**   New sources of revenue obtained within a specific time frame, net of cancellations and other revenue deductions. In private wealth management, it is a key measure of the effectiveness of Relationship Managers and other asset gatherers.

**Neuroticism**   A personality trait characterizing the degree to which a person displays emotional instability.

**No contest clause**   A provision included in an estate plan that disinherits any beneficiary who challenges the plan.

**Non-discretionary financial goals**   Encompass necessary expenses essential for sustaining the current lifestyle.

**Non-forfeiture clause**   Clause allowing policyholders of permanent life insurance to access a portion of their benefits even if they miss premium payments, provided this is done before the policy lapses.

**Non-grantor charitable lead trust**   A charitable lead trust where the donor is not a remainder beneficiary.

**Non-participating life insurance**   Insurance that offers policyholders fixed benefits that remain unaffected by the insurer's profits or performance.

**Offshore Financial Centers (OFCs)**   Jurisdictions that provide financial services to non-residents in a way that is more regulatory-efficient or tax-efficient than the client's home jurisdiction. These centers often attract capital flows seeking tax optimization, asset protection, or enhanced confidentiality.

**Offshore trust**   A trust established in a foreign jurisdiction, often a foreign tax haven.

**Openness**   A personality trait characterizing the willingness to be open to new experiences.

**Participating life insurance**   Insurance that enables policyholders to share in the insurer's profits via potential dividends above the guaranteed value.

**PATRIOT Act**   A US law enacted in 2001 which, among other goals, was aimed at preventing the funding of terrorist activities.

**Performance attribution**   The process of disaggregating a portfolio's return to determine the drivers of its performance.

**Permanent life insurance**   A type of life insurance that remains in force for the insured's entire lifetime, provided the premiums are consistently paid, and offers an accumulated cash value component.

**Personal umbrella liability policy**   Such an insurance offers specified limits and pays claims when the liability limits of the home or auto insurance are reached, thereby providing additional coverage.

**Polysemy**   Refers to the fact that value terms can have multiple meanings to different people.

**Postnuptial agreements**   Contracts signed after marriage that outline the division of assets, debts, and financial obligations in case of divorce or death.

**Power distance index**   A Hofstede cultural dimension that reflects the degree to which a society accepts that power in social groups is distributed unequally.

**Prenuptial agreements**   Contracts signed before marriage that outline the division of assets, debts, and financial obligations in case of divorce or death.

**Prepaid variable forward**   A contract that offers the asset owner an immediate cash payment, without immediate tax consequences, from a sale.

**Private grant-making foundation**   An independent legal entity created for charitable purposes in which the donor funds the foundation and receives a tax deduction, and the foundation must distribute at least 5% of its assets annually towards charitable endeavors.

**Private Placement Life Insurance (PPLI)**   A form of variable universal life insurance that offers more extensive investment choices and greater flexibility compared to traditional life insurance products. Often used by high-net-worth individuals for tax optimization and estate planning, PPLI policies are not publicly available and must be purchased through private placement. The policyholder can customize the asset allocation, which may include a range of investment options often not available in standard life insurance policies.

**Probability of ruin** The likelihood that an investor will deplete their financial assets before meeting a specific financial obligation or goal, including sustaining spending throughout retirement.

**Probate** A legal proceeding to confirm the validity of a will.

**Professional family office (PFO)** An institutionally backed entity that offers comprehensive services to its wealthy clients (also known as an institutional family office [IFO]).

**Property or wealth tax** Applies to property, real estate, financial, and other assets and is usually assessed annually.

**Prudent investor rule** The rule of law that governs trust investing.

**Publicly supported charitable organizations** Charities in the United States receive at least one-third of their support from the public, such as churches, hospitals, museums, and schools.

**Qualified charitable distribution** An income tax-free gift of up to USD 100,000 made via a required minimum distribution from a US retirement plan.

**Related-party, arm's-length transaction** A business arrangement between a company and its owners or executives made on terms that are comparable to what would be offered in the open market to unrelated parties under similar circumstances.

**Residence rules** The time a person can spend in a country without becoming a taxable resident.

**Resident** An individual or entity subject to tax in a specific country based on such factors as domicile or physical residence.

**Revocable trust** A trust that can be changed or revoked by the settlor.

**Risk acceptance** The decision of assuming specific risks and a strategy to mitigate the overall financial exposure based on one's financial capacity.

**Risk avoidance** The decision of avoiding specific risks and a strategy to mitigate the overall likelihood of significant loss by eliminating certain risks.

**Risk mitigation** Strategies implemented to mitigate the severity or probability of financial loss.

**Risk transfer** Strategies implemented to mitigate the impact of specific risks by transferring them to an insurance company.

**Robo-Advisers** Automated investment platforms that use algorithms to provide financial planning services with minimal human intervention. While they often serve retail clients, they are increasingly being integrated into wealth management offerings for more affluent clients.

**Rule against perpetuities** A common law rule that requires trusts to terminate or vest within 21 years after the date of death of a group of individuals who were alive when the trust was created or where a fixed date for termination or vesting is required.

**Selection effect** The impact of overweighting and underweighting individual securities relative to the benchmark on the return of the portfolio.

**Separate property** The regime in which each spouse can own and control property as an individual, enabling each to dispose of property as they wish.

**Separate property regimes** Regimes that consider pre-marital or post-marital gifts and inheritances as individual property.

**Settlor** A person who creates and funds a trust, also sometimes referred to as a grantor.

**Shari'a law** The law of Islam.

**Sharpe ratio** The ratio of mean excess return to standard deviation (excess return).

**Short sale against the box position** A hedging strategy that shorts a security that is held long.

**Single-family office (SFO)** A corporate structure owned by a single family and dedicated to the management of family assets and the fulfillment of individual and tailored needs of family members.

**Single-premium immediate annuity (SPIA)** An annuity converting a lump-sum investment into fixed annual income for a predetermined period or lifetime.

**Social desirability bias** A bias in which individuals give an answer that they believe is more socially acceptable than their genuine and authentic feeling.

**Socioemotional wealth (SEW)** A methodology to understand how family firms make decisions regarding the disposition of their business. It takes into account the fact that family business owners are often motivated by considerations other than profit.

**Source state** Jurisdiction where income originates—generally where the related economic activity takes place.

**Stamp duties** Taxes imposed on the purchase price of assets like shares or real estate.

**Stewardship of wealth** Refers to the responsible management of one's wealth to ensure a positive, lasting impact. It is typically manifested by wealthy individuals through philanthropy and aligning assets with values to benefit both family and society.

**Stiftung** A structure similar to an institution or foundation used in civil law jurisdictions for wealth transfer purposes.

**Supposedly irrelevant factors (SIFs)** A factor that is supposedly irrelevant to a decision being made. In practice, however, some SIFs have an outsized influence on decision making.

**Surplus** The difference between assets and liabilities, analogous to shareholders' equity on a corporate balance sheet.

**Tax avoidance** The practice of using legal means to reduce tax liability by conforming to both the spirit and the letter of the tax codes in relevant jurisdictions.

**Tax domicile** Country where an individual is considered a tax resident.

**Tax evasion** The illegal act of reducing tax liability by deliberately misreporting or concealing information from tax authorities.

**Tax haven** A country or independent region with no or very low tax rates for foreign investors.

**Tax lot** Represents the quantity, cost basis, and date of the security for tax purposes in a particular transaction.

**Tax-deferred account** Investment and contributions may be made on a pretax basis, and investment returns accumulate on a tax-deferred basis until funds are withdrawn, at which time they are typically taxed at ordinary income.

**Tax-exempt account** Taxes may or may not be assessed on the initial investment or contribution. Investment returns are typically allowed to grow and the proceeds withdrawn without tax.

**Tax-loss harvesting** A strategy used by investors to reduce their tax liability in taxable accounts by creating a tax offset, and involves selling securities at a loss to offset capital gains, thereby reducing the net tax liability in that period.

**Taxable account** The normal tax rules of the jurisdiction apply.

**Term life insurance**   A type of life insurance that provides coverage for a predetermined period but lacks a cash value component and becomes void if the insured individual either fails to pay the premiums or does not die within the policy term. Also called *temporary life insurance*.

**Territorial tax system**   A country that taxes income sourced within its borders; also known as source jurisdiction.

**Testamentary**   A provision in a will.

**Testamentary documents**   Documents such as a will or testamentary trust that take effect at death.

**Testamentary gratuitous transfer**   A gift by will.

**Testamentary trust**   A trust created under a will.

**Testator**   The person who creates a will.

**Tontine**   A pooled decumulation vehicle that allows longevity risk to the moderated by averaging.

**Transfer tax**   The tax imposed on the transfer of assets, including gift tax, estate tax, inheritance tax, and generation-skipping tax.

**Treaty shopping**   The attempt by a taxpayer to leverage treaty tax advantages without engaging in genuine economic activities in either country.

**Trust**   A structure whereby legal title to assets is held by one person (a trustee) who holds and manages the assets for the benefit of a third party or parties (the beneficiaries) who are the beneficial owners of the assets.

**Trust agreement**   The document that sets forth the terms of a trust.

**Trustee**   A person who has legal title to assets in the trust and who must administer the trust for the benefit of its beneficiaries.

**Unanchored inflation expectations**   The anticipation of rising inflation rates in the future, subsequently influencing economic decision-making for consumers, manufacturers, and service providers.

**Uncertainty avoidance index**   A Hofstede cultural dimension that considers the degree to which individuals are comfortable in ambiguous situations and tolerant of risk.

**Universal life insurance**   A flexible type of permanent life insurance that permits adjustable premiums and offers investment options for the accumulated cash value, remaining in effect as long as premiums are paid.

**Virtual family office (VFO)**   A legally organized business designed to manage, control, and facilitate both the financial and non-financial wealth and transactions of a family.

**Wash sale**   An investor sells a security at a loss and buys a very similar or substantially identical stock or security within a given time period before or after the sale.

**Wealth transfer tax**   Tax when assets are transferred from one owner to another through means other than a direct sale or purchase.

**Whole life insurance**   A life insurance policy that provides coverage for the insured's entire lifetime, with premiums usually paid annually. See *Permanent life insurance*.

**Will**   A legal document that becomes effective after a person's death that disposes of that person's property.

**Withholding taxes**   Imposed by countries for non-resident investors for interest and dividend payments. Depending on the jurisdictions involved, there may be tax treaties between the sending and receiving countries, which will impact the withholding tax rate.

**Worldwide tax systems**   Jurisdictions that tax all income no matter where it's earned.

**Zeroed-out CLAT**   A charitable lead annuity trust with an annuity so large that the actuarial remainder value is zero.